OUTRE-MER AND DRIFT-WOOD

BY

HENRY WADSWORTH LONGFELLOW

Published by Left of Brain Books

ISBN 978-1-396-31883-2

First Edition

Table of Contents

Introductory Note

In 1826 Mr. Longfellow made his first journey to Europe, and remained there for study and travel until the summer of 1829. It was toward the end of his residence abroad that he began the preparation of sketches for publication. "I am also writing a book," he wrote to his father from Göttingen, May 15, 1829,—"a kind of Sketch-Book of scenes in France, Spain, and Italy." Irving's *Sketch-Book* was at that time by far the most successful of American reports of the Old World, and it became the model for other books of the kind. It had been a great favorite with Mr. Longfellow, and in some of his juvenile productions he had taken it for a suggestion; but although he used the name when writing of his proposed book, he did not carry out his plans upon the lines of Irving's work.

After his return to America he was kept closely occupied by the duties of his professorship in Bowdoin College, and by the preparation of text-books for the use of his classes; but in 1831 he was asked by Mr. Joseph T. Buckingham to contribute to *The New England Magazine*. This magazine was one of the most promising of Mr. Buckingham's various ventures, and contained articles, sketches, and poems by Everett, Story, Hillard, Hildreth, Dr. Howe, Dr. Peabody, Epes Sargent, Holmes, and many of less repute. It was in this magazine that Dr. Holmes published a trial chapter of the Autocrat, but so completely had the title disappeared that nobody remembered it when he resumed it twenty-five years afterward, in the more mature wit and wisdom which made the early numbers of *The Atlantic Monthly* famous.

Mr. Longfellow responded to Mr. Buckingham's request by sending him some of the sketches which he had begun to write when abroad. He planned a framework for these sketches, and gave the series, which began with the first number of the magazine, that for July, 1831, the general title of *The Schoolmaster*. A motto from Franklin stood at the head: "My character, indeed, I would favor you with, but that I am cautious of praising myself, lest

I should be told my trumpeter's dead; and I cannot find in my heart at present to say anything to my own disadvantage."

The Schoolmaster is written in the first person and opens with a half-confidential disclosure to the reader. "I am a schoolmaster in the little village of Sharon. A son of New England, I have been educated in all her feelings and prejudices. To her maternal care I owe the little that is good within me; and upon her bosom I hope to repose hereafter when my worldly task is done, and my soul, like a rejoicing schoolboy, shall close its weary book, and burst forth from this earthly schoolhouse. My childhood was passed at my native village in the usual amusements and occupations of that age; but as I grew up I became satiated with the monotony of my life. A restless spirit prompted me to visit foreign countries. I said, with the cosmopolite, 'The world is a kind of book in which he who has seen his own country only has read but one page.' Guided by this feeling I became a traveller. I have traversed France on foot, smoked my pipe in a Flemish inn"—Here the words grow familiar, for the passage which follows is that beginning thus in *The Pilgrim of Outre-Mer. The Schoolmaster*, however, recovers its separate character, and for a page or two more one reads of the return of the narrator to his native village, and thenceforth of his travels by memory.

In September, 1831, appeared the second chapter of *The Schoolmaster*, which is substantially the same as *The Norman Diligence* in *Outre-Mer*. The motto, indeed, is that which in the book precedes *The Journey into Spain*, and the chapter in *The Schoolmaster* is longer. The slight mention of the cabaret in *Outre-Mer* is an abbreviation of a fuller and more detailed sketch in *The Schoolmaster*, where an old soldier and some wagoners have a half-operatic scene, and sing an apology for cider, an old French song of the fifteenth century; both the French and an English version of the song are given, and it is to be noted that in the revised edition of *Poets and Poetry of Europe*, Mr. Longfellow gave Oliver Basselin's modernized version of the song as translated by Oxenford, but said nothing of his own earlier rendering.

The third chapter of *The Schoolmaster*, published April, 1832, is *The Village of Auteuil*, and contains one or two interesting variations. The introductory paragraphs in *Outre-Mer* are new, and a happy little improvement is made, when, in place of the words in *The Schoolmaster*, "I took up my abode at a *maison de santé;* not that I was a valetudinarian, but because I there found society and good accommodations," *Outre-Mer* has, "Not that I was a valetudinarian, but because I there found some one to whom I could whisper, 'How sweet is solitude!' " Dr. Dardonville in *The Schoolmaster* becomes Dentdelion in *Outre-Mer*, and some details are given in the first form which do not appear in the second. In the *Outre-Mer* chapter, on the other hand, the account of the *fête patronale* is new. It would seem as if the author, in revising his chapters, removed them a little from a too literal transcript of his notebook, and threw over them a further air of refinement and imagination.

In July, 1832, the fourth chapter was printed, headed *Recollections of the Metropolis*, and consisting of a stroll through Paris with reference to certain historical sights. The fifth chapter, published in the October number of the same year, continues this imaginary walk, but is occupied chiefly with a romantic story from a chronicle of the time of Charles VI. The sixth chapter, in February, 1833, resumes the walk, interrupted by the story, and brings the reader finally to the gates of Père La Chaise.

With this number *The Schoolmaster* came to an abrupt close. Mr. Longfellow seems to have been disinclined to continue the fiction of the schoolmaster, and to have decided also to abandon the publication of his sketches in Mr. Bucking ham's magazine. In March, 1833, he wrote to George W. Greene: "I am writing a book,—a kind of Sketch-Book of France, Spain, Germany, and Italy; composed of descriptions, sketches of character, tales illustrating manners and customs, and tales illustrating nothing in particular. Whether the book will ever see the light is yet uncertain. If I conclude to publish it, I think I shall put it out in numbers or parts, and shall, of course, send you a copy as soon as it *peeps*. I find that it requires little courage to publish grammars and school books; but in the department of fine writing—or attempts at fine writing—it requires vastly more."

Later in the year appeared the first number of *Outre-Mer: A Pilgrimage Beyond the Sea;* it contained material used in the first three chapters of *The Schoolmaster*. As the publication in *The New England Magazine* was anonymous, so *Outre-Mer* also appeared without the name of the author; but there was no attempt at special secrecy, and when the second part appeared, a few months afterward, Professor Longfellow's name was openly connected with it. It is a little odd, however, that in the book notices of the September,

1833, number of *The New England Magazine* there is a very good-natured notice of the first part of *Outre-Mer* which closed with the chapter on Père La Chaise, but without a word that indicates a knowledge of the authorship, and several quotations from pages which had already formed part of *The Schoolmaster*. This innocence, to be sure, may have been assumed, though one would scarcely have predicated it from an acquaintance with more modern magazine editors. The last three chapters of *The Schoolmaster* were not reprinted, and the serial was not resumed.

The publication of *Outre-Mer* in parts was discontinued after the second number, and the entire work was published in 1835 by Messrs. Harper & Brothers. It was in two volumes, and contained some matter not retained by the author in subsequent editions. The chapter on The *Devotional Poetry of Spain* was headed *The Moral and Devotional Poetry of Spain*, and included the whole of the article, with a similar title, which the author contributed to the *North American Review* for April, 1832. That article, which was freely revised for the book, contained some passages from *Coplas de Manrique*, but in the book the entire poem was given as a separate section. After the chapter headed *Note Book*, the author inserted a revised copy of the article, *The Defence of Poetry*, which he contributed to the *North American Review* for January, 1832, the slight connection with the previous chapter being made through the reference to Holland, which permitted a passage over to Sir Philip Sidney. The chapter on *The Trouvères*, which had the additional heading, *The Ancient Lyric Poetry of the North of France*, incorporated some of the author's work in the first of his contributions to the *North American Review*, entitled *Origin* and *Progress of the French Language*, an article which appeared in April, 1831, but was never reprinted by the author.

When Mr. Longfellow went to Europe a second time, in 1835, he made arrangements for the publication of an English edition of *Outre-Mer* which was published in London, by Bentley, the same year. He took the opportunity, when thus reprinting, to insert after *The Sexagenarian* a chapter on *Old English Prose Romances*, which was, with a few changes, his article on that subject in the *North American Review* for October, 1833. The English edition gave the author as an American on the title-page, but neither in this edition nor in Harpers' was the date and place subscribed to the Epistle Dedicatory, as in recent revised forms of *Outre-Mer*. The re-issue of the work from time to time gave opportunity for revision of the text and many slight changes indicative of the author's carefulness of workmanship.

The reader of the *Life of Henry Wadsworth Longfellow* will find that his correspondence with friends at home, during his absence in Europe, coincides more or less fully with his sketches in *Outre-Mer*, but that there was a distinct access of literary form when he came to cast his material in shape for publication. His letters are free and have the undress of familiar converse; in the sketches, although he uses the first person singular in narration, it is the person of a literary composer.

It will be remembered that Mr. Longfellow was a professor in Bowdoin College when he published *Outre-Mer*. It was probably as a slight reflection of his position that he employed, in the first instance, the form of *The Schoolmaster* series for his sketches. In the first number of the series he assumed the guise of a teacher of young children in a village school, and looked upon his profession "in a far nobler and more elevated point of view than many do." "I take," he adds, "an inexpressible delight in watching the gradual dawn of intellect in the youthful mind." It is curious to compare his reflections at this time with those in which he indulged when writing *Kavanagh*, seventeen years later. At that time he was wearying of his routine of work at Cambridge, and he says of his schoolmaster: "Nature had made Mr. Churchill a poet, but destiny made him a schoolmaster. ... He was forced to teach grammar when he would fain have written poems; and from day to day and from year to year, the trivial things of life postponed the great designs which he felt capable of accomplishing, but never had the resolute courage to begin."

In one other instance Mr. Longfellow made use of the fiction of a schoolmaster, if fiction it can be called, where the writer's occupation agrees with his assumption. In the *Knickerbocker* for May, 1834, he began the publication of *The Blank Book of a Country Schoolmaster*, which consisted of brief passages taken apparently from his note book. He continued the series for three numbers, and afterward incorporated some of the passages in his prose writings.

OUTRE-MER, A PILGRIMAGE BEYOND THE SEA

I have passed manye landes and manye yles and contrees, and cherched manye fulle straunge places, and have ben in manye a fulle gods honourable companye. Now I am comen home to reste. And thus recordynge the tyme passed, I have fulfilled these thynges and putte hem wryten in this boke, as it woulde come into my mynde.

SIR JOHN MAUNDEVILLE.

THE EPISTLE DEDICATORY

The cheerful breeze sets fair; we fill our sail,
And scud before it. When the critic starts,
And angrily unties his bags of wind,
Then we lay to, and let the blast go by.

HURDIS.

WORTHY AND GENTLE READER,—

I DEDICATE this little book to thee with many fears and misgivings of heart. Being a stranger to thee, and having never administered to thy wants nor to thy pleasures, I can ask nothing at thy hands saving the common courtesies of life. Perchance, too, what I have written will be little to thy taste;—for it is little in accordance with the stirring spirit of the present age. If so, I crave thy forbearance for having thought that even the busiest mind might not be a stranger to those moments of repose when the clock of time clicks drowsily behind the door, and trifles become the amusement of the wise and great.

Besides, what perils await the adventurous author who launches forth into the uncertain current of public favor in so frail a bark as this! The very rocking of the tide may overset him; or peradventure some freebooting critic, prowling about the great ocean of letters, may descry his strange colors, hail him through a gray goose-quill, and perhaps sink him without more ado. Indeed, the success of an unknown author is as uncertain as the wind. "When a book is first to appear in the world," says a celebrated French writer, "one knows not whom to consult to learn its destiny. The stars preside not over its nativity. Their influences have no operation on it; and the most confident astrologers dare not foretell the diverse risks of fortune it must run."

It is from such considerations, worthy reader, that I would fain bespeak thy friendly offices at the outset. But in asking these I would not forestall thy good opinion too far, lest in the sequel I should disappoint thy kind wishes. I ask only a welcome and God-speed; hoping that when thou hast read these pages thou wilt say to me, in the words of Nick Bottom, the weaver, "I shall desire you of more acquaintance, good Master Cobweb."

Very sincerely thine,

THE AUTHOR.

BRUNSWICK, Maine, 1833.

The Pilgrim of Outre-Mer

I am a Palmer, as ye so,
Whiche of my lyfe muche part have spent
In many a fayre and farre cuntrie,
As pilgrims do of good intent.

The Four Ps.

"Lystenyth, ye godely gentylmen, and all that ben hereyn!" I am a pilgrim benighted on my way, and crave a shelter till the storm is over, and a seat by the fireside in this honorable company. As a stranger I claim this courtesy at your hands, and will repay your hospitable welcome with tales of the countries I have passed through in my pilgrimage.

This is a custom of the olden time. In the days of chivalry and romance, every baron bold, perched aloof in his feudal castle, welcomed the stranger to his halls and listened with delight to the pilgrim's tale and the song of the troubadour. Both pilgrim and troubadour had their tales of wonder from a distant land, embellished with the magic of Oriental exaggeration. Their salutation was,—

Lordyng lystnith to y tale,
That is meryer than the nightingale.

The soft luxuriance of the Eastern clime bloomed in the song of the bard; and the wild and romantic tales of regions so far off as to be regarded as almost a fairy land were well suited to the childish credulity of an age when what is now called the Old World was in its childhood. Those times have passed away. The world has grown wiser and less credulous, and the tales which then delighted delight no longer. But man has not changed his nature. He still retains the same curiosity, the same love of novelty, the same fondness for romance and tales by the chimney-corner, and the same desire of wearing out the rainy day and the long winter evening with the illusions of fancy and the fairy sketches of the poet's imagination. It is as true now as ever, that

Off talys, and tryfulles, many man tellys;
Sume byn trew, and sumo byn ellis;
A man may dryfe forthe the day that long tyms dwellis
Wyth harpyng, and pipyng, and other mery spellis, Wyth gle,
and wyth game.

The Pays d'Outre-Mer, or the Land beyond the Sea, is a name by which the pilgrims and crusaders of old usually designated the Holy Land. I, too, in a certain sense, have been a pilgrim of Outre-Mer; for to my youthful imagination the Old World was a kind of Holy Land, lying afar off beyond the blue horizon of the ocean; and when its shores first rose upon my sight, looming through the hazy atmosphere of the sea, my heart swelled with the deep emotions of the pilgrim, when he sees afar the spire which rises above the shrine of his devotion.

In this my pilgrimage, "I have passed many lands and countries, and searched many full strange places." I have traversed France from Normandy to Navarre; smoked my pipe in a Flemish inn; floated through Holland in a Trekschuit; trimmed my midnight lamp in a German university; wandered and mused amid the classic scenes of Italy; and listened to the gay guitar and merry castanet on the borders of the blue Guadalquivir. The recollection of many of the scenes I have passed through is still fresh in my mind, while the memory of others is fast fading away, or is blotted out forever. But now I will stay the too busy hand of time and call back the shadowy past. Perchance the old and the wise may accuse me of frivolity; but I see in this fair company the bright eye and listening ear of youth,—an age less rigid in its censure and more willing to be pleased. "To gentlewomen and their loves is consecrated all the wooing language, allusions to love-passions, and sweet embracements feigned by the muse amongst hills and rivers whatsoever tastes of description, battle, story, abstruse antiquity, and law of the kingdom, to the more severe reader. To the one be contenting enjoyments of their auspicious desires; to the other, happy attendance of their chosen Muses." [1]

And now, fair dames and courteous gentlemen, give me attentive audience:—

Lordyng lystnith to my tale,
That is meryer than the nightingale.

---

[1] Selden's Prefatory Discourse to the Notes in Drayton's *Poly-Olbion.*

The Norman Diligence

> The French guides, otherwise called the postilians, have one most diabolicall custome in their travelling upon the wayes. Diabolicall it may be well called; for whensoever their horses doe a little anger them, they will say, in their fury, *Allons, diable,*—that is, Go, thou divel. This I know by mine own experionce.
>
> CORYAT'S *Crudities.*

It was early in the "leafy month of June" that I travelled through the beautiful province of Normandy. As France was the first foreign country I visited, everything wore an air of freshness and novelty, which pleased my eye and kept my fancy constantly busy. Life was like a dream. It was a luxury to breathe again the free air after having been so long cooped up at sea; and, like a long-imprisoned bird let loose from its cage, I revelled in the freshness and sunshine of the morning landscape.

On every side, valley and hill were covered with a carpet of soft velvet green. The birds were singing merrily in the trees, and the landscape wore that look of gayety so well described in the quaint language of an old romance, making the "sad, pensive, and aching heart to rejoice, and to throw off mourning and sadness." Here and there a cluster of chestnut-trees shaded a thatch-roofed cottage, and little patches of vineyard were scattered on the slope of the hills, mingling their delicate green with the deep hues of the early summer grain. The whole landscape had a fresh, breezy look. It was not hedged in from the highways but lay open to the eye of the traveller, and seemed to welcome him with open arms. I felt less a stranger in the land; and as my eye traced the dusty road winding along through a rich cultivated country, skirted on either side with blossoming fruit-trees, and occasionally caught glimpses of a little farm-house resting in a green hollow and lapped in the bosom of plenty, I felt that I was in a prosperous, hospitable, and happy land.

I had taken my seat on top of the diligence, in order to have a better view of the country. It was one of those ponderous vehicles which totter slowly along the paved roads of France, laboring beneath a mountain of trunks and bales of all descriptions; and, like the Trojan horse, bearing a groaning multitude within it. It was a curious and cumbersome machine, resembling the bodies of three coaches placed upon one carriage, with a cabriolet on top for outside passengers. On the panels of each door were painted the fieurs-de-lis of France, and upon the side of the coach, emblazoned in golden characters, "*Exploitation Générale des Messageries Royales des Diligences pour le Havre, Rouen, et Paris.*"

It would be useless to describe the motley groups that filled the four quarters of this little world. There was the dusty tradesman with green coat and cotton umbrella; the sallow invalid in skull-cap and cloth shoes; the priest in his cassock; the peasant in his frock; and a whole family of squalling children. My fellow-travellers on top were a gay subaltern with fierce mustache, and a nut-brown village beauty of sweet sixteen. The subaltern wore a military undress and a little blue cloth cap, in the shape of a cow-bell, trimmed smartly with silver lace and cocked on one side of his head. The brunette was decked out with a staid white Norman cap, nicely starched and plaited and nearly three feet high, a rosary and cross about her neck, a linsey-woolsey gown, and wooden shoes.

The personage who seemed to rule this little world with absolute sway was a short, pursy man, with a busy, self-satisfied air and the sonorous title of *Monsieur le Conducteur*. As insignia of office he wore a little round fur cap and fur-trimmed jacket, and carried in his hand a small leathern portfolio, containing his way-bill. He sat with us on top of the diligence and with comic gravity issued his mandates to the postilion below, like some petty monarch speaking from his throne. In every dingy village we thundered through he had a thousand commissions to execute and to receive; a package to throw out on this side, and another to take in on that; a whisper for the landlady at the inn; a love-letter and a kiss for her daughter; and a wink or a snap of his fingers for the chambermaid at the window. Then there were so many questions to be asked and answered while changing horses! Everybody had a word to say. It was *Monsieur le Conducteur!* here; *Monsieur le Conducteur!* there. He was in complete bustle; till at length crying, *En route!* he ascended the dizzy height, and we lumbered away in a cloud of dust.

But what most attracted my attention was the grotesque appearance of the postilion and the horses. He was a comical-looking little fellow, already past the heyday of life, with a thin, sharp countenance, to which the smoke of tobacco and the fumes of wine had given the dusty look of parchment. He was equipped in a short jacket of purple velvet, set off with a red collar and adorned with silken cord. Tight breeches of bright yellow leather arrayed his pipe-stem legs, which were swallowed up in a huge pair of wooden boots, iron-fastened and armed with long, rattling spurs. His shirt-collar was of vast dimensions, and between it and the broad brim of his high, bell-crowned, varnished hat, projected an eel-skin queue, with a little tuft of frizzled hair like a powder-puff, at the end, bobbing up and down with the motion of the rider, and scattering a white cloud around him.

The horses which drew the diligence were harnessed to it with ropes and leather thongs, in the most uncouth manner imaginable. They were five in number, black, white, and gray, as various in size as in color. Their tails were braided and tied up with wisps of straw; and when the postilion mounted and cracked his heavy whip, off they started: one pulling this way, another that,—one on the gallop, another trotting, and the rest dragging along at a scrambling pace, between a trot and a walk. No sooner did the vehicle get comfortably in motion, than the postilion, throwing the reins upon his horse's neck, and drawing a flint and steel from one pocket and a short-stemmed pipe from another, leisurely struck fire and began to smoke. Ever and anon some part of the rope-harness would give way; *Monsieur le Conducteur* from on high would thunder forth an oath or two; a head would be popped out at every window; half a dozen voices exclaim at once, "What 's the matter?" and the postilion, apostrophizing the *diable* as usual, would thrust his long whip into the leg of his boot, leisurely dismount, and, drawing a handful of packthread from his pocket, quietly set himself to mend matters in the best way possible.

In this manner we toiled slowly along the dusty highway. Occasionally the scene was enlivened by a group of peasants, driving before them a little ass laden with vegetables for a neighboring market. Then we would pass a solitary shepherd sitting by the road-side with a shaggy dog at his feet, guarding his flock and making his scanty meal on the contents of his wallet; or perchance a little peasant girl in wooden shoes, leading a cow by a cord attached to her horns, to browse along the side of the ditch. Then we would all alight to ascend some formidable hill on foot, and be escorted up by a clamorous group of sturdy mendicants,—annoyed by the ceaseless importunity of worthless beggary, or moved to pity by the palsied limbs of the aged and the sightless eyeballs of the blind.

Occasionally, too, the postilion drew up in front of a dingy little cabaret, completely overshadowed by wide-spreading trees. A lusty grape-vine clambered up beside the door; and a pine-bough was thrust out from a hole in the wall, by way of tavern-bush. Upon the front of the house was generally inscribed in large black letters, "ICI ON DONNE À ROIRE ET À MANGER; ON LOGE À PIED ET À CHEVAL;" a sign which may be thus paraphrased,—"Good entertainment for man and beast;" but which was once translated by a foreigner, "Here they give to eat and drink; they lodge on foot and on horseback!"

Thus one object of curiosity succeeded another; hill, valley, stream, and woodland flitted by me like the shifting scenes of a magic lantern, and one train of thought gave place to another; till at length, in the after part of the day, we entered the broad and shady avenue of fine old trees which leads to the western gate of Rouen, and a few moments afterward were lost in the crowds and confusion of its narrow streets.

THE GOLDEN LION INN.

Monsieur Vinot. Je veux absolument un Lion d'Or; parce qu'on dit: Où allez-vous? Au Lion d'Or!—D'où venez-vous? Du Lion d'Or!—Où irons-nous? Au Lion d'Or!—Où y a-t-il de bon vin? Au Lion d'Or!

LA ROSE ROUGE.

THIS answer of Monsieur Vinot must have been running in my head as the diligence stopped at the Messagerie; for when the porter, who took my luggage, said:—

"Où allez-vous, Monsieur?"

I answered without reflection (for, be it said with all the veracity of a traveller, at that time I did not know there was a Golden Lion in the city),—

"Au Lion d' Or."

And so to the Lion d'Or we went.

The hostess of the Golden Lion received me with a curtsy and a smile, rang the house-bell for a servant, and told him to take the gentleman's things to number thirty-five. I followed him up-stairs. One, two, three, four, five, six, seven! Seven stories high, by Our Lady!—I counted them every one; and when I went down to remonstrate, I counted them again; so that there was no possibility of a mistake. When I asked for a lower room, the hostess told me the house was full; and when I spoke of going to another hotel, she said she should be so very sorry, so *désolée*, to have Monsieur leave her, that I marched up again to number thirty-five.

After finding all the fault I could with the chamber, I ended, as is generally the case with most men on such occasions, by being very well pleased with it. The only thing I could possibly complain of was my being lodged in the seventh story, and in the immediate neighborhood of a gentleman who was learning to play the French horn. But to remunerate me for these disadvantages, my window looked down into a market-place, and gave me a distant view of the towers of the cathedral and the ruins of the church and abbey of St. Ouen.

When I had fully prepared myself for a ramble through the city it was already sunset; and after the heat and dust of the day the freshness of the long evening twilight was delightful. When I enter a new city, I cannot rest till I have satisfied the first cravings of curiosity by rambling through its streets. Nor can I endure a cicerone, with his eternal "This way, Sir." I never desire to be led directly to an object worthy of a traveller's notice, but prefer a thousand times to find my own way and come upon it by surprise. This was particularly the case at Rouen. It was the first European city of importance that I visited. There was an air of antiquity about the whole city that breathed of the Middle Ages; and so strong and delightful was the impression that it made upon my youthful imagination, that nothing which I afterward saw could either equal or efface it. I have since passed through that city, but I did not stop. I was unwilling to destroy an impression which, even at this distant day, is as fresh upon my mind as if it were of yesterday.

With these delightful feelings I rambled on from street to street till at length, after threading a narrow alley, I unexpectedly came out in front of the magnificent cathedral. If it had suddenly risen from the earth the effect could not have been more powerful and instantaneous. It completely overwhelmed my imagination, and I stood for a long time motionless, gazing entranced upon the stupendous edifice. I had before seen no specimen of Gothic architecture; and the massive towers before me, the lofty windows of stained glass, the low portal, with its receding arches and rude statues, all produced upon my untravelled mind an impression of awful sublimity. When I entered the church, the impression was still more deep and solemn. It was the hour of vespers. The religious twilight of the place, the lamps that burned on the distant altar, the kneeling crowd, the tinkling bell, and the chant of the evening service that rolled along the vaulted roof in broken and repeated echoes, filled me with new and intense emotions. When I gazed on the stupendous architecture of the church, the huge columns that the eye followed up till they were lost in the gathering dusk of the arches above, the long and shadowy aisles, the statues of saints and martyrs that stood in every recess, the figures of armed knights upon the tombs, the uncertain light that stole through the painted windows of each little chapel, and the form of the cowled and solitary monk, kneeling at the shrine of his favorite saint or passing between the lofty columns of the church,—all I had read of, but had not seen,—I was transported back to the Dark Ages and felt as I can never feel again.

On the following day I visited the remains of an old palace, built by Edward the Third, now occupied as the Palais de Justice, and the ruins of the church and monastery of Saint Antoine. I saw the hole in the tower where the ponderous hell of the abbey fell through, and took a peep at the curious illuminated manuscript of Daniel d'Aubonne in the public library. The remainder of the morning was spent in visiting the ruins of the ancient abbey of St. Ouen, which is now trans formed into the Hotel de Ville, and in strolling through its beautiful gardens, dreaming of the present and the past, and given up to "a melancholy of my own."

At the *table d'hôte* of the Golden Lion, I fell into conversation with an elderly gentleman, who proved to be a great antiquarian and thoroughly read in all the forgotten lore of the city. As our tastes were somewhat similar, we were soon upon very friendly terms; and after dinner we strolled out to visit some remarkable localities, and took the *gloria* together at the Chevalier Bayard.

When we returned to the Golden Lion, he entertained me with many curious stories of the spots we had been visiting. Among others, be related the following singular adventure of a monk of the abbey of St. Antoine, which amused me so much that I cannot refrain from presenting it to my readers. I will not, however, vouch for the truth of the story for; that the antiquarian himself would not do. He said he found it in an ancient manuscript of the Middle Ages, in the archives of the public library; and I give it as it was told me, without note or comment.

MARTIN FRANC AND THE MONK OF SAINT ANTHONY.[2]

Seignor, oiez une merveille,
C'onques n' o'l'stes sa pareille,
Que je vos vueil dire et conter;
Or metes cuer a l'escouter.
FABLIAU DU BOUCRIER D'ABBEVILLE.

Lystyn Lordyngs to my tale,
And ye shall here of one story,
Is better than any wyne or ale,
That ever was made in this cuntry.
ANCIENT METRICAL ROMANCE.

IN times of old there lived in the city of Rouen a tradesman named Martin Franc, who by a series of misfortunes had been reduced from opulence to poverty. But poverty, which generally makes men humble and laborious, only served to make him proud and lazy; and in proportion as he grew poorer and poorer, he grew also prouder and lazier. He contrived, however, to live along from day to day, by now and then pawning a silken robe of his wife, or selling a silver spoon or some other trifle, saved from the wreck of his better for tunes; and passed his time pleasantly enough in loitering about the market-place, and walking up and down on the sunny side of the street.

[2] The outlines of the following tale were taken from a Norman Fabliau of the thirteenth century, entitled *Le Segretain Moine*. To judge by the numerous imitations of this story which still exist in old Norman poetry, it seems to have been a prodigious favorite of its day, and to have passed through as many hands as did the body of Friar Gui. It probably had its origin in "The Story of the Little Hunchback," a tale of the Arabian Nights; and in modern times has been imitated in the poetic tale of "The Knight and the Friar," by George Coleman. [This note appeared in the first edition of *Outre-Mer*, and contains the substance of a letter which Mr. Longfellow wrote to the New York *Atlas* in answer to a criticism which was printed in that paper after the appearance of the first of the two numbers of *Outre-Mer*.]

The fair Marguerite, his wife, was celebrated through the whole city for her beauty, her wit, and her virtue. She was a brunette, with the blackest eye, the whitest teeth, and the ripest nut-brown check in all Normandy; her figure was tall and stately, her hands and feet most delicately moulded, and her swimming gait like the motion of a swan. In happier days she had been the delight of the richest tradesmen in the city, and the envy of the fairest dames.

The friends of Martin Franc, like the friends of many a ruined man before and since, deserted him in the day of adversity. Of all that had eaten his dinners, and drunk his wine, and flattered his wife, none sought the narrow alley and humble dwelling of the broken tradesman save one, and that one was Friar Gui, the sacristan of the abbey of St. Anthony. He was a little, jolly, red-faced friar, with a leer in his eye and rather a doubtful reputation; but as he was a kind of travelling gazette, and always brought the latest news and gossip of the city, and besides was the only person that condescended to visit the house of Martin Franc,—in fine, for the want of a better, he was considered in the light of a friend.

In these constant assiduities, Friar Gui had his secret motives, of which the single heart of Martin Franc was entirely unsuspicious. The keener eye of his wife, however, soon discovered two faces under the hood but she persevered in misconstruing the friar's intentions, and in dexterously turning aside any expressions of gallantry that fell from his lips. In this way Friar Gui was for a long time kept at bay; and Martin Franc preserved in the day of poverty and distress that consolation of all this world's afflictions,—a friend. But, finally, things came to such a pass, that the honest tradesman opened his eyes and wondered he had been asleep so long. Whereupon he was irreverent enough to thrust Friar Gui into the street by the shoulders.

Meanwhile the times grew worse and worse. One family relic followed another,—the last silken robe was pawned, the last silver spoon sold until at length poor Martin Franc was forced to "drag the devil by the tail;" in other words, beggary stared him full in the face. But the fair Marguerite did not even then despair. In those days, a belief in the immediate guardianship of the saints was much more strong and prevalent than in these lewd and degenerate times; and as there seemed no great probability of improving their condition by any lucky change which could be brought about by mere human agency, she determined to try what could be done by intercession with the patron saint of her husband. Accordingly she repaired one evening to the abbey of St. Anthony, to place a votive candle, and offer her prayer at the altar which stood in the little chapel dedicated to St. Martin.

It was already sunset when she reached the church, and the evening service of the Virgin had commenced. A cloud of incense floated before the altar of the Madonna, and the organ rolled its deep melody along the dim arches of the church. Marguerite mingled with the kneeling crowd, and repeated the responses in Latin with as much devotion as the most learned clerk of the convent. When the service was over, she repaired to the chapel of St. Martin, and, lighting her votive taper at the silver lamp which burned before his altar, knelt down in a retired part of the chapel, and, with tears in her eyes, besought the saint for aid and protection. While she was thus engaged, the church became gradually deserted till she was left, as she thought, alone. But in this she was mistaken; for, when she arose to depart, the portly figure of Friar Gui was standing close at her elbow!

"Good evening, fair Marguerite," said he. "St. Martin has heard your prayer and sent me to relieve your poverty."

"Then," replied she, "the good saint is not very fastidious in the choice of his messengers."

"Nay, goodwife," answered the friar, not at all abashed by this ungracious reply, "if the tidings are good, what matters it who the messenger may be? And how does Martin Franc these days?"

"He is well," replied Marguerite; "and were he present, I doubt not would thank you heartily for the interest you still take in him and his poor wife."

"He has done me wrong," continued the friar. "But it is our duty to forgive our enemies, and so let the past be forgotten. I know that he is in want. Here, take this to him, and tell him I am still his friend."

So saying, he drew a small purse from the sleeve of his habit and proffered it to his companion. I know not whether it were a suggestion of St. Martin, but true it is that the fair wife of Martin Franc seemed to lend a more willing ear to the earnest whispers of the friar. At length she said,—

"Put up your purse; to-day I can neither deliver your gift nor your message. Martin Franc has gone from home."

"Then keep it for yourself."

"Nay," replied Marguerite, casting down her eyes; I can take no bribes here in the church, and in the very chapel of my husband's patron saint. You shall bring it to me at my house, if you will."

The friar put up the purse, and the conversation which followed was in a low and indistinct undertone, audible only to the ears for which it was intended. At length the interview ceased; and—O woman!—the last words that the virtuous Marguerite uttered, as she glided from the church, were,—

"To-night;—when the abbey-clock strikes twelve;—remember!"

It would be useless to relate how impatiently the friar counted the hours and the quarters as they chimed from the ancient tower of the abbey, while he paced to and fro along the gloomy cloister. At length the appointed hour approached; and just before the convent-bell sent forth its summons to call the friars of St. Anthony to their midnight devotions, a figure with a cowl stole out of a postern-gate, and, passing silently along the deserted streets, soon turned into the little alley which led to the dwelling of Martin Franc. It was none other than Friar Gui. He rapped softly at the tradesman's door, and casting a look up and down the street, as if to assure himself that his motions were unobserved, slipped into the house.

"Has Martin Franc returned?" inquired he in a whisper.

"No," answered the sweet voice of his wife; "he will not be back to-night."

"Then all good angels befriend us!" continued the monk, endeavoring to take her hand.

"Not so, good monk," said she, disengaging herself. "You forget the conditions of our meeting."

The friar paused a moment; and then, drawing a heavy leathern purse from his girdle, he threw it upon the table; at the same moment a footstep was heard behind him, and a heavy blow from a club threw him prostrate upon the floor. It came from the strong arm of Martin Franc himself!

It is hardly necessary to say that his absence was feigned. His wife had invented the story to decoy the monk, and thereby to keep her husband from beggary and to relieve herself, once for all, from the importunities of a false friend. At first Martin Franc would not listen to the proposition, but at length he yielded to the urgent entreaties of his wife; and the plan finally agreed upon was that Friar Gui, after leaving his purse behind him, should be sent back to the convent with a severer discipline than his shoulders had ever received from any penitence of his own.

The affair, however, took a more serious turn than was intended; for, when they tried to raise the friar from the ground,—he was dead. The blow aimed at his shoulders fell upon his shaven crown; and, in the excitement of the moment, Martin Franc had dealt a heavier stroke than he intended. Amid the grief and consternation which followed this discovery, the quick imagination of his wife suggested an expedient of safety. A bunch of keys at the friar's girdle caught her eye. Hastily unfastening the ring, she gave the keys to her husband, exclaiming,—

"For the holy Virgin's sake, be quick! One of these keys doubtless unlocks the gate of the convent-garden. Carry the body thither and leave it among the trees!"

Martin Franc threw the dead body of the monk across his shoulders, and with a heavy heart took the way to the abbey. It was a clear, starry night; and though the moon had not yet risen, her light was in the sky and came reflected down in a soft twilight upon earth. Not a sound was heard through all the long and solitary streets, save at intervals the distant crowing of a cock, or the melancholy hoot of an owl from the lofty tower of the abbey. The silence weighed like an accusing spirit upon the guilty conscience of Martin Franc. He started at the sound of his own breathing, as he panted under the heavy burden of the monk's body; and if, perchance, a bat flitted near him on drowsy wings, he paused and his heart beat audibly with terror. At length he reached the garden-wall of the abbey, opened the postern-gate with the key, and bearing the monk into the garden, seated him upon a stone bench by the edge of the fountain, with his head resting against a column, upon which was sculptured an image of the Madonna. He then replaced the bunch of keys at the monk's girdle and returned home with hasty steps.

When the prior of the convent, to whom the repeated delinquencies of Friar Gui were but too well known, observed that he was again absent from his post at midnight prayers, he waxed exceedingly angry; and no sooner were the duties of the chapel finished than he sent a monk in pursuit of the truant sacristan, summoning him to appear immediately at his cell. By chance it happened that the monk chosen for this duty was an enemy of Friar Gui; and very shrewdly supposing that the sacristan had stolen out of the garden-gate on some midnight adventure, he took that direction in pursuit. The moon was just climbing the convent-wall, and threw its silvery light through the trees of the garden, and on the sparkling waters of the fountain that fell with a soft lulling sound into the deep basin below. As the monk passed on his way, he stopped to quench his thirst with a draught of cool water, and was turning to depart, when his eye caught the motionless form of the sacristan, sitting erect in the shadow of the stone column.

"How is this, Friar Gui?" quoth the monk. "Is this a place to be sleeping at midnight, when the brotherhood are all at their prayers?"

Friar Gui made no answer.

"Up, up! thou eternal sleeper, and do penance for thy negligence. The prior calls for thee at his cell!" continued the monk, growing angry, and shaking the sacristan by the shoulder.

But still no answer.

"Then, by Saint Anthony, I'll wake thee!"

And saying this, he dealt the sacristan a heavy box on the ear. The body bent slowly forward from its erect position, and, giving a headlong plunge, sank with a heavy splash into the basin of the fountain. The monk waited a few moments in expectation of seeing Friar Gui rise dripping from his cold bath; but he waited in vain; for he lay motionless at the bottom of the basin,—his eyes open, and his ghastly face distorted by the ripples of the water. With a beating heart the monk stooped down, and, grasping the skirt of the sacristan's habit, at length succeeded in drawing him from the water. All efforts, however, to resuscitate him were unavailing. The monk was filled with terror, not doubting that the friar had died untimely by his hand; and as the animosity between them was no secret in the convent, he feared that when the deed was known he should be accused of murder. He therefore looked round for an expedient to relieve himself from the dead body; and the well-known character of the sacristan soon suggested one. He determined to carry the body to the house of the most noted beauty of Rouen, and leave it on the door-step; so that all suspicion of the murder might fall upon the shoulders of some jealous husband. The beauty of Martin Franc's wife had penetrated even the thick walls of the convent, and there was not a friar in the whole abbey of Saint Anthony who had not done penance for his truant imagination. Accordingly, the dead body of Friar Gui was laid upon the monk's brawny shoulders, carried back to the house of Martin Franc, and placed in an erect position against the door. The monk knocked loud and long; and then, gliding through a by-lane, stole back to the convent.

A troubled conscience would not suffer Martin Franc and his wife to close their eyes; but they lay awake, lamenting the doleful events of the night. The knock at the door sounded like a death-knell in their ears. It still continued at intervals, rap—rap—rap!—with a dull, low sound, as if something heavy were swinging against the panel; for the wind had risen during the night, and every angry gust that swept down the alley swung the arms of the lifeless sacristan against the door. At length Martin Franc mustered courage enough to dress himself and go down, while his wife followed him with a lamp in her hand but no sooner had he lifted the latch, than the ponderous body of Friar Gui fell stark and heavy into his arms.

"Jesu Maria!" exclaimed Marguerite, crossing herself; "here is the monk again!"

"Yes, and dripping wet, as if he had just been dragged out of the river!"

"Oh, we are betrayed!" exclaimed Marguerite in agony.

"Then the Devil himself has betrayed us," replied Martin Franc, disengaging himself from the embrace of the sacristan; "for I met not a living being the whole city was as silent as the grave."

"Saint Martin defend us!" continued his terrified wife. "Here, take this scapulary to guard you from the Evil One; and lose no time. You must throw the body into the river, or we are lost! Holy Virgin! How bright the moon shines!"

Saying this, she threw round his neck a scapulary, with the figure of a cross on one end and an image of the Virgin on the other; and Martin Franc again took the dead friar upon his shoulders, and with fearful misgivings departed on his dismal errand. He kept as much as possible in the shadow of the houses, and had nearly reached the quay, when suddenly he thought he heard foot steps behind him. He stopped to listen; it was no vain imagination; they came along the pavement, tramp, tramp! and every step grew louder and nearer. Martin Franc tried to quicken his pace,—but in vain: his knees smote together, and he staggered against the wall. His hand relaxed its grasp, and the monk slid from his back and stood ghastly and straight beside him, supported by chance against the shoulder of his bearer. At that moment a man came round the corner, tottering beneath the weight of a huge sack. As his head was bent downwards, he did not perceive Martin Franc till he was close upon him; and when, on looking up, he saw two figures standing motionless in the shadow of the wall, he thought himself waylaid, and, without waiting to be assaulted, dropped the sack from his shoulders and ran off at full speed. The sack fell heavily on the pavement, and directly at the feet of Martin Franc. In the fall the string was broken; and out came the bloody head, not of a dead monk, as it first seemed to the excited imagination of Martin Franc, but of a dead hog! When the terror and surprise caused by this singular event had a little subsided, an idea came into the mind of Martin Franc, very similar to what would have come into the mind of almost any person in similar circumstances. He took the hog out of the sack, and putting the body of the monk into its place, secured it well with the remnants of the broken string, and then hurried homeward with the animal upon his shoulders.

He was hardly out of sight when the man with the sack returned, accompanied by two others. They were surprised to find the sack still lying on the ground, with no one near it, and began to jeer the former bearer, telling him he had been frightened at his own shadow on the wall. Then one of them took the sack upon his shoulders without the least suspicion of the change that had been made in its contents, and all three disappeared.

Now it happened that the city of Rouen was at that time infested by three street robbers, who walked in darkness like the pestilence, and always carried the plunder of their midnight marauding to the Tête-de-Bœuf, a little tavern in one of the darkest and narrowest lanes of the city. The host of the Tête-de-Bœuf was privy to all their schemes, and had an equal share in the profits of their nightly excursions. He gave a helping hand, too, by the length of his bills, and by plundering the pockets of any chance traveller that was luckless enough to sleep under his roof.

On the night of the disastrous adventure of Friar Gui, this little marauding party had been prowling about the city until a late hour, without finding anything to reward their labors. At length, however, they chanced to spy a hog hanging under a shed in a butcher's yard, in readiness for the next day's market; and as they were not very fastidious in selecting their plunder, but, on the contrary, rather addicted to taking whatever they could lay their hands on, the hog was straightway purloined, thrust into a large sack, and sent to the

Tête-de-Bœuf on the shoulders of one of the party, while the other two continued their nocturnal excursion. It was this person who had been so terrified at the appearance of Martin Franc and the dead monk; and as this encounter had interrupted any further operations of the party, the dawn of day being now near at hand, they all repaired to their gloomy den in the Tête-de-Bœuf. The host was impatiently waiting their return; and, asking what plunder they had brought with them, proceeded without delay to remove it from the sack. The first thing that presented itself, on untying the string, was the monk's hood.

"The devil take the devil!" cried the host, as he opened the neck of the sack; "what's this? Your hog wears a cowl!"

"The poor devil has become disgusted with the world, and turned monk!" said he who held the light, a little surprised at seeing the head covered with a coarse gray cloth.

"Sure enough he has," exclaimed another, starting back in dismay, as the shaven crown and ghastly face of the friar appeared. "Holy St. Benedict be with us! It is a monk stark dead!"

"A dead monk, indeed!" said a third, with an incredulous shake of the head; "how could a dead monk get into this sack? No, no; there is some sorcery in this. I have heard it said that Satan can take any shape he pleases; and you may rely upon it this is Satan himself, who has taken the shape of a monk to get us all hanged."

"Then we had better kill the devil than have the devil kill us!" replied the host, crossing himself; "and the sooner we do it the better for it is now daylight, and the people will soon be passing in the street."

"So say I," rejoined the man of magic; "and my advice is, to take him to the butcher's yard, and hang him up in the place where we found the hog."

This proposition so pleased the others that it was executed without delay. They carried the friar to the butcher's house, and, passing a strong cord round his neck, suspended him to a beam in the shed, and there left him.

When the night was at length past, and daylight began to peep into the eastern windows of the city, the butcher arose and prepared himself for market. He was casting up in his mind what the hog would bring at his stall, when, looking upward, lo! in its place he recognized the dead body of Friar Gui.

"By St. Denis!" quoth the butcher. "I always feared that this friar would not die quietly in his cell; but I never thought I should find him hanging under my own roof. This must not be; it will be said that I murdered him, and I shall pay for it with my life. I must contrive some way to get rid of him."

So saying, he called his man, and, showing him what had been done, asked him how he should dispose of the body so that he might not be accused of murder. The man, who was of a ready wit, reflected a moment, and then answered,—

"This is indeed a difficult matter, but there is no evil without its remedy. We will place the friar on horseback"—

"What! a dead man on horseback?—impossible!" interrupted the butcher. "Who ever heard of a dead man on horseback!"

"Hear me out, and then judge. We must place the body on horseback as well as we may and bind it fast with cords; and then set the horse loose in the street, and pursue him, crying out that the monk has stolen the horse. Thus all who meet him will strike him with their staves as he passes, and it will be thought that he came to his death in that way."

Though this seemed to the butcher rather a mad project, yet, as no better one offered itself at the moment, and there was no time for reflection, mad as the project was, they determined to put it into execution. Accordingly the butcher's horse was brought out, and the friar was bound upon his back, and with much difficulty fixed in an upright position. The butcher then gave the horse a blow upon the crupper with his staff, which set him into a smart gallop down the street, and he and his man joined in pursuit, crying,—

"Stop thief! Stop thief! The friar has stolen my horse!"

As it was now sunrise, the streets were full of people,—peasants driving their goods to market, citizens going to their daily avocations. When they saw the friar dashing at full speed down the street, they joined in the cry of "Stop thief!—Stop thief!" and many who endeavored to seize the bridle, as the friar passed them at full speed, were thrown upon the pavement, and trampled under foot; others joined in the halloo and the pursuit; but this only served to quicken the gallop of the frightened steed, who dashed down one street and up another like the wind, with two or three mounted citizens clattering in full cry at his heels. At length they reached the market-place. The people scattered right and left in dismay; and the steed and rider dashed onward, overthrowing in their course men and women, and stalls, and piles of merchandise, and sweeping away like a whirl wind. Tramp—tramp—tramp! they clattered on; they had distanced all pursuit. They reached the quay; the wide pavement was cleared at a bound,—one more wild leap,—and splash!—both horse and rider sank into the rapid current of the river,—swept down the stream,—and were seen no more!

The Village of Auteuil

Il n'est tel Plaisir
Que d'estre a gésir
Parmy les beaux champs,
L'herbe verde choisir,
Et prendre bon temps.
MARTIAL D'AUVERGNE.

THE sultry heat of summer always brings with it, to the idler and the man of leisure, a longing for the leafy shade and the green luxuriance of the country. It is pleasant to interchange the din of the city, the movement of the crowd, and the gossip of society, with the silence of the hamlet, the quiet seclusion of the grove, and the gossip of a woodland brook. As is sung in the old ballad of Robin Hood,—

In somer, when the shawes be sheyn,
And leves be large and long,
Hit is full mery in feyre forests,
To here the foulys song;
To se the dere draw to the dale
And leve the hilles hee,
And shadow hem in the loves grene
Vnder the grene wode tre.

It was a feeling of this kind that prompted me, during my residence in the North of France, to pass one of the summer months at Auteuil, the pleasantest of the many little villages that lie in the immediate vicinity of the metropolis. It is situated on the outskirts of the Bois de Boulogne, a wood of some extent, in whose green alleys the dusty cit enjoys the luxury of an evening drive, and gentlemen meet in the morning to give each other satisfaction in the usual way. A cross-road, skirted with green hedge-rows and overshadowed by tall poplars, leads you from the noisy highway of St. Cloud and Versailles to the still retirement of this suburban hamlet. On either side the eye discovers old châteaux amid the trees, and green parks, whose pleasant shades recall a thousand images of La Fontaine, Racine, and Molière; and on an eminence, overlooking the windings of the Seine, and giving a beautiful though distant view of the domes and gardens of Paris, rises the village of Passy, long the residence of our countrymen, Franklin and Count Rumford.

I took up my abode at a *maison de santé*; not that I was a valetudinarian, but because I there found some one to whom I could whisper, "How sweet is solitude!" Behind the house was a garden filled with fruit-trees of various kinds, and adorned with gravel-walks and green arbors, furnished with tables and rustic seats, for the repose of the invalid and the sleep of the indolent. Here the inmates of the rural hospital met on common ground, to breathe the invigorating air of morning, and while away the lazy noon or vacant evening with tales of the sick-chamber.

The establishment was kept by Dr. Dentdelion, a dried-up little fellow, with red hair, a sandy complexion, and the physiognomy and gestures of a monkey. His character corresponded to his out ward lineaments, for he had all a monkey's busy and curious impertinence. Nevertheless, such as he was, the village Æsculapius strutted forth the little great man of Auteuil. The peasants looked up to him as to an oracle; he contrived to be at the head of everything, and laid claim to the credit of all public improvements in the village; in fine, he was a great man on a small scale.

It was within the dingy walls of this little potentate's imperial palace that I chose my country residence. I had a chamber in the second story, with a solitary window, which looked upon the street and gave me a peep into a neighbor's garden. This I esteemed a great privilege for, as a stranger, I desired to see all that was passing out of doors; and the sight of green trees, though growing on another's ground, is always a blessing. Within doors—had I been disposed to quarrel with my household gods—I might have taken some objection to my neighborhood; for on one side of me was a consumptive patient, whose graveyard cough drove me from my chamber by day; and on the other, an English colonel, whose incoherent ravings, in the delirium of a high and obstinate fever, often broke my slumbers by night; but I found ample amends for these inconveniences in the society of those who were so little indisposed as hardly to know what ailed them, and those who, in health themselves, had accompanied a friend or relative to the shades of the country in pursuit of it. To these I am indebted for much courtesy; and particularly to one who, if these pages should ever meet her eye, will not, I hope, be unwilling to accept this slight memorial of a former friendship.

It was, however, to the Bois de Boulogne that I looked for my principal recreation. There I took my solitary walk, morning and evening; or, mounted on a little mouse-colored donkey, paced demurely along the woodland pathway. I had a favorite seat beneath the shadow of a venerable oak, one of the few hoary patriarchs of the wood which had survived the bivouacs of the allied armies. It stood upon the brink of a little glassy pool, whose tranquil bosom was the image of a quiet and secluded life, and stretched its parental arms over a rustic bench, that had been constructed beneath it for the accommodation of the foot-traveller, or, perchance, some idle dreamer like myself. It seemed to look round with a lordly air upon its old hereditary domain, whose stillness was no longer broken by the tap of the martial drum, nor the discordant clang of arms; and, as the breeze whispered among its branches, it seemed to be holding friendly colloquies with a few of its venerable contemporaries, who stooped from the opposite bank of the pool, nodding gravely now and then, and gazing at themselves, with a sigh, in the mirror below.

In this quiet haunt of rural repose I used to sit at noon, hear the birds sing, and "possess myself in much quietness." Just at my feet lay the little silver pool, with the sky and the woods painted in its mimic vault, and occasionally the image of a bird, or the soft, watery outline of a cloud, floating silently through its sunny hollows. The water-lily spread its broad, green leaves on the surface, and rocked to sleep a little world of insect life in its golden cradle. Sometimes a wandering leaf came floating and wavering downward, and settled on the water; then a vagabond insect would break the smooth surface into a thousand ripples, or a green-coated frog slide from the bank, and, plump! dive headlong to the bottom.

I entered, too, with some enthusiasm, into all the rural sports and merrimakes of the village. The holidays were so many little eras of mirth and good feeling; for the French have that happy and sunshiny temperament—that merry-go-mad character—which renders all their social meetings scenes of enjoyment and hilarity. I made it a point never to miss any of the *fêtes champêtres,* or rural dances, at the wood of Boulogne; though I confess it sometimes gave me a momentary uneasiness to see my rustic throne beneath the oak usurped by a noisy group of girls, the silence and decorum of my imaginary realm broken by music and laughter, and, in a word, my whole kingdom turned topsy-turvy with romping, fiddling, and dancing. But I am naturally, and from principle, too, a lover of all those innocent amusements which cheer the laborer's toil, and, as it were, put their shoulders to the wheel of life and help the poor man along with his load of cares. Hence I saw with no small delight the rustic swain astride the wooden horse of the *carrousel*, and the village maiden whirling round and round in its dizzy car; or took my stand on a rising ground that overlooked the dance, an idle spectator in a busy throng. It was just where the village touched the outward border of the wood. There a little area had been levelled beneath the trees, surrounded by a painted rail, with a row of benches inside. The music was placed in a slight balcony, built around the trunk of a large tree in the centre; and the lamps, hanging from the branches above, gave a gay, fantastic, and fairy look to the scene. How often in such moments did I recall the lines of Goldsmith, describing those "kinder skies" beneath which "France displays her bright domain," and feel how true and masterly the sketch:

Alike all ages; dames of ancient days
Have led their children through the mirthful maze;
And the gray grandsire, skilled in gestic lore,
Has frisked beneath the burthen of threescore.

Nor must I forget to mention the *fête patronale,*—a kind of annual fair, which is held at midsummer in honor of the patron saint of Auteuil. Then the principal street of the village is filled with booths of every description; strolling players, and rope-dancers, and jugglers, and giants, and dwarfs, and wild beasts, and all kinds of wonderful shows, excite the gaping curiosity of the throng; and in dust, crowds, and confusion, the village rivals the capital itself. Then the goodly dames of Passy descend into the village of Auteuil; then the brewers of Billancourt and the tanners of Sèvres dance lustily under the greenwood tree; and then, too, the sturdy fishmongers of Brétigny and Saint-Yon regale their wives with an airing in a swing, and their customers with eels and crawfish; or, as is more poetically set forth in an old Christmas carol,—

Vous eussiez vu venir
    Tous ceux de Saint-Yon,
Et ceux de Brétigny
    Apportant du poisson,
Les barbeaux et gardons,
Anguilles et carpettes
    Etaient à bon marché,
        Croyez,
    A cette journée-là,
        Là, là,
Et aussi les perchettes.

I found another source of amusement in observing the various personages that daily passed and repassed beneath my window. The character which most of all arrested my attention was a poor blind fiddler, whom I first saw chanting a doleful ballad at the door of a small tavern near the gate of the village. He wore a brown coat, out at elbows, the fragment of a velvet waistcoat, and a pair of tight nankeen trousers, so short as hardly to reach below his calves. A little foraging-cap, that had long since seen its best days, set off an open, good-humored countenance, bronzed by sun and wind. He was led about by a brisk, middle-aged woman, in straw hat and wooden shoes; and a little barefooted boy, with clear, blue eyes and flaxen hair, held a tattered hat in his hand, in which he collected eleemosynary sous. The old fellow had a favorite song, which he used to sing with great glee to a merry, joyous air, the burden of which ran, *"Chantons l'amour et le plaisir!"* I often thought it would have been a good lesson for the crabbed and discontented rich man to have heard this remnant of humanity,—poor, blind, and in rags, and dependent upon casual charity for his daily bread,—singing in so cheerful a voice the charms of existence, and, as it were, fiddling life away to a merry tune.

I was one morning called to my window by the sound of rustic music. I looked out and beheld a procession of villagers advancing along the road, attired in gay dresses, and marching merrily on in the direction of the church. I soon perceived that it was a marriage-festival. The procession was led by a long orang-outang of a man, in a straw hat and white dimity bob-coat, playing on an asthmatic clarionet, from which he contrived to blow unearthly sounds, ever and anon squeaking off at right angles from his tune, and winding up with a grand flourish on the guttural notes. Behind him, led by his little boy, came the blind fiddler, his honest features glowing with all the hilarity of a rustic bridal, and, as he stumbled along, sawing away upon his fiddle till he made all crack again. Then came the happy bridegroom, dressed in his Sunday suit of blue, with a large nosegay in his button-hole; and close beside him his blushing bride, with downcast eyes, clad in a white robe and slippers, and wearing a wreath of white roses in her hair. The friends and relatives brought up the procession; and a troop of village urchins came shouting along in the rear, scrambling among themselves for the largess of sons and sugar-plums, that now and then issued in large handfuls from the pockets of a lean man in black, who seemed to officiate as master of ceremonies on the occasion. I gazed on the procession till it was out of sight; and when the last wheeze of the clarionet died upon my ear, I could not help thinking how happy were they who were thus to dwell together in the peaceful bosom of their native village, far from the gilded misery and the pestilential vices of the town.

On the evening of the same day, I was sitting by the window, enjoying the freshness of the air and the beauty and stillness of the hour, when I heard the distant and solemn hymn of the Catholic burial-service, at first so faint and indistinct that it seemed an illusion. It rose mournfully on the hush of evening,—died gradually away,—then ceased. Then it rose again, nearer and more distinct, and soon after a funeral procession appeared, and passed directly beneath my window. It was led by a priest, bearing the banner of the church, and followed by two boys holding long flambeaux in their hands. Next came a double file of priests in their surplices, with a missal in one hand and a lighted wax taper in the other, chanting the funeral dirge at intervals,—now pausing, and then again taking up the mournful burden of their lamentation, accompanied by others, who played upon a rude kind of bassoon, with a dismal and wailing sound. Then followed various symbols of the church, and the bier borne on the shoulders of four men. The coffin was covered with a velvet pall, and a chaplet of white flowers lay upon it, indicating that the deceased was unmarried. A few of the villagers came behind, clad in mourning robes, and bearing lighted tapers. The procession passed slowly along the same street that in the morning had been thronged by the gay bridal company. A melancholy train of thought forced itself home upon my mind. The joys and sorrows of this world are so strikingly mingled! Our mirth and grief are brought so mournfully in contact! We laugh while others weep,—and others rejoice when we are sad! The light heart and the heavy walk side by side and go about together! Beneath the same roof are spread the wedding-feast and the burial-pall! The bridal-song mingles with the funeral-hymn! One goes to the marriage-bed, another to the grave; and all is mutable, uncertain, and transitory.

It is with sensations of pure delight that I recur to the brief period of my existence which was passed in the peaceful shades of Auteuil. There is one kind of wisdom which we learn from the world, and another kind which can be acquired in solitude only. In cities we study those around us; but in the retirement of the country we learn to know ourselves. The voice within us is more distinctly audible in the stillness of the place; and the gentler affections of our nature spring up more freshly in its tranquillity and sunshine,—nurtured by the healthy principle which we inhale with the pure air, and invigorated by the genial influences which descend into the heart from the quiet of the sylvan solitude around, and the soft serenity of the sky above.

JACQUELINE.

> Death lies on her, like an untimely frost
> Upon the sweetest flower of all the field.
>
> SHAKESPEARE.

"DEAR mother, is it not the bell I hear?"

"Yes, my child; the bell for morning prayers. It is Sunday to-day."

"I had forgotten it. But now all days are alike to me. Hark! it sounds again,—louder,—louder. Open the window, for I love the sound. The sunshine and the fresh morning air revive me. And the church-bell,—O mother,—it reminds me of the holy Sunday mornings by the Loire,—so calm, so hushed, so beautiful! Now give me my prayer-book, and draw the curtain back, that I may see the green trees and the church-spire. I feel better to-day, dear mother."

It was a bright, cloudless morning in August. The dew still glistened on the trees, and a slight breeze wafted to the sick-chamber of Jacqueline the song of the birds, the rustle of the leaves, and the solemn chime of the church-bells. She had been raised up in bed, and, reclining upon the pillow, was gazing wistfully upon the quiet scene without. Her mother gave her the prayer-book and then turned away to hide a tear that stole down her cheek.

At length the bells ceased. Jacqueline crossed herself, kissed a pearl crucifix that hung around her neck, and opened the silver clasps of her missal. For a time she seemed wholly absorbed in her devotions. Her lips moved, but no sound was audible. At intervals the solemn voice of the priest was heard at a distance, and then the confused responses of the congregation dying away in inarticulate murmurs. Erelong the thrilling chant of the Catholic service broke upon the ear. At first it was low, solemn, and indistinct; then it became more earnest and entreating, as if interceding and imploring pardon for sin; and then arose louder and louder, full, harmonious, majestic, as it wafted the song of praise to heaven-and suddenly ceased. Then the sweet tones of the organ were heard,—trembling, thrilling, and rising higher and higher, and filling the whole air with their rich, melodious music. What exquisite accords!—what noble harmonies!—what touching pathos! The soul of the sick girl seemed to kindle into more ardent devotion, and to be rapt away to heaven in the full, harmonious chorus, as it swelled onward, doubling and redoubling, and rolling upward in a full burst of rapturous devotion! Then all was hushed again. Once more the low sound of the bell smote the air, and announced the elevation of the host. The invalid seemed entranced in prayer. Her book had fallen beside her,—her hands were clasped,—her eyes closed,—her soul retired within its secret chambers. Then a more triumphant peal of bells arose. The tears gushed from her closed and swollen lids; her check was flushed she opened her dark eyes, and fixed them with an expression of deep adoration and penitence upon an image of the Saviour on the cross, which hung at the foot of her bed, and her lips again moved in prayer. Her countenance expressed the deepest resignation. She seemed to ask only that she might die in peace, and go to the bosom of her Redeemer.

The mother was kneeling by the window, with her face concealed in the folds of the curtain. She arose, and going to the bedside of her child threw her arms around her and burst into tears.

"My dear mother, I shall not live long; I feel it here. This piercing pain,—at times it seizes me, and I cannot—cannot breathe."

"My child, you will be better soon."

"Yes, mother, I shall be better soon. All tears, and pain, and sorrow will be over. The hymn of adoration and entreaty I have just heard, I shall never hear again on earth. Next Sunday, mother, kneel again by that window as to-day. I shall not be here, upon this bed of pain and sickness; but when you hear the solemn hymn of worship and the beseeching tones that wing the spirit up to God, think, mother, that I am there, with my sweet sister who has gone before us,—kneeling at our Saviour's feet, and happy,—oh, how happy!"

The afflicted mother made no reply; her heart was too full to speak.

"You remember, mother, how calmly Amie died. She was so young and beautiful! I always pray that I may die as she did. I do not fear death, as I did before she was taken from us. But, oh,—this pain,—this cruel pain!—it seems to draw my mind back from heaven. When it leaves me I shall die in peace."

"My poor child! God's holy will be done!"

The invalid soon sank into a quiet slumber. The excitement was over, and exhausted nature sought relief in sleep.

The persons between whom this scene passed were a widow and her sick daughter, from the neighborhood of Tours. They had left the banks of the Loire to consult the more experienced physicians of the metropolis, and had been directed to the *maison de santé* at Auteuil for the benefit of the pure air. But all in vain. The health of the uncomplaining patient grew worse and worse, and it soon became evident that the closing scene was drawing near.

Of this Jacqueline herself seemed conscious, and towards evening she expressed a wish to receive the last sacraments of the church. A priest was sent for, and erelong the tinkling of a little bell in the street announced his approach. He bore in his hand a silver chalice containing the consecrated wafer, and a small vessel filled with the holy oil of the extreme unction hung from his neck. Before him walked a boy carrying a little bell, whose sound announced the passing of these symbols of the Catholic faith. In the rear, a few of the villagers, bearing lighted wax tapers, formed a short and melancholy procession. They soon entered the sick-chamber, and the glimmer of the tapers mingled with the red light of the setting sun that shot his farewell rays through the open window. The vessel of oil and the silver chalice were placed upon the table in front of a crucifix that hung upon the wall, and all present, excepting the priest, threw themselves upon their knees. The priest then approached the bed of the dying girl, and said, in a slow and solemn tone,—

"The King of kings and Lord of lords has passed thy threshold. Is thy spirit ready to receive him?"

"It is, father."

"Hast thou confessed thy sins?"

"Holy father, no."

"Confess thyself, then, that thy sins may be forgiven, and thy name recorded in the book of life."

And, turning to the kneeling crowd around, he waved his hand for them to retire, and was left alone with the sick girl. He seated himself beside her pillow, and the subdued whisper of the confession mingled with the murmur of the evening air, which lifted the heavy folds of the curtains and stole in upon the holy scene. Poor Jacqueline had few sins to confess,—a secret thought or two towards the pleasures and delights of the world,—a wish to live, unuttered, but which, to the eye of her self-accusing spirit, seemed to resist the wise providence of God;—no more. The confession of a meek and lowly heart is soon made. The door was again opened; the attendants entered and knelt around the bed, and the priest proceeded,—

"And now prepare thyself to receive with contrite heart the body of our blessed Lord and Redeemer. Dost thou believe that our Lord Jesus Christ was conceived by the Holy Spirit, and born of the Virgin Mary?"

"I believe."

And all present joined in the solemn response,—

"I believe."

"Dost thou believe that the Father is God, that the Son is God, and that the Holy Spirit is God,—three persons and one God?"

"I believe."

"Dost thou believe that the Son is seated on the right hand of the Majesty on high, whence he shall come to judge the quick and the dead?"

"I believe."

"Dost thou believe that by the holy sacraments of the church thy sins are forgiven thee, and that thus thou art made worthy of eternal life?"

"I believe."

"Dost thou pardon, with all thy heart, all who have offended thee in thought, word, or deed?"

"I pardon them."

"And dost thou ask pardon of God and thy neighbor for all offences thou hast committed against them, either in thought, word, or deed?"

"I do."

"Then repeat after me,—O Lord Jesus, I am not worthy, nor do I merit, that thy divine majesty should enter this poor tenement of clay; but, according to thy holy promises, be my sins forgiven, and my soul washed white from all transgression."

Then, taking a consecrated wafer from the vase, he placed it between the lips of the dying girl, and, while the assistant sounded the little silver bell, said,—

"Corpus Domini nostri Jesu Christi custodiat animam tuam in vitam eternam."

And the kneeling crowd smote their breasts and responded in one solemn voice,—

"Amen!"

The priest then took a little golden rod, and, dipping it in holy oil, anointed the invalid upon the hands, feet, and breast in the form of the cross. When these ceremonies were completed the priest and his attendants retired, leaving the mother alone with her dying child, who, from the exhaustion caused by the preceding scene, sank into a death-like sleep.

> Between two worlds life hovered like a star,
> 'Twixt night and morn, upon the horizon's verge.

The long twilight of the summer evening stole on; the shadows deepened without, and the night-lamp glimmered feebly in the sick-chamber; but still she slept. She was lying with her hands clasped upon her breast,—her pallid cheek resting upon the pillow, and her bloodless lips apart, but motionless and silent as the sleep of death. Not a breath interrupted the silence of her slumber. Not a movement of the heavy and sunken eyelid, not a trembling of the lip, not a shadow on the marble brow, told when the spirit took its flight. It passed to a better world than this:—

> There's a perpetual spring,—perpetual youth;
> No joint-benumbing cold, nor scorching heat,
> Famine, nor age, have any being there.

The Sexagenarian

> Do you set down your name in the scroll of youth, that are written down old, with all the characters of age? Have you not a moist eye, a dry hand, a yellow cheek, a white beard, a decreasing leg?
>
> SHAKESPARE.

THERE he goes, in his long russet surtout, sweeping down yonder gravel-walk, beneath the trees, like a yellow leaf in autumn wafted along by a fitful gust of wind. Now he pauses,—now seems to be whirled round in an eddy,—and now rustles and brushes onward again. He is talking to himself in an undertone, as usual, and flourishes a pinch of snuff between his forefinger and his thumb, ever and anon drumming on the cover of his box, by way of emphasis, with a sound like the tap of a woodpecker. He always takes a morning walk in the garden,—in fact, I may say he passes the greater part of the day there, either strolling up and down the gravel-walks, or sitting on a rustic bench in one of the leafy arbors. He always wears that same dress, too; a bell-crowned hat, a frilled bosom, and white dimity waistcoat soiled with snuff,—light nankeen breeches, and, over all, that long and flowing surtout of russet-brown Circassian, hanging in wrinkles round his slender body, and toying with his thin, rakish legs. Such is his constant garb, morning and evening; and it gives him a cool and breezy look, even in the heat of a noonday in August.

The personage sketched in the preceding paragraph is Monsieur d'Argentville, a sexagenarian, with whom I became acquainted during my residence at the *maison de santé* of Auteuil. I found him there, and left him there. Nobody knew when he came,—he had been there from time immemorial; nor when he was going away,—for he himself did not know; nor what ailed him,—for though he was always complaining, yet he grew neither better nor worse, never consulted the physician, and ate voraciously three times a day. At table he was rather peevish, troubled his neighbors with his elbows, and uttered the monosyllable *pouah!* rather oftener than good-breeding and a due deference to the opinions of others seemed to justify. As soon as he seated himself at table, he breathed into his tumbler, and wiped it out with a napkin; then wiped his plate, his spoon, his knife and fork in succession, and each with great care. After this he placed the napkin under his chin; and, these preparations being completed, gave full swing to an appetite which was not inappropriately denominated, by one of our guests, *"une faim canine."*

The old gentleman's weak side was an affectation of youth and gallantry. Though "written down old, with all the characters of age," yet at times he seemed to think himself in the heyday of life; and the assiduous court he paid to a fair countess, who was passing the summer at the *maison de santé*, was the source of no little merriment to all but himself. He loved, too, to recall the golden age of his amours; and would discourse with prolix eloquence, and a faint twinkle in his watery eye, of his *bonnes fortunes* in times of old, and the rigors that many a fair dame had suffered on his account. Indeed, his chief pride seemed to be to make his hearers believe that he had been a dangerous man in his youth, and was not yet quite safe.

As I also was a peripatetic of the garden, we encountered each other at every turn. At first our conversation was limited to the usual salutations of the day, but erelong our casual acquaintance ripened into a kind of intimacy. Step by step I won my way,—first into his society,—then into his snuff-box,—and then into his heart. He was a great talker, and he found in me what he found in no other inmate of the house,—a good listener, who never interrupted his long stories, nor contradicted his opinions. So he talked down one alley and up another,—from breakfast till dinner,—from dinner till midnight,—at all times and in all places, when he could catch me by the button, till at last he had confided to my ear all the important and unimportant events of a life of sixty years.

Monsieur d'Argentville was a shoot from a wealthy family of Nantes. Just before the Revolution, he went up to Paris to study law at the University, and, like many other wealthy scholars of his age, was soon involved in the intrigues and dissipation of the metropolis. He first established himself in the Rue de l'Université; but a roguish pair of eyes at an opposite window soon drove from the field such heavy tacticians as Hugues Doneau and Gui Coquille. A flirtation was commenced in due form; and a flag of truce, offering to capitulate, was sent in the shape of a billet-doux. In the meantime he regularly amused his leisure hours by blowing kisses across the street with an old pair of bellows. One afternoon, as he was occupied in this way, a tall gentleman with whiskers stepped into the room, just as he had charged the bellows to the muzzle. He muttered something about an explanation,—his sister,—marriage,—and the satisfaction of a gentleman! Perhaps there is no situation in life so awkward to a man of real sensibility as that of being awed into matrimony or a duel by the whiskers of a tall brother. There was but one alternative; and the next morning a placard at the window of the Bachelor of Love, with the words "Furnished Apartment to Let," showed that the former occupant had found it convenient to change lodgings.

He next appeared in the Chaussée d'Antin, where he assiduously prepared himself for future exigencies by a course of daily lessons in the use of the small-sword. He soon after quarrelled with his best friend about a little actress on the Boulevard, and had the satisfaction of being jilted, and then run through the body at the Bois de Boulogne. This gave him new éclat in the fashionable world, and consequently he pursued pleasure with a keener relish than ever. He next had the *grande passion*, and narrowly escaped marrying an heiress of great expectations and a countless number of chateaux. Just before the catastrophe, however, he had the good fortune to discover that the lady's expectations were limited to his own pocket, and that, as for her chateaux, they were all Chateaux en Espagne.

About this time his father died, and the hopeful son was hardly well established in his inheritance when the Revolution broke out. Unfortunately he was a firm upholder of the divine right of kings, and had the honor of being among the first of the proscribed. He narrowly escaped the guillotine by jumping on board a vessel bound for America, and arrived at Boston with only a few francs in his pocket; but as he knew how to accommodate himself to circumstances, he contrived to live by teaching fencing and French, and keeping a dancing-school.

At the restoration of the Bourbons, he returned to France; and from that time to the day of our acquaintance had been engaged in a series of vexatious lawsuits, in the hope of recovering a portion of his property, which had been intrusted to a friend for safe-keeping at the commencement of the Revolution. His friend, however, denied all knowledge of the transaction, and the assignment was very difficult to prove. Twelve years of unsuccessful litigation had completely soured the old gentleman's temper, and made him peevish and misanthropic; and he had come to Auteuil merely to escape the noise of the city, and to brace his shattered nerves with pure air and quiet amusements. There he idled the time away, sauntering about the garden of the *maison de santé*, talking to himself when he could get no other listener, and occasionally reinforcing his misanthropy with a dose of the Maxims of La Rochefoucauld, or a visit to the scene of his duel in the Bois de Boulogne.

Poor Monsieur d'Argentville! What a miserable life he led,—or rather dragged on, from day to day! A petulant, broken-down old man, who had outlived his fortune, and his friends, and his hopes,—yea, everything but the sting of bad passions and the recollection of a life ill-spent! Whether he still walks the earth or slumbers in its bosom, I know not; but a lively recollection of him will always mingle with my reminiscences of Auteuil.

PÈRE LA CHAISE

> Our fathers find their graves in our short memories, and sadly tell us how we may be buried in our survivors.
>
> Oblivion is not to be hired. The greater part must be content to be as though they had not been,—to be found in the register of God, not in the record of man.
>
> SIR THOMAS BROWNE'S URN BURIAL.

THE cemetery of Père la Chaise is the Westminster Abbey of Paris. Both are the dwellings of the dead; but in one they repose in green alleys and beneath the open sky,—in the other their resting-place is in the shadowy aisle, and beneath the dim arches of an ancient abbey. One is a temple of nature; the other a temple of art. In one, the soft melancholy of the scene is rendered still more touching by the warble of birds and the shade of trees, and the grave receives the gentle visit of the sunshine and the shower: in the other, no sound but the passing footfall breaks the silence of the place; the twilight steals in through high and dusky windows; and the damps of the gloomy vault lie heavy on the heart, and leave their stain upon the mouldering tracery of the tomb.

Père la Chaise stands just beyond the Barrière d'Aulney, on a hillside looking towards the city. Numerous gravel-walks, winding through shady avenues and between marble monuments, lead up from the principal entrance to a chapel on the summit. There is hardly a grave that has not its little enclosure planted with shrubbery; and a thick mass of foliage half conceals each funeral stone. The sighing of the wind as the branches rise and fall upon it, the occasional note of a bird among the trees, and the shifting of light and shade upon the tombs beneath have a soothing effect upon the mind; and I doubt whether any one can enter that enclosure, where repose the dust and ashes of so many great and good men, without feeling the religion of the place steal over him, and seeing something of the dark and gloomy expression pass off from the stern countenance of death.

It was near the close of a bright summer afternoon that I visited this celebrated spot for the first time. The first object that arrested my attention, on entering, was a monument in the form of a small Gothic chapel, which stands near the entrance, in the avenue leading to the right hand. On the marble couch within are stretched two figures, carved in stone and dressed in the antique garb of the Middle Ages. It is the tomb of Abélard and Héloïse. The history of these unfortunate lovers is too well known to need recapitulation; but perhaps it is not so well known how often their ashes were disturbed in the slumber of the grave. Abélard died in the monastery of Saint Marcel, and was buried in the vaults of the church. His body afterwards was removed to the convent of the Paraclet, at the request of Héloïse, and at her death her own was deposited in the same tomb. Three centuries they reposed together; after which they were separated to different sides of the church, to calm the delicate scruples of the lady-abbess of the convent. More than a century afterward, they were again united in the same tomb; and when at length the Paraclet was destroyed, these mouldering remains were transported to the church of Nogent-sur-Seine. They were next deposited in an ancient cloister at Paris; and now repose near the gateway of the cemetery of Père la Chaise. What a singular destiny was theirs! that, after a life of such passionate and disastrous love,—such sorrows, and tears, and penitence,—their very dust should not he suffered to rest quietly in the grave!—that their death should so much resemble their life in its changes and vicissitudes, its partings and its meetings, its inquietudes and its persecutions!—that mistaken zeal should follow them down to the very tomb,—as if earthly passion could glimmer, like a funeral lamp, amid the damps of the charnel-house, and "even in their ashes burn their wonted fires!"

As I gazed on the sculptured forms before me, and the little chapel, whose Gothic roof seemed to protect their marble sleep, my busy memory swung back the dark portals of the past, and the picture of their sad and eventful lives came up before me in the gloomy distance. What a lesson for those who are endowed with the fatal gift of genius! It would seem, indeed, that He who "tempers the wind to the shorn lamb" tempers also his chastisements to the errors and infirmities of a weak and simple mind,—while the transgressions of him upon whose nature are more strongly marked the intellectual attributes of the Deity are followed, even upon earth, by severer tokens of the Divine displeasure. He who sins in the darkness of a benighted intellect sees not so clearly, through the shadows that surround him, the countenance of an offended God; but he who sins in the broad noonday of a clear and radiant mind, when at length the delirium of passion has subsided, and the cloud flits away from before the sun, trembles beneath the searching eye of that accusing power which is strong in the strength of a godlike intellect. Thus the mind and the heart are closely linked together, and the errors of genius bear with them their own chastisement, even upon earth. The history of Abélard and Héloïse is an illustration of this truth. But at length they sleep well. Their lives are like a tale that is told; their errors are "folded up like a book;" and what mortal hand shall break the seal that death has set upon them?

Leaving this interesting tomb behind me, I took a pathway to the left, which conducted me up the hillside. I soon found myself in the deep shade of heavy foliage, where the branches of the yew and willow mingled, interwoven with the tendrils and blossoms of the honeysuckle. I now stood in the most populous part of this city of tombs. Every step awakened a new train of thrilling recollections; for at every step my eye caught the name of some one whose glory had exalted the character of his native land, and resounded across the waters of the Atlantic. Philosophers, historians, musicians, warriors, and poets slept side by side around me; some beneath the gorgeous monument, and some beneath the simple headstone. But the political intrigue, the dream of science, the historical research, the ravishing harmony of sound, the tried courage, the inspiration of the lyre,—where are they? With the living, and not with the dead! The right hand has lost its cunning in the grave; but the soul, whose high volitions it obeyed, still lives to reproduce itself in ages yet to come.

Among these graves of genius I observed here and there a splendid monument, which had been raised by the pride of family over the dust of men who could lay no claim either to the gratitude or remembrance of posterity. Their presence seemed like an intrusion into the sanctuary of genius. What had wealth to do there? Why should it crowd the dust of the great? That was no thoroughfare of business,—no mart of gain! There were no costly banquets there; no silken garments, nor gaudy liveries, nor obsequious attendants! "What servants," says Jeremy Taylor, "shall we have to wait upon us in the grave? what friends to visit us? what officious people to cleanse away the moist and un wholesome cloud reflected upon our faces from the sides of the weeping vaults, which are the longest weepers for our funerals?" Material wealth gives a factitious superiority to the living, but the treasures of intellect give a real superiority to the dead; and the rich man, who would not deign to walk the street with the starving and penniless man of genius, deems it an honor, when death has redeemed the fame of the neglected, to have his own ashes laid beside him, and to claim with him the silent companionship of the grave.

I continued my walk through the numerous winding paths, as chance or curiosity directed me. Now I was lost in a little green hollow, overhung with thick-leaved shrubbery, and then came out upon an elevation, from which, through an opening in the trees, the eye caught glimpses of the city, and the little esplanade, at the foot of the hill, where the poor lie buried. There poverty hires its grave, and takes but a short lease of the narrow house. At the end of a few months, or at most of a few years, the tenant is dislodged to give place to another, and he in turn to a third. "Who," says Sir Thomas Browne, "knows the fate of his bones, or how often he is to be buried? Who hath the oracle of his ashes, or whither they are to be scattered?"

Yet, even in that neglected corner, the hand of affection had been busy in decorating the hired house. Most of the graves were surrounded with a slight wooden paling, to secure them from the passing footstep; there was hardly one so deserted as not to be marked with its little wooden cross, and decorated with a garland of flowers; and here and there I could perceive a solitary mourner, clothed in black, stooping to plant a shrub on the grave, or sitting in a motionless sorrow beside it.

As I passed on, amid the shadowy avenues of the cemetery, I could not help comparing my own impressions with those which others have felt when walking alone among the dwellings of the dead. Are, then, the sculptured urn and storied monument nothing more than symbols of family pride? Is all I see around me a memorial of the living more than of the dead, an empty show of sorrow which thus vaunts itself in mournful pageant and funeral parade? Is it indeed true, as some have said, that the simple wild-flower, which springs spontaneously upon the grave, and the rose, which the hand of affection plants there, are fitter objects wherewith to adorn the narrow house? No! I feel that it is not so! Let the good and the great be honored even in the grave. Let the sculptured marble direct our footsteps to the scene of their long sleep;

let the chiselled epitaph repeat their names, and tell us where repose the nobly good and wise! It is not true that all are equal in the grave. There is no equality even there. The mere handful of dust and ashes,—the mere distinction of prince and beggar,—of a rich winding—sheet and a shroudless burial,—of a solitary grave and a family vault,—were this all,—then, indeed, it would be true that death is a common leveller. Such paltry distinctions as those of wealth and poverty are soon levelled by the spade and mattock; the damp breath of the grave blots them out forever. But there are other distinctions which even the mace of death cannot level or obliterate. Can it break down the distinction of virtue and vice? Can it confound the good with the bad? the noble with the base? all that is truly great, and pure, and godlike, with all that is scorned, and sinful, and degraded? No! Then death is not a common leveller! Are all alike beloved in death and honored in their burial? Is that ground holy where the bloody hand of the murderer sleeps from crime? Does every grave awaken the same emotions in our hearts? and do the footsteps of the stranger pause as long beside each funeral-stone? No! Then all are not equal in the grave! And as long as the good and evil deeds of men live after them, so long will there be distinctions even in the grave. The superiority of one over another is in the nobler and better emotions which it excites; in its more fervent admonitions to virtue; in the livelier recollections which it awakens of the good and the great, whose bodies are crumbling to dust beneath our feet!

If, then, there are distinctions in the grave, surely it is not unwise to designate them by the external marks of honor. These outward appliances and memorials of respect,—the mournful urn,—the sculptured bust, the epitaph eloquent in praise,—cannot indeed create these distinctions, but they serve to mark them. It is only when pride or wealth builds them to honor the slave of mammon or the slave of appetite, when the voice from the grave rebukes the false and pompous epitaph, and the dust and ashes of the tomb seem struggling to maintain the superiority of mere worldly rank, and to carry into the grave the bawbles of earthly vanity,—it is then, and then only, that we feel how utterly worthless are all the devices of sculpture, and the empty pomp of monumental brass!

After rambling leisurely about for some time, reading the inscriptions on the various monuments which attracted my curiosity, and giving way to the different reflections they suggested, I sat down to rest myself on a sunken tombstone. A winding gravel-walk, overshaded by an avenue of trees, and lined on both sides with richly sculptured monuments, had gradually conducted me to the summit of the hill, upon whose slope the cemetery stands. Beneath me in the distance, and dim-discovered through the misty and smoky atmosphere of evening, rose the countless roofs and spires of the city. Beyond, throwing his level rays athwart the dusky landscape, sank the broad red sun. The distant murmur of the city rose upon my ear, and the toll of the evening bell came up, mingled with the rattle of the paved street and the confused sounds of labor. What an hour for meditation! What a contrast between the metropolis of the living and the metropolis of the dead! I could not help calling to my mind that allegory of mortality, written by a hand which has been many a long year cold:—

Earth goeth upon earth as man upon mould,
Like as earth upon earth never go should,
Earth goeth upon earth as glistening gold,
And yet shall earth unto earth rather than he would.

Lo, earth on earth, consider thou may,
How earth cometh to earth naked alway,
Why shall earth upon earth go stout or gay,
Since earth out of earth shall pass in poor array.[3]

---

[3] I subjoin this relic of old English verse entire, and in its antiquated language, for those of my readers who may have antiquarian taste. It is copied from a book whose title I have forgotten, and of which I have but a single leaf, containing the poem. In describing the antiquities of the church of Stratford-upon-Avon, the writer gives the following account of a very old painting upon the wall, and of the poem which served as its motto. The painting is no longer visible, having been effaced in repairing the church.

"Against the west wall of the nave, on the south side of the arch, was painted the martyrdom of Thomas-à-Becket, while kneeling at the altar of St. Benedict in Canterbury cathedral; below this was the figure of an angel, probably St. Michael, supporting a long scroll, upon which were seven stanzas in old English, being an allegory of mortality:—

Erthe outs of Erthe ys wondurly wroght
Erth hath gotyn uppon erth a dygnyte of noght

Before I left the graveyard the shades of evening had fallen, and the objects around me grown dim and indistinct. As I passed the gateway, I turned to take a parting look. I could distinguish only the chapel on the summit of the hill, and here and there a lofty obelisk of snow-white marble, rising from the black and heavy mass of foliage around, and pointing upward to the gleam of the departed sun, that still lingered in the sky, and mingled with the soft starlight of a summer evening.

Erth ypon erth sett all hys thowht
How erth apon erth may be hey browght

Erth apon erth wold be a kyng
But how that erth got to erth he thyngkys nothyng
When erth byddys erth hys rentys whom bryng
Then schall erth apon erth have a hard ptyng

Erth apon erth wynnys castellys and towrys
Then seth erth unto erth thys ys all owrys
When erth upon erth hath bylde hys bowrys
Then schall erth for erth suffur many hard schowrys

Erth goth apon erth as man apon mowld
Lyke as erth apon erth never goo schold
Erth goth apon erth as gelsteryng gold
And yet schall erth unto erth rather than he wold

Why that erth loveth erth wondur me thynke
Or why that erth wold for erth other swett or swynke
When erth apon erth ys broght wt. yn the brynke
Than schall erth apon erth have a fowl stynke

Lo erth on erth consedur thow may
How erth comyth to erth nakyd all way
Why schall erth apon erth goo stowte or gay
Seth erth owt of erth schall passe yn poor aray

I counsill erth apon erth that ys wondurly wrogt
The whyl yt. erth ys apon erth to torne hys thowht
And pray to god upon erth yt. all erth wroght
That all crystyn soullys to ye. blys may be broght

"Beneath were two men, holding a scroll over a body wrapped in a winding-sheet, and covered with some emblems of mortality," etc.

The Valley of the Loire

Je ne conçois qu'nne manière do voyager plus agréable que d'aller à cheval; c'est d'aller à pied. On part à son moment, on s'arrfite à sa volonté, on fait tant et si peu d'exercise qu'on veut.

Quand on ne veut qu'arriver, on peut courir en chaise de poste; mais quand on veut voyager, il faut aller à pied.

ROUSSEAU.

IN the beautiful month of October, I made a foot excursion along the banks of the Loire, from Orléans to Tours. This luxuriant region is justly called the garden of France. From Orléans to Blois, the whole valley of the Loire is one continued vineyard. The bright green foliage of the vine spreads, like the undulations of the sea, over all the landscape, with here and there a silver flash of the river, a sequestered hamlet, or the towers of an old chateau, to enliven and variegate the scene.

The vintage had already commenced. The peasantry were busy in the fields,—the song that cheered their labor was on the breeze, and the heavy wagon tottered by, laden with the clusters of the vine. Everything around me wore that happy look which makes the heart glad. In the morning I arose with the lark, and at night I slept where sunset overtook me. The healthy exercise of foot-travelling, the pure, bracing air of autumn, and the cheerful aspect of the whole landscape about me, gave fresh elasticity to a mind not overburdened with care, and made me forget not only the fatigue of walking, but also the consciousness of being alone.

My first day's journey brought me at evening to a village, whose name I have forgotten, situated about eight leagues from Orléans. It is a small, obscure hamlet, not mentioned in the guide-book, and stands upon the precipitous banks of a deep ravine, through which a noisy brook leaps down to turn the ponderous wheel of a thatch-roofed mill. The village inn stands upon the highway, but the village itself is not visible to the traveller as he passes. It is completely hidden in the lap of a wooded valley, and so embowered in trees that not a roof nor a chimney peeps out to betray its hiding place. It is like the nest of a ground-swallow, which the passing footstep almost treads upon, and yet it is not seen. I passed by without suspecting that a village was near, and the little inn had a look so uninviting that I did not even enter it.

After proceeding a mile or two farther, I perceived, upon my left, a village spire rising over the vineyards. Towards this I directed my footsteps, but it seemed to recede as I advanced, and at last quite disappeared. It was evidently many miles distant; and as the path I followed descended from the highway, it had gradually sunk beneath a swell of the vine-clad landscape. I now found myself in the midst of an extensive vine-yard. It was just sunset, and the last golden rays lingered on the rich and mellow scenery around me. The peasantry were still busy at their task, and the occasional bark of a dog and the distant sound of an evening bell gave fresh romance to the scene. The reality of many a day-dream of childhood, of many a poetic revery of youth, was before me. I stood at sunset amid the luxuriant vineyards of France!

The first person I met was a poor old woman, a little bowed down with age, gathering grapes into a large basket. She was dressed like the poorest class of peasantry, and pursued her solitary task alone, heedless of the cheerful gossip and the merry laugh which came from a band of more youthful vintagers at a short distance from her. She was so intently engaged in her work that she did not perceive my approach until I bade her good-evening. On hearing my voice, she looked up from her labor and returned the salutation; and, on my asking her if there were a tavern or a farm-house in the neighborhood where I could pass the night, she showed me the pathway through the vineyard that led to the village, and then added, with a look of curiosity,—

"You must be a stranger, sir, in these parts."

"Yes; my home is very far from here."

"How far?"

"More than a thousand leagues."

The old woman looked incredulous.

"I came from a distant land beyond the sea."

"More than a thousand leagues!" at length repeated she; "and why have you come so far from home?"

"To travel;—to see how you live in this country."

"Have you no relations in your own?"

"Yes; I have both brothers and sisters, a father and"—

"And a mother?"

"Thank Heaven, I have."

"And did you leave *her*?"

Here the old woman gave me a piercing look of reproof, shook her head mournfully, and, with a deep sigh, as if some painful recollections had been awakened in her bosom, turned again to her solitary task. I felt rebuked, for there is something almost prophetic in the admonitions of the old. The eye of age looks meekly into my heart! the voice of age echoes mournfully through it! the hoary head and palsied hand of age plead irresistibly for its sympathies! I venerate old age, and I love not the man who can look without emotion upon the sunset of life, when the dusk of evening begins to gather over the watery eye, and the shadows of twilight grow broader and deeper upon the understanding!

I pursued the pathway which led towards the village, and the next person I encountered was an old man, stretched lazily beneath the vines upon a little strip of turf, at a point where four paths met, forming a crossway in the vineyard. He was clad in a coarse garb of gray, with a pair of long gaiters or spatter-dashes. Beside him lay a blue cloth cap, a staff, and an old weather-beaten knap sack. I saw at once that he was a foot-traveller like myself, and therefore, without more ado, entered into conversation with him. From his language, and the peculiar manner in which he now and then wiped his upper lip with the back of his hand, as if in search of the mustache which was no longer there, I judged that he had been a soldier. In this opinion I was not mistaken. He had served under Napoleon, and had followed the imperial eagle across the Alps, and the Pyrenees, and the burning sands of Egypt. Like every *vieille moustache*, he spake with enthusiasm of the Little Corporal, and cursed the English, the Germans, the Spanish, and every other race on earth, except the Great Nation,—his own.

"I like," said he, "after a long day's march, to lie down in this way upon the grass, and enjoy the cool of the evening. It reminds me of the bivouacs of other days, and of old friends who are now up there."

Here he pointed with his finger to the sky.

“They have reached the last *étape* before me, in the long march. But I shall go soon. We shall all meet again at the last roll-call. *Sacré nom de*—! There’s a tear!”

He wiped it away with his sleeve.

Here our colloquy was interrupted by the approach of a group of vintagers, who were returning homeward from their labor. To this party I joined myself, and invited the old soldier to do the same; but he shook his head.

“I thank you; my pathway lies in a different direction.”

“But there is no other village near, and the sun has already set.”

“No matter, I am used to sleeping on the ground. Good-night.”

I left the old man to his meditations, and walked on in company with the vintagers. Following a well-trodden pathway through the vine yards, we soon descended the valley’s slope, and I suddenly found myself in the bosom of one of those little hamlets from which the laborer rises to his toil as the skylark to his song. My companions wished me a good-night, as each entered his own thatch-roofed cottage, and a little girl led me out to the very in which an hour or two before I had disdained to enter.

When I awoke in the morning, a brilliant autumnal sun was shining in at my window. The merry song of birds mingled sweetly with the sound of rustling leaves and the gurgle of the brook. The vintagers were going forth to their toil; the wine-press was busy in the shade, and the clatter of the mill kept time to the miller’s song. I loitered about the village with a feeling of calm delight. I was unwilling to leave the seclusion of this sequestered hamlet; but at length, with reluctant step, I took the cross-road through the vineyard, and in a moment the little village had sunk again, as if by enchantment, into the bosom of the earth.

I breakfasted at the town of Mer; and, leaving the high-road to Blois on the right, passed down to the banks of the Loire, through a long, broad avenue of poplars and sycamores. I crossed the river in a boat, and in the after part of the day I found myself before the high and massive walls of the chateau of Chambord. This chateau is one of the finest specimens of the ancient Gothic castle to be found in Europe. The little river Cosson fills its deep and ample moat, and above it the huge towers and heavy battlements rise in stem and solemn grandeur, moss-grown with age, and blackened by the storms of three centuries. Within, all is mournful and deserted. The grass has overgrown the pavement of the courtyard, and the rude sculpture upon the walls is broken and defaced. From the courtyard I entered the central tower, and, ascending the principal staircase, went out upon the battlements. I seemed to have stepped back into the precincts of the feudal ages; and, as I passed along through echoing corridors and vast, deserted halls, stripped of their furniture and mouldering silently away, the distant past came back upon me; and the times when the clang of arms, and the tramp of mail-clad men, and the sounds of music and revelry and wassail, echoed along those high-vaulted and solitary chambers!

My third day's journey brought me to the ancient city of Blois, the chief town of the department of Loire-et-Cher. This city is celebrated for the purity with which even the lower classes of its inhabitants speak their native tongue. It rises precipitously from the northern bank of the Loire, and many of its streets are so steep as to be almost impassable for carriages. On the brow of the hill, overlooking the roofs of the city, and commanding a fine view of the Loire and its noble bridge, and the surrounding country sprinkled with cottages and chateaux, runs an ample terrace, planted with trees and laid out as a public walk. The view from this terrace is one of the most beautiful in France. But what most strikes the eye of the traveller at Blois is an old, though still unfinished castle. Its huge parapets of hewn stone stand upon either side of the street; but they have walled up the wide gateway, from which the colossal drawbridge was to have sprung high in air, connecting together the main towers of the building, and the two hills upon whose slope its foundations stand. The aspect of this vast pile is gloomy and desolate. It seems as if the strong hand of the builder had been arrested in the midst of his task by the stronger hand of death; and the unfinished fabric stands a lasting monument both of the power and weakness of man,—of his vast de sires, his sanguine hopes, his ambitious purposes,—and of the unlooked-for conclusion, where all these desires and hopes and purposes are so often arrested. There is also at Blois another ancient chateau, to which some historic interest is attached, as being the scene of the massacre of the Duke of Guise.

On the following day, I left Blois for Amboise, and, after walking several leagues along the dusty highway, crossed the river in a boat to the little village of Moines, which lies amid luxuriant vineyards upon the southern bank of the Loire. From Moines to Amboise the road is truly delightful. The rich lowland scenery, by the margin of the river, is verdant even in October; and occasionally the landscape is diversified with the picturesque cottages of the vintagers, cut in the rock along the road side, and overhung by the thick foliage of the vines above them.

At Amboise I took a cross-road, which led me to the romantic borders of the Cher and the chateau of Chenonceau. This beautiful chateau, as well as that of Chambord, was built by the gay and munificent Francis the First. One is a specimen of strong and massive architecture,—a dwelling for a warrior; but the other is of a lighter and more graceful construction, and was destined for those soft languishments of passion with which the fascinating Diane de Poitiers had filled the bosom of that voluptuous monarch.

The chateau of Chenonceau is built upon arches across the river Cher, whose waters are made to supply the deep moat at each extremity. There is a spacious courtyard in front, from which a draw-bridge conducts to the outer hall of the castle. There the armor of Francis the First still hangs upon the wall,—his shield and helm and lance,—as if the chivalrous prince had just exchanged them for the silken robes of the drawing-room. From this hall a door opens into a long gallery, extending the whole length of the building across the Cher. The walls of the gallery are hung with the faded portraits of the long line of the descendants of Hugh Capet; and the windows, looking up and down the stream, command a fine reach of pleasant river scenery. This is said to be the only chateau in France in which the ancient furniture of its original age is preserved. In one part of the building you are shown the bed-chamber of Diane de Poitiers, with its antique chairs covered with faded damask and embroidery, her bed, and a portrait of the royal favorite hanging over the mantelpiece. In another you see the apartment of the infamous Catherine de' Medici; a venerable arm-chair and an autograph letter of Henry the Fourth; and in an old laboratory, among broken crucibles, and neckless retorts, and drums, and trumpets, and skins of wild beasts, and other ancient lumber, of various kinds, are to be seen the bed-posts of Francis the First! Doubtless the naked walls and the vast solitary chambers of an old and desolate chateau inspire a feeling of greater solemnity and awe; but when the antique furniture of the olden time remains,—the faded tapestry on the walls, and the arm-chair by the fireside,—the effect upon the mind is more magical and delightful. The old inhabitants of the place, long gathered to their fathers, though living still in history, seem to have left their halls for the chase or the tournament; and, as the heavy door swings upon its reluctant hinge, one almost expects to see the gallant princes and courtly dames enter those halls again, and sweep in stately procession along the silent corridors.

Rapt in such fancies as these, and gazing on the beauties of this noble edifice and the soft scenery around it, I lingered, unwilling to depart, till the rays of the setting sun, streaming through the dusty windows, admonished me that the day was drawing rapidly to a close. I sallied forth from the southern gate of the chateau, and crossing the broken drawbridge, pursued a pathway along the bank of the river, still gazing back upon those towering walls, now bathed in the rich glow of sunset, till a turn in the road and a clump of woodland at length shut them out from my sight.

A short time after candle-lighting, I reached the little tavern of the Boule d'Or, a few leagues from Tours, where I passed the night. The following morning was lowering and sad. A veil of mist hung over the landscape, and ever and anon a heavy shower burst from the overburdened clouds, that were driving by before a high and piercing wind. This unpropitious state of the weather detained me until noon, when a cabriolet for Tours drove up; and taking a seat within it, I left the hostess of the Boule d'Or in the middle of a long story about a rich countess, who always alighted there when she passed that way. We drove leisurely along through a beautiful country, till at length we came to the brow of a steep hill which commands a fine view of the city of Tours and its delightful environs. But the scene was shrouded by the heavy drifting mist, through which I could trace but indistinctly the graceful sweep of the Loire and the spires and roofs of the city far below me.

The city of Tours and the delicious plain in which it lies have been too often described by other travellers to render a new description, from so listless a pen as mine, either necessary or desirable. After a sojourn of two cloudy and melancholy days, I set out on my return to Paris, by the way of Vendôme and Chartres. I stopped a few hours at the former place, to examine the ruins of a chateau built by Jeanne d'Albret, mother of Henry the Fourth. It stands upon the summit of a high and precipitous hill, and almost overhangs the town beneath. The French Revolution has completed the ruin that time had already begun; and nothing now remains but a broken and crumbling bastion, and here and there a solitary tower dropping slowly to decay. In one of these is the grave of Jeanne d'Albret. A marble entablature in the wall above contains the inscription, which is nearly effaced, though enough still remains to tell the curious traveller that there lies buried the mother of the "Bon Henri." To this is added a prayer that the repose of the dead may be respected.

Here ended my foot excursion. The object of my journey was accomplished; and, delighted with this short ramble through the valley of the Loin, I took my seat in the diligence for Paris, and on the following day was again swallowed up in the crowds of the metropolis, like a drop in the bosom of the sea.

THE TROUVÈRES

Quant recommence et revient biaux estez,
  Que foille et flor resplendit par boschage,
Que li froiz tanz de l'hyver est passez,
  Et cil oisel chantent en lor langage,
    Lors chanterai
    Et envoisiez serai
    De cuer vorai.

JAQUES DE CHISON.

THE literature of France is peculiarly rich in poetry of the olden time. We can trace up the stream of song until it is lost in the deepening shadows of the Middle Ages. Even there it is not a shallow tinkling rill; but it comes like a mountain stream, rushing and sounding onward through the enchanted regions of romance, and mingles its voice with the tramp of steeds and the brazen sound of arms.

The glorious reign of Charlemagne,[4] at the close of the eighth and the commencement of the ninth century, seems to have breathed a spirit of learning as well as of chivalry throughout all France. The monarch established

---

[4] The following amusing description of this Restorer of Letters, as his biographers call him, is taken from the fabulous *Chronicle of John Turpin*, chap. xx.

"The Emperor was of a ruddy complexion, with brown hair; of a well-made, handsome form, but a stern visage. His height was about eight of his own feet, which were very long. He was of a strong, robust make; his legs and thighs very stout, and his sinews firm. His face was thirteen inches long; his beard a palm; his nose half a palm; his forehead a foot over. His lion-like eyes flashed fire like carbuncles his eyebrows were half a palm over. When he was angry, it was a terror to look upon him. He required eight spans for his girdle beside what hung loose. He ate sparingly of bread but a whole quarter of lamb, two fowls, a goose, or a large portion of pork; a peacock, a crane, or a whole hare. He drank moderately of wine and water. He was so strong that he could at a single blow cleave asunder an armed soldier on horseback, from the head to the waist, and the horse likewise. He easily vaulted over four horses harnessed together; and could raise an armed man from the ground to his head, as he stood erect upon his hand."

schools and academies in different parts of his realm, and took delight in the society and conversation of learned men. It is amusing to see with what evident self-satisfaction some of the magi whom he gathered around him speak of their exertions in widening the sphere of human knowledge, and pouring in light upon the darkness of their age. "For some," says Alcuin, the director of the school of St. Martin de Tours, "I cause the honey of the Holy Scriptures to flow; I intoxicate others with the old wine of ancient history; these I nourish with the fruits of grammar, gathered by my own hands; and those I enlighten by pointing out to them the stars, like lamps attached by the vaulted ceiling of a great palace!"

Besides this classic erudition of the schools, the age had also its popular literature. Those who were untaught in scholastic wisdom were learned in traditionary lore; for they had their ballads, in which were described the valor and achievements of the early kings of the Franks. These ballads, of which a collection was made by order of Charlemagne, animated the rude soldier as he rushed to battle, and were sung in the midnight bivouacs of the camp. "Perhaps it is not too much to say," observes the literary historian Schlegel, "that we have still in our possession, if not the original language and form, at least the substance, of many of those ancient poems which were collected by the orders of that prince;—I refer to the Nibelungenlied, and the collection which goes by the name of the Heldenbuch."

When at length the old Tudesque language, which was the court language of Charlemagne, had given place to the Langue d'Oil, the northern dialect of the French Romance, these ancient ballads passed from the memories of the descendants of the Franks, and were succeeded by the romances of Charlemagne and his Twelve Peers,—of Rowland, and Olivir, and the other paladins who died at Roncesvalles. Robert Wace, a Norman Trouvère of the twelfth century, says in one of his poems that a minstrel named Taillefer, mounted on a swift horse, went in front of the Norman army at the battle of Hastings, singing these ancient poems.

These *Chansons de Geste*, or old historic romances of France, are epic in their character, though, without doubt, they were written to be chanted to the sound of an instrument. To what period many of them belong, in their present form, has never yet been fully determined; and should it finally be proved by philological research that they can claim no higher antiquity than the twelfth or thirteenth century, still there can be little doubt that in their original form many of them reached far back into the ninth or tenth. The long prevalent theory, that the romances of the Twelve Peers of France all originated in the fabulous chronicle of Charlemagne and Rowland, written by the Archbishop Turpin in the twelfth century, if not as yet generally exploded, is nevertheless fast losing ground.

To the twelfth and thirteenth centuries also belong most of the Fabliaux, or metrical tales of the Trouvères. Many of these compositions are remarkable for the inventive talent they display, but as poems they have, generally speaking, little merit, and at times exhibit such a want of refinement, such open and gross obscenity, as to be highly offensive.

It is a remarkable circumstance in the literary history of France that, while her antiquarians and scholars have devoted themselves to collecting and illustrating the poetry of the Troubadours, the early lyric poets of the South, that of the Trouvères, or the Troubadours of the North, has been almost entirely neglected. By a singular fatality, too, what little time and attention have hitherto been bestowed upon the fathers of French poetry have been so directed as to save from oblivion little of the most valuable portions of their writings; while the more tedious and worthless parts have been brought forth to the public eye, as if to deaden curiosity and put an end to further research. The ancient historic romances of the land have, for the most part, been left to slumber unnoticed; while the lewd and tiresome Fabliaux have been ushered into the world as fair specimens of the ancient poetry of France. This has created unjust prejudices in the minds of many against the literature of the olden time, and has led them to regard it as nothing more than a confused mass of coarse and vulgar fictions, adapted to a rude and inelegant state of society.

Of late, however, a more discerning judgment has been brought to the difficult task of ancient research; and, in consequence of this, the long established prejudices against the crumbling monuments of the national literature of France during the Middle Ages is fast disappearing. Several learned men are engaged in rescuing from oblivion the ancient poetic romances of Charlemagne and the Twelve Peers of France, and their labors seem destined to throw new light, not only upon the state of literature, but upon the state of society, during the twelfth and thirteenth centuries.

Among the voluminous remains of Troubadour literature, little else has yet been discovered than poems of a lyric character. The lyre of the Troubadour seems to have responded to the impulse of momentary feelings only,—to the touch of local and transitory circumstances. His song was a sudden burst of excited feeling;—it ceased when the passion was subdued, or rather when its first feverish excitement passed away; and, as the liveliest feelings are the most transitory, the songs which embodied them are short, but full of spirit and energy. On the other hand, the great mass of the poetry of the Trouvères is of a narrative or epic character. The genius of the North seems always to have delighted in romantic fiction; and whether we attribute the origin of modern romance to the Arabians or to the Scandinavians, this at least is certain, that there existed marvellous tales in the Northern languages, and from these, in part at least, the Trouvères imbibed the spirit of narrative poetry. There are no traces of lyric compositions among their writings till about the commencement of the thirteenth century; and it seems probable that the spirit of song-writing was imbibed from the Troubadours of the South.

Unfortunately, the neglect which has so long attended the old historic and heroic romances of the North of France has also befallen in some degree its early lyric poetry. Little has yet been done to discover and bring forth its riches; and doubtless many a sweet little ballad and melancholy complaint lies buried in the dust of the thirteenth century. It is not, however, my object, in this paper, to give an historical sketch of this ancient and almost forgotten poetry, but simply to bring forward a few specimens which shall exhibit its most striking and obvious characteristics.

In these examples it would be in vain to look for high-wrought expression suited to the prevailing taste of the present day. Their most striking peculiarity, and perhaps their greatest merit, consists in the simple and direct expression of feeling which they contain. This feeling, too, is one which breathes the languor of that submissive homage which was paid to beauty in the days of chivalry; and I am aware that, in this age of masculine and matter of fact thinking, the love conceits of a more poetic state of society are generally looked upon as extremely trivial and puerile. Nevertheless I shall venture to present one or two of these simple poems, which, by recalling the distant age wherein they were composed, may peradventure please by the power of contrast.

I have just remarked that one of the greatest beauties of these ancient ditties is *naïveté* of thought and simplicity of expression. These I shall endeavor to preserve as far as possible in the translation, though I am fully conscious how much the sparkling beauty of an original loses in being filtered through the idioms of a foreign language.

The favorite theme of the ancient lyric poets of the North of France is the wayward passion of love. They all delight to sing *"les douces dolors et li mal plaisant define amor."* With such feelings the beauties of the opening spring are naturally associated. Almost every love-ditty of the old poets commences with some such exordium as this: "When the snows of winter have passed away, when the soft and gentle spring returns, and the flower and leaf shoot in the groves, and the little birds warble to their mates in their own sweet language,—then will I sing my lady-love!"

Another favorite introduction to these little rhapsodies of romantic passion is the approach of morning and its sweet-voiced herald, the lark. The minstrel's song to his lady-love frequently commences with an allusion to the hour.

When the rosebud opes its een,
  And the bluebells droop and die,
And upon the leaves so green
  Sparkling dew-drops lie.

The following is at once the simplest and prettiest piece of this kind which I have met with among the early lyric poets of the North of France. It is taken from an anonymous poem, entitled "The Paradise of Love." A lover, having passed the "livelong night in tears, as he was wont," goes forth to beguile his sorrows with the fragrance and beauty of morning. The carol of the vaulting skylark salutes his ear, and to this merry musician he makes his complaint.

  Hark! Hark!
  Pretty lark!
Little heedest thou my pain!
But if to these longing arms
Pitying Love would yield the charms
  Of the fair
  With smiling air,
Blithe would beat my heart again.

Hark! hark!
Pretty lark!
Little heedest thou my pain!
Love may force me still to bear,
While he lists, consuming care;
But in anguish,
Though I languish,
Faithful shall my heart remain.

Hark! hark!
Pretty lark!
Little heedest thou my pain!
Then cease, Love, to torment me so;
But rather than all thoughts forego
Of the fair
With flaxen hair,
Give me back her frowns again.

Hark! hark!
Pretty lark!
Little heedest thou my pain!

Besides the "woful ballad made to his mistress's eyebrow," the early lyric poet frequently indulges in more calmly analyzing the philosophy of love, or in questioning the object and destination of a sigh. Occasionally these quaint conceits are prettily expressed, and the little song flutters through the page like a butterfly. The following is an example:—

And whither goest thou, gentle sigh,
Breathed so softly in my ear?
Say, dost thou bear his fate severe
To Love's poor martyr doomed to die?
Come, tell me quickly,—do not lie;
What secret message bring'st thou here?
And whither goest thou, gentle sigh,
Breathed so softly in my ear?

May Heaven conduct thee to thy will,
And safely speed thee on thy way;

This only I would humbly pray,—
Pierce deep,—but oh! forbear to kill.
And whither goest thou, gentle sigh,
Breathed so softly in my ear?

The ancient lyric poets of France are generally spoken of as a class, and their beauties and defects referred to them collectively, and not individually. In truth, there are few characteristic marks by which any individual author can be singled out and ranked above the rest. The lyric poets of the thirteenth and fourteenth centuries stand upon nearly the same level. But in the fifteenth century there were two who surpassed all their contemporaries in the beauty and delicacy of their sentiments; and in the sweetness of their diction, and the structure of their verse, stand far in advance of the age in which they lived. These are Charles d'Orléans and Clotilde de Surville.

Charles, Duke of Orléans, the father of Louis the Twelfth, and uncle of Francis the First, was born in 1391. In the general tenor of his life, the peculiar character of his mind, and his talent for poetry, there is a striking resemblance between this noble poet and James the First of Scotland, his contemporary. Both were remarkable for learning and refinement; both passed a great portion of their lives in sorrow and imprisonment; and both cheered the solitude of their prison-walls with the charms of poetry. Charles d'Orléans was taken prisoner at the battle of Agincourt, in 1415, and carried into England, where he remained twenty-five years in captivity. It was there that he composed the greater part of his poetry.

The poems of this writer exhibit a singular delicacy of thought and sweetness of expression. The following little *Renouveaux*, or songs on the return of spring, are full of delicacy and beauty.

Now Time throws off his cloak again
Of ermined frost, and wind, and rain,
And clothes him in the embroidery
Of glittering sun and clear blue sky.
With beast and bird the forest rings,
Each in his jargon cries or sings;
And Time throws off his cloak again
Of ermined frost, and wind, and rain.

River, and fount, and tinkling brook
Wear in their dainty livery
Drops of silver jewelry;
In new-made suit they merry look;
And Time throws off his cloak again
Of ermined frost, and wind, and rain.

The second upon the same subject presents a still more agreeable picture of the departure of winter and the return of spring.

Gentle spring!—in sunshine clad,
 Well dost thou thy power display!
For winter maketh the light heart sad,
 And thou,—thou makest the sad heart gay.
He sees thee, and calls to his gloomy train,
The sleet, and the snow, and the wind, and the rain;
And they shrink away, and they flee in fear,
 When thy merry step draws near.

Winter giveth the fields and the trees so old
 Their beards of icicles and snow;
And the rain, it raineth so fast and cold,
 We must cower over the embers low;
And, snugly housed from the wind and weather,
Mope like birds that are changing feather.
But the storm retires, and the sky grows clear,
 When thy merry step draws near.

Winter maketh the sun in the gloomy sky
 Wrap him round in a mantle of cloud;
But, Heaven be praised, thy step is nigh;
 Thou tearest away the mournful shroud,
And the earth looks bright,—and winter surly,
Who has toiled for naught both late and early,
Is banished afar by the new-born year,
 When thy merry step draws near.

The only person of that age who can dispute the laurel with Charles d'Orléans is Clotilde de Surville. This poetess was born In the Bas Vivarais, in the year 1405. Her style is singularly elegant and correct; and the reader who will take the trouble to decipher her rude provincial orthography will find her writings full of quiet beauty. The following lines, which breathe the very soul of maternal tenderness, are part of a poem to her first-born.

Sweet babe! true portrait of thy father's face,
  Sleep on the bosom that thy lips have pressed!
Sleep, little one; and closely, gently place
  Thy drowsy eyelid on thy mother's breast!

Upon that tender eye, my little friend,
  Soft sleep shall come that cometh not to me!
I watch to see thee, nourish thee, defend;—
  'T is sweet to watch for thee,—alone for thee!

His arms fall down; sleep sits upon his brow;
  His eye is closed; he sleeps,—how still and calm!
Wore not his cheek the apple's ruddy glow,
  Would you not say he slept on Death's cold arm?

Awake, my boy!—I tremble with affright!
  Awake, and chase this fatal thought!—unclose
Thine eye but for one moment on the light!
  Even at the price of thine, give me repose!

Sweet error!—he but slept;—I breathe again;
  Come, gentle dream, the hour of sleep beguile!
Oh, when shall he for whom I sigh in vain
  Beside me watch to see thy waking smile?

But upon this theme I have written enough, perhaps too much.

"This may be poetry, for aught I know,"
  Says an old worthy friend of mine, while leaning
Over my shoulder as I write,—"although
  I can' t exactly comprehend its meaning."

I have touched upon the subject before me in a brief and desultory manner, and have purposely left my remarks unencumbered by learned reference and far-sought erudition; for these are ornaments which would ill become so trivial a pen as this wherewith I write, though, perchance, the want of them will render my essay unsatisfactory to the scholar and the critic. But I am emboldened thus to skim with a light wing over this poetic lore of the past, by the reflection, that the greater part of my readers belong not to that grave and serious class who love the deep wisdom which lies in quoting from a quaint, forgotten tome, and who are ready on all occasions to say, "Commend me to the owl!"

The Baptism of Fire.

> The more you mow us down, the thicker we rise; the Christian blood you spill is like the seed you sow,—it springs from the earth again and fructifies the more.
>
> Tertullian.

As day was drawing to a close, and the rays of the setting sun climbed slowly up the dungeon wall, the prisoner sat and read in a tome with silver clasps. He was a man in the vigor of his days, with a pale and noble countenance, that wore less the marks of worldly care than of high and holy thought. His temples were already bald; but a thick and curling beard bespoke the strength of manhood and his eye, dark, full, and eloquent, beamed with all the enthusiasm of a martyr.

The book before him was a volume of the early Christian Fathers. He was reading the Apologetic of the eloquent Tertullian, the oldest and ablest writer of the Latin Church. At times he paused, and raised his eyes to heaven as if in prayer, and then read on again in silence. At length a passage seemed to touch his inmost soul. He read aloud:—

"Give us, then, what names you please; from the instruments of cruelty you torture us by, call us Sarmenticians and Semaxians, because you fasten us to trunks of trees, and stick us about with fagots to set us on fire; yet let me tell you, when we are thus begirt and dressed about with fire, we are then in our most illustrious apparel. These are our victorious palms and robes of glory; and, mounted on our funeral pile, we look upon ourselves as in our triumphal chariot. No wonder, then, such passive heroes please not those they vanquish with such conquering sufferings. And therefore we pass for men of despair, and violently bent upon our own destruction. However, what you are pleased to call madness and despair in us are the very actions which, under virtue's standard, lift up your sons of fame and glory, and emblazon them to future ages."

He arose and paced the dungeon to and fro, with folded arms and a firm step. His thoughts held communion with eternity.

"Father which art in heaven!" he exclaimed, "give me strength to die like those holy men of old, who scorned to purchase life at the expense of truth. That truth has made me free; and though condemned on earth, I know that I am absolved in heaven!"

He again seated himself at his table, and read in that tome with silver clasps.

This solitary prisoner was Anne Du Bourg, a man who feared not man; once a merciful judge in that august tribunal upon whose voice hung the life and death of those who were persecuted for conscience' sake, he was now himself an accused, a convicted heretic, condemned to the Baptism of Fire, because he would not unrighteously condemn others. He had dared to plead the cause of suffering humanity before that dread tribunal, and, in the presence of the king himself, to declare that it was an offence to the majesty of God to shed man's blood in his name. Six weary months—from June to December—he had lain a prisoner in that dungeon, from which a death by fire was soon to set him free. Such was the clemency of Henry the Second!

As the prisoner read, his eyes were filled with tears. He still gazed upon the printed page, but it was a blank before his eyes. His thoughts were far away amid the scenes of his childhood, amid the green valleys of Riom and the Golden Mountains of Auvergne. Some simple word had called up the vision of the past. He was a child again. He was playing with the pebbles of the brook,—he was shouting to the echo of the hills,—he was praying at his mother's knee, with his little hands clasped in hers.

This dream of childhood was broken by the grating of bolts and bars, as the jailer opened his prison-door. A moment afterward, his former colleague, De Harley, stood at his side.

"Thou here!" exclaimed the prisoner, surprised at the visit. "Thou in the dungeon of a heretic! On what errand hast thou come?"

"On an errand of mercy," replied De Harley. "I come to tell thee"—

"That the hour of my death draws near?"

"That thou mayst still be saved."

"Yes; if I will bear false witness against my God,—barter heaven for earth,—an eternity for a few brief days of worldly existence. Lost, thou shouldst say,—lost, not saved!"

"No! saved!" cried De Harley with warmth; "saved from a death of shame and an eternity of woe! Renounce this false doctrine,—this abominable heresy,—and return again to the bosom of the church which thou dost rend with strife and dissension."

"God judge between thee and me, which has embraced the truth."

"His hand already smites thee."

"It has fallen more heavily upon those who so justly persecute me. Where is the king?—he who said that with his own eyes he would behold me perish at the stake?—he to whom the un daunted Du Faur cried, like Elijah to Ahab, 'It is thou who troublest Israel!'—Where is the king? Called, through a sudden and violent death, to the judgment-seat of Heaven!—Where is Minard, the persecutor of the just? Slain by the hand of an assassin! It was not without reason that I said to him, when standing before my accusers, 'Tremble! believe the word of one who is about to appear before God; thou likewise shalt stand there soon,—thou that sheddest the blood of the children of peace.' He has gone to his account before me."

"And that menace has hastened thine own condemnation. Minard was slain by the Huguenots, and it is whispered that thou wast privy to his death."

"This, at least, might have been spared a dying man!" replied the prisoner, much agitated by so unjust and so unexpected an accusation "As I hope for mercy hereafter, I am innocent of the blood of this man and of all knowledge of so foul a crime. But tell me, hast thou come here only to embitter my last hours with such an accusation as this? If so, I pray thee, leave me. My moments are precious. I would be alone."

"I came to offer thee life, freedom, and happiness."

"Life,—freedom,—happiness! At the price thou hast set upon them, I scorn them all! Had the apostles and martyrs of the early Christian Church listened to such paltry bribes as these, where were now the faith in which we trust? These holy men of old shall answer for me. Hear what Justin Martyr says, in his earnest appeal to Antonine the Pious, in behalf of the Christians who in his day were unjustly loaded with public odium and oppression."

He opened the volume before him and read:—

"I could wish you would take this also into consideration, that what we say is really for your own good; for it is in our power at any time to escape your torments by denying the faith, when you question us about it: but we scorn to purchase life at the expense of a lie; for our souls are winged with a desire of a life of eternal duration and purity, of an immediate conversation with God, the Father and Maker of all things. We are in haste to be confessing and finishing our faith; being fully persuaded that we shall arrive at this blessed state, if we approve ourselves to God by our works, and by our obedience express our passion for that divine life which is never interrupted by any clashing evil."

The Catholic and the Huguenot reasoned long and earnestly together, but they reasoned in vain. Each was firm in his belief, and they parted to meet no more on earth.

On the following day, Du Bourg was summoned before his judges to receive his final sentence. He heard it unmoved, and with a prayer to God that he would pardon those who had condemned him according to their consciences. He then addressed his judges in an oration full of power and eloquence. It closed with these words:—

"And now, ye judges, if, indeed, you hold the sword of God as ministers of his wrath, to take vengeance upon those who do evil, beware, I charge you, beware how you condemn us. Consider well what evil we have done; and, before all things, decide whether it be just that we should listen unto you rather than unto God. Are you so drunken with the wine-cup of the great sorceress that you drink poison for nourishment? Are you not those who make the people sin by turning them away from the service of God? And if you regard more the opinion of men than that of Heaven, in what esteem are you held by other nations, and principalities, and powers, for the martyrdoms you have caused in obedience to this blood-stained Phalaris? God grant, thou cruel tyrant, that by thy miserable death thou mayst put an end to our groans!

"Why weep ye? What means this delay? Your hearts are heavy within you,—your consciences are haunted by the judgment of God. And thus it is that the condemned rejoice in the fires you have kindled, and think they never live better than in the midst of consuming flames. Torments affright them not,—insults enfeeble them not; their honor is redeemed by death,—he that dies is the conqueror, and the conquered he that mourns.

"No! whatever snares are spread for us, whatever suffering we endure, you cannot separate us from the love of Christ. Strike, then,—slay,—grind us to powder! Those that die in the Lord shall live again; we shall all be raised together. Condemn me as you will,—I am a Christian; yes, I am a Christian, and am ready to die for the glory of our Lord,—for the truth of the Evangelists.

"Quench, then, your fires! Let the wicked abandon his way, and return unto the Lord, and he will have compassion on him. Live,—be happy,—and meditate on God, ye judges! As for me, I go rejoicing to my death. What wait ye for? Lead me to the scaffold!"

They bound the prisoner's hands, and, leading him forth from the council-chamber, placed him upon the cart that was to hear him to the Place de Grève. Before and behind marched a guard of five hundred soldiers; for Du Bourg was beloved by the people, and a popular tumult was apprehended. The day was overcast and sad, and ever and anon the sound of the tolling bell mingled its dismal clang with the solemn notes of the funeral march. They soon reached the place of execution, which was already filled with a dense and silent crowd. In the centre stood the gallows, with a pile of fagots beneath it, and the executioner with a burning torch in his hand. But this funeral apparel inspired no terror in the heart of Du Bourg. A look of triumph beamed from his eye, and his countenance shone like that of an angel. With his own hands he divested himself of his outer garments, and, gazing round upon the breathless and sympathizing crowd, exclaimed,—

"My friends, I come not hither as a thief or a murderer; but it is for the Gospel's sake!"

A cord was then fastened round his waist, and he was drawn up into the air. At the same moment the burning torch of the executioner was applied to the fagots beneath, and the thick volumes of smoke concealed the martyr from the horror-stricken crowd. One stifled groan arose from all that vast multitude, like the moan of the sea, and all was hushed again, save the crackling of the fagots, and at intervals the funeral knell, that smote the very soul. The quivering flames darted upward and around, and an agonizing cry broke from the murky cloud,—

"My God! my God! forsake me not, that I forsake not thee!"

The wind lifted the reddening smoke like a veil, and the form of the martyr was seen to fall into the fire beneath. In a moment it rose again, its garments all in flame; and again the faint, half smothered cry of agony was heard,—

"My God! my God! forsake me not, that I forsake not thee!"

Once more the quivering body descended into the flames; and once more it was lifted into the air, a blackened, burning cinder. Again and again this fiendish mockery of baptism was repeated; till the martyr, with a despairing, suffocating voice, exclaimed,—

"O God! I cannot die!"

The executioner came forward, and, either in mercy to the dying man, or through fear of the populace, threw a noose over his neck, and strangled the almost lifeless victim. At the same moment the cord which held the body was loosened, and it fell into the fire to rise no more. And thus was consummated the martyrdom of the Baptism of Fire.

COQ-À-L'ÂNE

My brain, methinks, is like an hour-glass,
Wherein my imaginations run like sands,
Filling up time; but then are turned, and turned,
So that I know not what to stay upon
And less to put in art.

BEN JONSON.

A RAINY and gloomy winter was just drawing to its close, when I left Paris for the South of France. We started at sunrise, and as we passed along the solitary streets of the vast and silent metropolis, drowsily one by one its clanging horologues chimed the hour of six. Beyond the city gates the wide landscape was covered with a silvery network of frost; a wreath of vapor overhung the windings of the Seine; and every twig and shrub, with its sheath of crystal, flashed in the level rays of the rising sun. The sharp, frosty air seemed to quicken the sluggish blood of the old postilion and his horses;—a fresh team stood ready in harness at each stage and notwithstanding the slippery pavement of the causeway, the long and tedious climbing of the hillside, and the equally long and tedious descent with chained wheels and the drag, just after nightfall the lumbering vehicle of Vincent Caillard stopped at the gateway of the "Three Emperors," in the famous city of Orléans.

I cannot pride myself much upon being a good travelling-companion, for the rocking of a coach always lulls me into forgetfulness of the present; and no sooner does the hollow, monotonous rumbling of the wheels reach my ear, than, like Nick Bottom, "I have an exposition of sleep come upon me." It is not, however, the deep, sonorous slumber of a laborer, "stuffed with distressful bread," but a kind of day-dream, wherein the creations of fancy seem realities, and the real world, which swims dizzily before the half-shut, drowsy eye, becomes mingled with the imaginary world within. This is doubtless a very great failing in a traveller; and I confess, with all humility, that at times the line of demarcation between truth and fiction is rendered thereby so indefinite and indistinct, that I cannot always determine, with unerring certainty, whether an event really happened to me, or whether I only dreamed it.

On this account I shall not attempt a detailed description of my journey from Paris to Bordeaux. I was travelling like a bird of passage, and five weary days and four weary nights I was on the way. The diligence stopped only to change horses, and for the travellers to take their meals and by night I slept with my head under my wing in a snug corner of the coach.

Strange as it may appear to some of my readers, this night-travelling is at times far from being disagreeable; nay, if the country is flat and uninteresting, and you are favored with a moon, it may be very pleasant. As the night advances, the conversation around you gradually dies away and is imperceptibly given up to some garrulous traveller who finds himself belated in the midst of a long story; and when at length he puts out his feelers in the form of a question, discovers, by the silence around him, that the breathless attention of his audience is owing to their being asleep. All is now silent. You let down the window of the carriage, and the fresh night-air cools your flushed and burning cheek. The landscape, though in reality dull and uninteresting, seems beautiful as it floats by in the soft moonshine. Every ruined hovel is changed by the magic of night to a trim cottage, every straggling and dilapidated hamlet becomes as beautiful as those we read of in poetry and romance. Over the lowland hangs a silver mist; over the hills peep the twinkling stars. The keen night-air is a spur to the postilion and his horses. In the words of the German ballad,—

Halloo! halloo! away they go,
Unheeding wet or dry,
And horse and rider snort and blow,
sparkling pebbles fly.
And all on which the moon doth shine
Behind them flees afar,
And backward sped, scud overhead,
The sky and every star.

Anon you stop at the relay. The drowsy hostler crawls out of the stable-yard; a few gruff words and strange oaths pass between him and the postilion,—then there is a coarse joke in *patois*, of which you understand the ribaldry only, and which is followed by a husky laugh, a sound between a hiss and a growl;—and then you are off again in a crack. Occasionally a way-traveller is uncaged, and a new-comer takes the vacant perch at your elbow. Meanwhile your busy fancy speculates upon all these things, and you fall asleep amid its thousand vagaries. Soon you wake again and snuff the morning air. It was but a moment, and yet the night is gone. The gray of twilight steals into the window and gives a ghastly look to the countenances of the sleeping group around you. One sits bolt upright in a corner, offending none, and stiff and motionless as an Egyptian mummy; another sits equally straight and immovable, but snores like a priest; the head of a third is dangling over his shoulder, and the tassel of his nightcap tickles his neighbor's ear; a fourth has lost his hat,—his wig is awry, and his under-lip hangs lolling about like an idiot's. The whole scene is a living caricature of man, presenting human nature in some of the grotesque attitudes she assumes when that pragmatical schoolmaster, Propriety, has fallen asleep in his chair, and the unruly members of his charge are freed from the thraldom of the rod.

On leaving Orléans, instead of following the great western mail-route through Tours, Poitiers, and Angoulême, and thence on to Bordeaux, I struck across the departments of the Indre, Haute-Vienne, and the Dordogne, passing through the provincial capitals of Châteauroux, Limoges, and Périgueux. South of the Loire the country assumes a more mountainous aspect, and the landscape is broken by long sweeping hills and fertile valleys. Many a fair scene invites the traveller's foot to pause; and his eye roves with delight over the picturesque landscape of the valley of the Creuse, and the beautiful highland scenery near Périgueux. There are also many objects of art and antiquity which arrest his attention. Argenton boasts its Roman amphitheatre, and the ruins of an Old castle built by King Pepin; at Chalus the tower beneath which Richard Cœur-de-Lion was slain is still pointed out to the curious traveller; and Périgueux is full of crumbling monuments of the Middle Ages.

Scenes like these, and the constant chatter of my fellow-travellers, served to enlighten the tedium of a long and fatiguing journey. The French are preëminently a talking people, and every new object afforded a topic for light and animated discussion. The affairs of church and state were, however, the themes oftenest touched upon. The bill for the suppression of the liberty of the press was then under discussion in the Chamber of Peers, and excited the most lively interest through the whole kingdom. Of course it was a subject not likely to be forgotten in a stage-coach.

"Ah! mon Dieu!" said a brisk little man, with snow-white hair and a blazing red face, at the same time drawing up his shoulders to a level with his ears; "the ministry are determined to carry their point at all events. They mean to break down the liberty of the press, cost what it will."

"If they succeed," added the person who sat opposite, "we may thank the Jesuits for it. It is all their work. They rule the mind of our imbecile monarch, and it is their miserable policy to keep the people in darkness."

"No doubt of that," rejoined the first speaker. "Why, no longer ago than yesterday I read in the 'Figaro' that a printer had been prosecuted for publishing the moral lessons of the Evangelists without the miracles."

"Is it possible?" said I. "And are the people so stupid as thus patiently to offer their shoulders to the pack-saddle?"

"Most certainly not! We shall have another revolution."

"If history speaks true, you have had revolutions enough, during the last century or two, to satisfy the most mercurial nation on earth. You have hardly been quiet a moment since the day of the Barricades and the memorable war of the *pots-de-chambre* in the times of the Grand Condé."

"You are pleased to speak lightly of our revolutions, sir," rejoined the politician, growing warm. "You must, however, confess that each successive one has brought us nearer to our object. Old institutions, whose foundations lie deep in the prejudices of a great nation, are not to be toppled down by the springing of a single mine. You must confess, too, that our national character is much improved since the days you speak of. The youth of the present century are not so frivolous as those of the last. They have no longer that unbounded levity and light-heartedness so generally ascribed to them. From this circumstance we have everything to hope. Our revolutions, likewise, must necessarily change their character and secure to us more solid advantages than heretofore."

"Luck makes pluck, as the Germans say. You go on bravely; but it gives me pain to see religion and the church so disregarded."

"Superstition and the church, you mean," said the gray-headed man. "Why, sir, the church is nothing nowadays but a tumble-down, dilapidated tower for rocks and daws, and such silly birds, to build their nests in!"

It was now very evident that I had unearthed a radical; and there is no knowing when his harangue would have ended, had not his voice been drowned by the noise of the wheels, as we entered the paved street of the city of Limoges.

A breakfast of boiled capon stuffed with truffes, and accompanied by a *Pâté de Périgueux*, a dish well known to French gourmands, restored us all to good-humor. While we were at breakfast a personage stalked into the room, whose strange appearance arrested my attention and gave subject for future conversation to our party. He was a tall, thin figure, armed with a long whip, brass spurs, and black whiskers. He wore a bell-crowned, varnished hat, a blue frock-coat with standing collar, a red waistcoat, a pair of yellow leather breeches, and boots that reached to the knees. I at first took him for a postilion, or a private courier; but, upon inquiry, I found that he was only the son of a notary-public, and that be dressed in this strange fashion to please his own fancy.

As soon as we were comfortably seated in the diligence, I made some remark on the singular costume of the personage whom I had just seen at the tavern.

"These things are so common with us," said the politician, "that we hardly notice them."

"What you want in liberty of speech, then, you make up in liberty of dress?"

"Yes; in this, at least, we are a free people."

"I had not been long in France, before I discovered that a man may dress as he pleases, without being stared at. The most opposite styles of dress seem to be in vogue at the same moment. No strange garment nor desperate hat excites either ridicule or surprise. French fashions are known and imitated all the world over."

"Very true, indeed," said a little man in gosling green. "We give fashions to all other nations."

"Fashions!" said the politician, with a kind of growl,—"fashions! Yes, sir, and some of us are simple enough to boast of it, as if we were a nation of tailors."

Here the little man in gosling-green pulled up the horns of his cotton shirt-collar.

"I recollect," said I, "that your Madame de Pompadour in one of her letters says something to this effect: 'We furnish our enemies with hair dressers, ribbons, and fashions; and they furnish us with laws.'"

"That is not the only silly thing she said in her lifetime. Ah! these Pompadours and Maintenons and Montespans were the authors of much woe to France. Their follies and extravagances exhausted the public treasury, and made the nation poor. They built palaces, and covered themselves with jewels, and ate from golden plate; while the people who toiled for them had hardly a crust to keep their own children from starvation! And yet they preach to us the divine right of kings!"

My radical had got upon his high horse again, and I know not whither it would have carried him, had not a thin man with a black, seedy coat, who sat at his elbow, at that moment crossed his path by one of those abrupt and sudden transitions which leave you aghast at the strange association of ideas in the speaker's mind.

"Apropos de bottes!" I exclaimed he, "speaking of boots, and notaries public, and such matters,—excuse me for interrupting you, sir,—a little story has just popped into my head which may amuse the company; and as I am not very fond of political discussions,—no offence, sir,—I will tell it, for the sake of changing the conversation."

Whereupon, without further preamble or apology, he proceeded to tell his story in, as nearly as may be, the following words.

THE NOTARY OF PÉRIGUEUX

Do not trust thy body with a physician. He'll make thy foolish bones go without flesh in a fortnight, and thy soul walk without a body a sennight after.

SHIRLEY.

YOU must know, gentlemen, that there lived some years ago, in the city of Périgueux, an honest notary-public, the descendant of a very ancient and broken-down family, and the occupant of one of those old weather-beaten tenements which remind you of the times of your great-grandfather. He was a man of an unoffending, quiet disposition; the father of a family, though not the head of it,—for in that family "the hen overcrowed the cock," and the neighbors, when they spake of the notary, shrugged their shoulders, and ex claimed, "Poor fellow! his spurs want sharpening." In fine,—you understand me, gentlemen,—he was henpecked.

Well, finding no peace at home, he sought it elsewhere, as was very natural for him to do, and at length discovered a place of rest, far beyond the cares and clamors of domestic life. This was a little *Café Estaminet*, a short way out of the city, whither he repaired every evening to smoke his pipe, drink sugar-water, and play his favorite game of domino. There he met the boon companions he most loved; heard all the floating chitchat of the day; laughed when he was in merry mood; found consolation when he was sad; and at all times gave vent to his opinions, without fear of being snubbed short by a flat contradiction.

Now, the notary's bosom-friend was a dealer in claret and cognac, who lived about a league from the city, and always passed his evenings at the *Estaminet*. He was a gross, corpulent fellow, raised from a full-blooded Gascon breed, and sired by a comic actor of some reputation in his way. He was remarkable for nothing but his good-humor, his love of cards, and a strong propensity to test the quality of his own liquors by comparing them with those sold at other places.

As evil communications corrupt good manners, the bad practices of the wine-dealer won insensibly upon the worthy notary; and before he was aware of it, he found himself weaned from domino and sugar-water, and addicted to piquet and spiced wine. Indeed, it not unfrequently happened, that, after a long session at the *Estaminet*, the two friends grew so urbane, that they would waste a full half-hour at the door in friendly dispute which should conduct the other home. Though this course of life agreed well enough with the sluggish, phlegmatic temperament of the wine-dealer, it soon began to play the very deuce with the more sensitive organization of the notary, and finally put his nervous system completely out of tune. He lost his appetite, became gaunt and haggard, and could get no sleep. Legions of blue-devils haunted him by day, and by night strange faces peeped through his bed-curtains, and the night mare snorted in his ear. The worse he grew, the more he smoked and tippled; and the more he smoked and tippled,—why, as a matter of course, the worse he grew. His wife alternately stormed, remonstrated, entreated; but all in vain. She made the house too hot for him,—he retreated to the tavern; she broke his long-stemmed pipes upon the andirons,—he substituted a short stemmed one, which, for safe-keeping, he carried in his waistcoat-pocket.

Thus the unhappy notary ran gradually down at the heel. What with his bad habits and his domestic grievances, he became completely hipped. He imagined that he was going to die, and suffered in quick succession all the diseases that ever beset mortal man. Every shooting pain was an alarming symptom,—every uneasy feeling after dinner a sure prognostic of some mortal disease. In vain did his friends endeavor to reason, and then to laugh him out of his strange whims; for when did ever jest or reason cure a sick imagination? His only answer was, "Do let me alone; I know better than you what ails me."

Well, gentlemen, things were in this state, when, one afternoon in December, as he sat moping in his office, wrapped in an overcoat, with a cap on his head and his feet thrust into a pair of furred slippers, a cabriolet stopped at the door and a loud knocking without aroused him from his gloomy revery. It was a message from his friend the wine-dealer, who had been suddenly attacked with a violent fever, and growing worse and worse, had now sent in the greatest haste for the notary to draw up his last will and testament. The case was urgent and admitted neither excuse nor delay; and the notary, tying a handkerchief round his face, and buttoning up to the chin, jumped into the cabriolet, and suffered himself, though not without some dismal presentiments and misgivings of heart, to be driven to the wine-dealer's house.

When he arrived, he found everything in the greatest confusion. On entering the house, he ran against the apothecary, who was coming downstairs, with a face as long as your arm; and a few steps farther he met the housekeeper—for the wine-dealer was an old bachelor—running up and down, and wringing her hands, for fear that the good man should die without making his will. He soon reached the chamber of his sick friend, and found him tossing about in a paroxysm of fever and calling aloud for a draught of cold water. The notary shook his head; he thought this a fatal symptom; for ten years back the wine-dealer had been suffering under a species of hydrophobia, which seemed suddenly to have left him.

When the sick man saw who stood by his bedside, he stretched out his hand and exclaimed,—

"Ah! my dear friend! have you come at last? You see it is all over with me. You have arrived just in time to draw up that-that passport of mine. Ah, *grand diable*! how hot it is here! Water,—water,—water! Will nobody give me a drop of cold water?"

As the case was an urgent one, the notary made no delay in getting his papers in readiness; and in a short time the last will and testament of the wine-dealer was drawn up in due form, the notary guiding the sick man's hand as he scrawled his sig nature at the bottom.

As the evening were away, the wine-dealer grew worse and worse, and at length became delirious, mingling in his incoherent ravings the phrases of the Credo and Paternoster with the shibboleth of the dram-shop and the card-table.

"Take care! take care! There, now—*Credo in*—Pop! ting-a-ling-ling! give me some of that. Cent-é-dize! Why, you old publican, this wine is poisoned,—I know your tricks!—*Sanctam ecclesiam catholicam*—Well, well, we shall see. Imbecile! to have a tierce-major and a seven of hearts, and discard the seven! By St. Anthony, capot! You are lurched,—ha! ha! I told you so. I knew very well,—there,—there,—don't interrupt me—*Carnis resurrectionem et vitam eternam*!"

With these words upon his lips, the poor wine dealer expired. Meanwhile the notary sat cowering over the fire, aghast at the fearful scene that was passing before him, and now and then striving to keep up his courage by a glass of cognac. Already his fears were on the alert; and the idea of contagion flitted to and fro through his mind. In order to quiet these thoughts of evil import, he lighted his pipe and began to prepare for returning home. At that moment the apothecary turned round to him and said,—

"Dreadful sickly time this! The disorder seems to be spreading."

"What disorder?" exclaimed the notary, with a movement of surprise.

"Two died yesterday, and three to-day," continued the apothecary, without answering the question. "Very sickly time, sir,—very."

"But what disorder is it? What disease has carried off my friend here so suddenly?"

"What disease? Why, scarlet fever, to be sure."

"And is it contagious?"

"Certainly!"

"Then I am a dead man!" exclaimed the notary, putting his pipe into his waistcoat-pocket, and beginning to walk up and down the room in despair. "I am a dead man! Now, don't deceive me,—don't, will you? What—what are the symptoms?"

"A sharp burning pain in the right side," said the apothecary.

"Oh, what a fool I was to come here!"

In vain did the housekeeper and the apothecary strive to pacify him;—he was not a man to be reasoned with; he answered that he knew his own constitution better than they did, and insisted upon going home without delay. Unfortunately, the vehicle he came in had returned to the city, and the whole neighborhood was shed and asleep. What was to be done? Nothing in the world but to take the apothecary's horse, which stood hitched at the door, patiently waiting his master's will.

Well, gentlemen, as there was no remedy, our notary mounted this raw-boned steed and set forth upon his homeward journey. The night was cold and gusty, and the wind right in his teeth. Over head the leaden clouds were beating to and fro, and through them the newly risen moon seemed to be tossing and drifting along like a cock-boat in the surf; now swallowed up in a huge billow of cloud, and now lifted upon its bosom and dashed with silvery spray. The trees by the roadside groaned with a sound of evil omen, and before him lay three mortal miles, beset with a thousand imaginary perils. Obedient to the whip and spur, the steed leaped forward by fits and starts, now dashing away in a tremendous gallop, and now relaxing into a long, hard trot; while the rider, filled with symptoms of disease and dire presentiments of death, urged him on, as if he were fleeing before the pestilence.

In this way, by dint of whistling and shouting, and beating right and left, one mile of the fatal three was safely passed. The apprehensions of the notary had so far subsided, that he even suffered the poor horse to walk up hill; but these apprehensions were suddenly revived again with tenfold violence by a sharp pain in the right side, which seemed to pierce him like a needle.

"It is upon me at last!" groaned the fear-stricken man. "Heaven be merciful to me, the greatest of sinners! And must I die in a ditch, after all? He! get up,—get up!"

And away went horse and rider at full speed,—hurry-scurry,—up hill and down,—panting and blowing like a whirlwind. At every leap the pain in the rider's side seemed to increase. At first it was a little point like the prick of a needle,—then it spread to the size of a half-franc piece,—then covered a place as large as the palm of your hand. It gained upon him fast. The poor man groaned aloud in agony; faster and faster sped the horse over the frozen ground,—farther and farther spread the pain over his side. To complete the dismal picture, the storm commenced,—snow mingled with rain. But snow and rain and cold were naught to him; for, though his arms and legs were frozen to icicles, he felt it not; the fatal symptom was upon him he was deemed to die,—not of cold, but of scarlet fever!

At length, he knew not how, more dead than alive, he reached the gate of the city. A band of ill-bred dogs, that were serenading at a corner of the street, seeing the notary dash by, joined in the hue and cry, and ran barking and yelping at his heels. It was now late at night, and only here and there a solitary lamp twinkled from an upper story. But on went the notary, down this street and up that, till at last he reached his own door. There was a light in his wife's bedroom. The good woman came to the window, alarmed at such a knocking, and howling, and clattering at her door so late at night and the notary was too deeply absorbed in his own sorrows to observe that the lamp cast the shadow of two heads on the window-curtain.

"Let me in! let me in! Quick! quick!" he exclaimed, almost breathless from terror and fatigue.

"Who are you, that come to disturb a lone woman at this hour of the night?" cried a sharp voice from above. "Begone about your business, and let quiet people sleep."

"Come down and let me in! I am your husband. Don't you know my voice? Quick, I beseech you, for I am dying here in the street!"

After a few moments of delay and a few more words of parley, the door was opened, and the notary stalked into his domicile, pale and haggard in aspect, and as stiff and straight as a ghost. Cased from head to heel in an armor of ice, as the glare of the lamp fell upon him, he looked like a knight-errant mailed in steel. But in one place his armor was broken. On his right side was a circular spot, as large as the crown of your hat, and about as black!

"My dear wife!" he exclaimed, with more tenderness than he had exhibited for many years. "Reach me a chair. My hours are numbered. I am a dead man!"

Alarmed at these exclamations, his wife stripped off his overcoat. Something fell from beneath it, and was dashed to pieces on the hearth. It was the notary's pipe! He placed his hand upon his side, and, lo! it was bare to the skin! Coat, waistcoat, and linen were burnt through and through, and there was a blister on his side as large as your hand!

The mystery was soon explained, symptom and all. The notary had put his pipe into his pocket without knocking out the ashes! And so my story ends.

"Is that all" asked the radical, when the story teller had finished.

"That is all."

"Well, what does your story prove?"

"That is more than I can tell. All I know is that the story is true."

"And did he die?" said the nice little man in gosling-green.

"Yes, he died afterwards," replied the story teller, rather annoyed by the question.

"And what did he die of?" continued gosling-green, following him up.

"What did he die of? why, he died—of a sudden!"

THE JOURNEY INTO SPAIN.

A l'issue de l'yver que le joly temps de primavère commence, at qu'on voit arbres verdoyer, fleurs espanouir, et qu'on oit les oisillons chanter en toute joie et doulceur, tant que les verts bocages retentissent de leurs sons et que cœurs tristes pensifs y dolens s'en esjouissent, s'émeuvent à delaisser deuil et toute tristesse, et se parforcent à valoir mieux.

LA PLAISANTE HISTOIRE DE GUERIN DE MONGLAVE.

SOFT-BREATHING Spring! how many pleasant thoughts, how many delightful recollections, does thy name awaken in the mind of a traveller! Whether he has followed thee by the banks of the Loire or the Guadalquivir, or traced thy footsteps slowly climbing the sunny slope of Alp or Apennine, the thought of thee shall summon up sweet visions of the past, and thy golden sunshine and soft vapory atmosphere become a portion of his day-dreams and of him. Sweet images of thee, and scenes that have oft inspired the poet's song, shall mingle in his recollections of the past. The shooting of the tender leaf,—the sweetness and elasticity of the air,—the blue sky,—the fleet-drifting cloud,—and the flocks of wild fowl wheeling in long-drawn phalanx through the air, and screaming from their dizzy height,—all these shall pass like a dream before his imagination.

And gently o'er his memory come at times
A glimpse of joys that had their birth in thee,
Like a brief strain of some forgotten tune.

It was at the opening of this delightful season of the year that I passed through the South of France, and took the road of St. Jean de Luz for the Spanish frontier. I left Bordeaux amid all the noise and gayety of the last scene of Carnival. The streets and public walks of the city were full of merry groups in masks,—at every corner crowds were listening to the discordant music of the wandering ballad-singer; and grotesque figures, mounted on high stilts, and dressed in the garb of the peasants of the Landes of Gascony, were stalking up and down like so many long-legged cranes; others were amusing themselves with the tricks and grimaces of little monkeys, disguised like little men, bowing to the ladies, and figuring away in red coats and ruffles; and here and there a band of chimney-sweeps were staring in stupid wonder at the miracles of a showman's box. In a word, all was so full of mirth and merrimake, that even beggary seemed to have forgotten that it was wretched, and gloried in the ragged masquerade of one poor holiday.

To this scene of noise and gayety succeeded the silence and solitude of the Landes of Gascony. The road from Bordeaux to Bayonne winds along immense pine-forests and sandy plains, spotted here and there with a dingy little hovel, and the silence is interrupted only by the dismal hollow roar of the wind among the melancholy and majestic pines. Occasionally, however, the way is enlivened by a market-town or a straggling village; and I still recollect the feelings of delight which I experienced, when, just after sunset, we passed through the romantic town of Roquefort, built upon the sides of the green valley of the Douze, which has scooped out a verdant hollow for it to nestle in, amid those barren tracts of sand.

On leaving Bayonne, the scene assumes a character of greater beauty and sublimity. To the vast forests of the Landes of Gascony succeeds a scene of picturesque beauty, delightful to the traveller's eye. Before him rise the snowy Pyrenees,—a long line of undulating hills,—

> Bounded afar by peak aspiring bold,
> Like giant capped with helm of burnished gold.

To the left, as far as the eye can reach, stretch the delicious valleys of the Nive and Adour; and to the right the sea flashes along the pebbly margin of its silver beach, forming a thousand little bays and inlets, or comes tumbling in among the cliffs of a rock-bound coast, and beats against its massive barriers with a distant, hollow, continual roar.

Should these pages meet the eye of any solitary traveller who is journeying into Spain by the road I here speak of, I would advise him to travel from Bayonne to St. Jean de Luz on horseback. At the gate of Bayonne he will find a steed ready caparisoned for him, with a dark-eyed Basque girl for his companion and guide, who is to sit beside him upon the same horse. This style of travelling is, I believe, peculiar to the Basque provinces; at all events, I have seen it nowhere else. The saddle is constructed with a large frame-work extending on each side, and covered with cushions; and the traveller and his guide, being placed on the opposite extremities, serve as a balance to each other. We overtook many travellers mounted in this way, and I could not help thinking it a mode of travelling far preferable to being cooped up in a diligence. The Basque girls are generally beautiful, and there was one of these merry guides we met upon the road to Bidart whose image haunts me still. She had large and expressive black eyes, teeth like pearls, a rich and sunburnt complexion, and hair of a glossy blackness, parted on the forehead, and falling down behind in a large braid, so long as almost to touch the ground with the little ribbon that confined it at the end. She wore the common dress of the peasantry of the South of France, and a large gypsy straw hat was thrown back over her shoulder, and tied by a ribbon about her neck. There was hardly a dusty traveller in the coach who did not envy her companion the seat he occupied beside her.

Just at nightfall we entered the town of St. Jean de Luz, and dashed down its narrow streets at full gallop. The little madcap postilion cracked his knotted whip incessantly, and the sound echoed back from the high dingy walls like the report of a pistol. The coach-wheels nearly touched the houses on each side of us; the idlers in the street jumped right and left to save themselves; window-shutters flew open in all directions; a thousand heads popped out from cellar and upper story; *"Sacr-r-ré mâtin!"* shouted the postilion,—and we rattled on like an earthquake.

St. Jean de Luz is a smoky little fishing-town, situated on the low grounds at the mouth of the Nivelle, and a bridge connects it with the faubourg of Sibourne, which stands on the opposite bank of the river. I had no time, however, to note the peculiarities of the place, for I was whirled out of it with the same speed and confusion with which I had been whirled in, and I can only recollect the sweep of the road across the Nivelle,—the church of Sibourne by the water's edge,—the narrow streets,—the smoky-looking houses with red window-shutters, and "a very ancient and fish-like smell."

I passed by moonlight the little river Bidasoa, which forms the boundary between France and Spain; and when the morning broke, found myself far up among the mountains of San Salvador, the most westerly links of the great Pyrenean chain. The mountains around me were neither rugged nor precipitous, but they rose one above another in a long, majestic swell, and the trace of the ploughshare was occasionally visible to their summits. They seemed entirely destitute of trees; and as the season of vegetation had not yet commenced, their huge outlines lay black, and barren, and desolate against the sky. But it was a glorious morning, and the sun rose up into a cloudless heaven, and poured a flood of gorgeous splendor over the mountain landscape, as if proud of the realm he shone upon. The scene was enlivened by the dashing of a swollen mountain-brook, whose course we followed for miles down the valley, as it leaped onward to its journey's end, now breaking into a white cascade, and now foaming and chafing beneath a rustic bridge. Now and then we drove through a dilapidated town, with a group of idlers at every corner, wrapped in tattered brown cloaks, and smoking their little paper cigars in the sun; then would succeed a desolate tract of country, cheered only by the tinkle of a mule-bell, or the song of a muleteer; then we would meet a solitary traveller mounted on horseback, and wrapped in the ample folds of his cloak, with a gun hanging at the pommel of his saddle. Occasionally, too, among the bleak, inhospitable hills, we passed a rude little chapel, with a cluster of ruined cottages around it; and whenever our carriage stopped at the relay, or loitered slowly up the hillside, a crowd of children would gather around us, with little images and crucifixes for sale, curiously ornamented with ribbons and bits of tawdry finery.

A day's journey from the frontier brought us to Vitoria, where the diligence stopped for the night. I spent the scanty remnant of daylight in rambling about the streets of the city, with no other guide than the whim of the moment. Now I plunged down a dark and narrow alley, now emerged into a wide street or a spacious market place, and now aroused the drowsy echoes of a church or cloister with the sound of my intruding footsteps. But descriptions of churches and public squares are dull and tedious matters for those readers who are in search of amusement, and not of instruction; and if anyone has accompanied me thus far on my fatiguing journey towards the Spanish capital, I will readily excuse him from the toil of an evening ramble through the streets of Vitoria.

On the following morning we left the town, long before daybreak, and during our forenoon's journey the postilion drew up at an inn, on the southern slope of the Sierra de San Lorenzo, in the province of Old Castile. The house was an old, dilapidated tenement, built of rough stone, and coarsely plastered upon the outside. The tiled roof had long been the sport of wind and rain, the motley coat of plaster was broken and time-worn, and the whole building sadly out of repair; though the fanciful mouldings under the caves, and the curiously carved wood-work that supported the little balcony over the principal entrance, spoke of better days gone by. The whole building reminded me of a dilapidated Spanish Don, down at the heel and out at elbows, but with here and there a remnant of former magnificence peeping through the loopholes of his tattered cloak.

A wide gateway ushered the traveller into the interior of the building, and conducted him to a low-roofed apartment, paved with round stones, and serving both as a court-yard and a stable. It seemed to be a neutral ground for man and beast,—a little republic, where horse and rider had common privileges, and mule and muleteer lay check by jowl. In one corner a poor jackass was patiently devouring a bundle of musty straw,—in another, its master lay sound asleep, with his saddle-cloth for a pillow; here a group of muleteers were quarrelling over a pack of dirty cards, and there the village barber, with a self-important air, stood laving the Alcalde's chin from the helmet of Mambrino. On the wall, a little taper glimmered feebly before an image of St. Anthony; directly opposite these a leathern wine-bottle hung by the neck from a pair of ox-horns; and the pavement below was covered with a curious med ley of boxes, and bags, and cloaks, and pack-saddles, and sacks of grain, and skins of wine, and all kinds of lumber.

A small door upon the right led us into the inn kitchen. It was a room about ten feet square, and literally all chimney; for the hearth was in the centre of the floor, and the walls sloped upward in the form of a long, narrow pyramid, with an opening at the top for the escape of the smoke. Quite round this little room ran a row of benches, upon which sat one or two grave personages smoking paper cigars. Upon the hearth blazed a handful of fagots, whose bright flame danced merrily among a motley congregation of pets and kettles, and a long wreath of smoke wound lazily up through the huge tunnel of the roof above. The walls were black with soot, and ornamented with sundry legs of bacon and festoons of sausages; and as there were no windows in this dingy abode, the only light which cheered the darkness within came flickering from the fire upon the hearth and the smoky sunbeams that peeped down the long necked chimney.

I had not been long seated by the fire, when the tinkling of mule-bells, the clatter of hoofs, and the hoarse voice of a muleteer in the outer apartment announced the arrival of new guests. A few moments afterward the kitchen-door opened, and a person entered, whose appearance strongly arrested my attention. It was a tall, athletic figure, with the majestic carriage of a grandee, and a dark, sunburnt countenance, that indicated an age of about fifty years. His dress was singular, and such as I had not before seen. He wore a round hat with wide, flapping brim, from beneath which his long, black hair hung in curls upon his shoulders; a leather jerkin, with cloth sleeves, descended to his hips; around his waist was closely buckled a leather belt, with a cartouch-box on one side; a pair of loose trousers of black serge hung in ample folds to the knees, around which they were closely gathered by embroidered garters of blue silk; and black broadcloth leggins, buttoned close to the calves, and strapped over a pair of brown leather shoes, completed the singular dress of the stranger. He doffed his hat as he entered, and, saluting the company with a *"Dios guarde á Ustedes, caballeros"* (God guard you, Gentlemen), took a seat by the fire, and entered into conversation with those around him. As my curiosity was not a little excited by the peculiar dress of this person, I inquired of a travelling companion, who sat at my elbow, who and what this new-comer was. From him I learned that he was a muleteer of the Maragatería,—a name given to a cluster of small towns which lie in the mountainous country between Astorga and Villafranca, in the western corner of the kingdom of Leon.

"Nearly every province in Spain," said he, "has its peculiar costume, as you will see, when you have advanced farther into our country. For instance, the Catalonians wear crimson caps, hanging down upon the shoulder like a sack; wide pantaloons of green velvet, long enough in the waistband to cover the whole breast; and a little strip of a jacket, made of the same material, and so short as to bring the pocket directly under the armpit. The Valencians, on the contrary, go almost naked: a linen shirt, white linen trousers, reaching no lower than the knees, and a pair of coarse leather sandals complete their simple garb; it is only in midwinter that they indulge in the luxury of a jacket. The most beautiful and expensive costume, however, is that of Andalusia; it consists of a velvet jacket, faced with rich and various-colored embroidery, and covered with tassels and silken cord; a waistcoat of some gay color; a silken handkerchief round the neck, and a crimson sash round the waist; breeches that button down each side; gaiters and shoes of white leather; and a handkerchief of bright-colored silk wound about the head like a turban, and surmounted by a velvet cap or a little round hat, with a wide band, and an abundance of silken loops and tassels. The Old Castilians are more grave in their attire they wear a leather breastplate instead of a jacket, breeches and leggins, and a montera cap. This fellow is a Maragato; and in the villages of the Maragatería the costume varies a little from the rest of Leon and Castile."

"If he is indeed a Maragato," said I, jestingly, "who knows but he may be a descendant of the muleteer who behaved so naughtily at Cacabelos, as related in the second chapter of the veracious history of Gil Blas de Santillana?"

"*¿Quien sabe?*" was the reply. "Notwithstanding the pride which even the meanest Castilian feels in counting over a long line of good-for-nothing ancestors, the science of genealogy has become of late a very intricate study in Spain."

Here our conversation was cut short by the *Mayoral* of the diligence, who came to tell us that the mules were waiting; and before many hours had elapsed we were scrambling through the square of the ancient city of Burgos. On the morrow we crossed the river Duero and the Guadarrama Mountains, and early in the afternoon entered the "Heróica Villa" of Madrid, by the Puerta de Fuencarral.

SPAIN.

Santiago y cierra España! — SPANISH WAR-CRY.

IT is a beautiful morning in June;—so beautiful, that I almost fancy myself in Spain. The tessellated shadow of the honeysuckle lies motionless upon the floor, as if it were a figure in the carpet; and through the open window comes the fragrance of the wild-brier and the mock-orange, reminding me of that soft, sunny clime where the very air is laden, like the bee, with sweetness, and the south wind

Comes over gardens, and the flowers
That kissed it are betrayed.

The birds are carolling in the trees, and their shadows flit across the window as they dart to and fro in the sunshine, while the murmur of the bee, the cooing of doves from the eaves, and the whir ring of a little humming-bird that has its nest in the honeysuckle, send up a sound of joy to meet the rising sun! How like the climate of the South! How like a summer morning in Spain!

My recollections of Spain are of the most lively and delightful kind. The character of the soil and of its inhabitants,—the stormy mountains and free spirits of the North,—the prodigal luxuriance and gay voluptuousness of the South,—the history and traditions of the past, resembling more the fables of romance than the solemn chronicle of events, a soft and yet majestic language that falls like martial music on the ear, and a literature rich in the attractive lore of poetry and fiction,—these, but not these alone, are my reminiscences of Spain. With these I recall the thousand little circumstances and enjoyments which always give a coloring to our recollections of the past; the clear sky, the pure, balmy air,—the delicious fruits and flowers,—the wild-fig and the aloe, and the olive by the wayside,—all, all that makes existence so joyous, and renders the sons and daughters of that clime the children of impulse and sensation.

As I write these words, a shade of sadness steals over me. When I think what that glorious land might be, and what it is,—what nature intended it should be, and what man has made it,—my very heart sinks within me. My mind instinctively reverts from the degradation of the present to the glory of the past; or, looking forward with strong misgivings, but with yet stronger hopes, interrogates the future.

The burnished armor of the Cid stands in the archives of the royal museum of Madrid, and there, too, is seen the armor of Ferdinand and of Isabel, of Guzman the Good and of Gonzalo de Córdova, and other early champions of Spain; but what hand shall now wield the sword of the Campeador, or lift up the banner of Leon and Castile? The ruins of Christian castle and Moorish alcázar still look forth from the hills of Spain; but where, oh where is the spirit of freedom that once fired the children of the Goth? Where is the spirit of Bernardo del Carpio, and Perez de Vargas, and Alonzo de Aguilar? Shall it forever sleep? Shall it never again beat high in the hearts of their sons? Shall the descendants of Pelayo bow forever beneath an iron yoke, "like cattle whose despair is dumb"?

The dust of the Cid lies mingling with the dust of Old Castile, but his spirit is not buried with his ashes. It sleeps, but is not dead. The day will come, when the foot of the tyrant shall be shaken from the neck of Spain; when a brave and generous people, though now ignorant, degraded, and much abused, "shall know their rights, and knowing dare maintain."

Of the national character of Spain I have brought away this impression: that its prominent traits are a generous pride of birth, a superstitious devotion to the dogmas of the Church, and an innate dignity, which exhibits itself even in the common and every-day employments of life. Castilian pride is proverbial. A beggar wraps his tattered cloak around him with all the dignity of a Roman senator, and a muleteer bestrides his beast of burden with the air of a grandee.

I have thought, too, that there was a tinge of sadness in the Spanish character. The national music of the land is remarkable for its melancholy tone, and at times the voice of a peasant, singing amid the silence and solitude of the mountains, falls upon the car like a funeral chant. Even a Spanish holiday wears a look of sadness,—a circumstance which some writers attribute to the cruel and overbearing spirit of the municipal laws. "On the greatest festivals," says Jovellanos, "instead of that boisterous merriment and noise which should bespeak the joy of the inhabitants, there reigns throughout the streets and market-places a slothful inactivity, a gloomy stillness, which cannot be remarked without mingled emotions of surprise and pity. The few persons who leave their houses seem to be driven from them by listlessness, and dragged as far as the threshold, the market, or the church-door; there, muffled in their cloaks, leaning against a corner, seated on a bench, or lounging to and fro, without object, aim, or purpose, they pass their hours, their whole evenings, without mirth, recreation, or amusement. When you add to this picture the dreariness and filth of the villages, the poor and slovenly dress of the inhabitants, the gloominess and silence of their air, the laziness, the want of concert and union so striking everywhere, who but would be astonished, who but would be afflicted by so mournful a phenomenon? This is not, indeed, the place to expose the errors which conspire to produce it; but, whatever those errors may be, one point is clear,—that they are all to be found in the laws!"[5]

Of the same serious, sombre character is the favorite national sport,—the bull-fight. It is a barbarous amusement, but of all others the most exciting, the most spirit-stirring, and in Spain the most popular. "If Rome lived content with bread and arms," says the author I have just quoted, in a spirited little discourse entitled *Pan y Toros*, "Madrid lives content with bread and bulls."

Shall I describe a Spanish bull-fight? No. It has been so often and so well described by other pens that mine shall not undertake it, though it is a tempting theme. I cannot, however, refuse myself the pleasure of quoting here a few lines from one of the old Spanish ballads upon this subject. It is entitled "The Bull-fight of Ganzul." The description of the bull, which is contained in the passage I here extract, is drawn with a master's hand. It is rather a paraphrase than a translation, by Mr. Lockhart.

From Guadiana comes he not, he comes not from Xenil,
From Guadalarif of the plain, or Barves of the hill;
But where from out the forest burst Xarama's waters clear,
Beneath the oak-trees was he nursed, this proud and stately steer.

---

[5] Informe dado á la Real Academia de Historia sobre Juegos, Espectáculos, y Diversiones Públicas.

Dark is his hide on either side, but the blood within doth boil,
And the dun hide glows, as if on fire, as he paws to the turmoil.
His eyes are jet, and they are set in crystal rings of snow;
But now they stare with one red glare of brass upon the foe.

Upon the forehead of the bull the horns stand close and near,
From out the broad and wrinkled skull like daggers they appear;
His neck is massy, like the trunk of some old knotted tree,
Whereon the monster's shaggy mane, like billows curled, ye see.

His legs are short, his hams are thick, his hoofs are black as night;
Like a strong flail he holds his tail, in fierceness of his might;
Like something molten out of iron, or hewn from forth the rock,
Harpado of Xarama stands, to hide the Alcayde's shock.

Now stops the drum,—close, close they come; thrice meet, and thrice give back;
The white foam of Harpado lies on the charger's breast of black—
The white foam of the charger on Harpado's front of dun;—
Once more advance upon his lance—once more, then fearless one!

There are various circumstances closely connected with the train of thought I have here touched upon; but I forbear to mention them, for fear of drawing out this chapter to too great a length. Some of them will naturally find a place hereafter. Meanwhile let us turn the leaf to a new chapter, and to subjects of a livelier nature.

A Tailor's Drawer.

Nedyls, threde, thyrnbell, shers, and all suche knackes.

THE FOUR PS.

I.

A TAILOR'S drawer, did you say?

Yes, a tailor's drawer. It is, indeed, rather a quaint rubric for a chapter in the pilgrim's breviary; albeit it well befits the motley character of the following pages. It is a title which the Spaniards give to a desultory discourse, wherein various and discordant themes are touched upon, and which is crammed full of little shreds and patches of erudition; and certainly it is not inappropriate to a chapter whose contents are of every shape and hue, and "do no more adhere and keep pace together than the hundredth psalm to the tune of Green Sleeves."

II.

It is recorded in the Adventures of Gil Blas de Santillana, that, when this renowned personage first visited the city of Madrid, he took lodgings at the house of Mateo Melandez, in the Puerta del Sol. In choosing a place of abode in the Spanish court, I followed, as far as practicable, this illustrious example; but, as the kind-hearted Mateo had been long gathered to his fathers, I was content to take up my residence in the hired house of Valentin Gonzalez, at the foot of the Calle de la Montera. My apartments were in the third story, above the dust, though not beyond the rattle, of the street; and my balconies looked down into the Puerta del Sol, the heart of Madrid, through which circulates the living current of its population at least once every twenty-four hours.

The Puerta del Sol is a public square, from which diverge the five principal streets of the metropolis. It is the great rendezvous of grave and gay,—of priest and layman,—of gentle and simple,—the mart of business and of gossip,—the place where the creditor seeks his debtor, where the lawyer seeks his client, where the stranger seeks amusement, where the friend seeks his friend, and the foe his foe; where the idler seeks the sun in winter, and the shade in summer, and the busybody seeks the daily news, and picks up the crumbs of gossip to fly away with them in his beak to the *tertulia* of Doña Paquita!

Tell me, ye who have sojourned in foreign lands, and know in what bubbles a traveller's happiness consists,—is it not a blessing to have your window overlook a scene like this?

III.

There,—take that chair upon the balcony, and let us look down upon the busy scene beneath us. What a continued roar the crowded thoroughfare sends up! Though three stories high, we can hardly hear the sound of our own voices! The London cries are whispers, when compared with the cries of Madrid.

See,—yonder stalks a gigantic peasant of New Castile, with a montera cap, brown jacket and breeches, and coarse blue stockings, forcing his way through the crowd and leading a donkey laden with charcoal, whose sonorous bray is in unison with the harsh voice of his master. Close at his elbow goes a rosy-checked damsel, selling calico. She is an Asturian from the mountains of Santander. How do you know? By her short yellow petticoats,—her blue bodice,—her coral neck lace and ear-rings. Through the middle of the square struts a peasant of Old Castile, with his yellow leather jerkin strapped about his waist,—his brown leggins and his blue garters,—driving before him a flock of gabbling turkeys, and crying at the top of his voice, *"Pao, pao, pavitos, paos!"* Next comes a Valencian, with his loose linen trousers and sandal shoon, holding a huge sack of watermelons upon his shoulder with his left hand, and with his right balancing high in air a specimen of the luscious fruit, upon which is perched a little pyramid of the crimson pulp, while he tempts the passers-by with *"A cala, y calando; una sandia vendo-o-o. Si esto es sangre!"* (By the slice,—come and try it,—watermelon for sale. This is blood!) His companion near him has a pair of scales thrown over his shoulder, and holds both arms full of muskmelons. He chimes into the harmonious ditty with

"Melo—melo-o-o—meloncitos agui está el azúcarl!" (Melons, melons; here is the sugar!) Behind them creeps a slow-moving Asturian, in heavy wooden shoes, crying water-cresses; and a peasant woman from the Guadarrama Mountains, with a montera cocked up in front, and a blue kerchief tied under her chin, swings in each hand a bunch of live chickens, that hang by the claws, head downwards, fluttering, scratching, crowing with all their might, while the good woman tries to drown their voices in the discordant cry of *"¿Quien me compra un gallo,—un par de gallinas?"* (Who buys a cock,—a pair of fowls?) That tall fellow in blue, with a pot of flowers upon his shoulder, is a wag, beyond all dispute. See how cunningly he cocks his eye up at us, and cries, *"Si yo tuviera balcon!"* (If I only had a balcony!)

What next? A Manchego with a sack of oil under his arm; a Gallego with a huge water-jar upon his shoulders; an Italian pedler with images of saints and madonnas; a razor-grinder with his wheel; a mender of pets and kettles, making music, as he goes, with a shovel and a frying-pan; and, in fine, a noisy, patchwork, ever-changing crowd, whose discordant cries mingle with the rumbling of wheels, the clatter of hoofs, and the clang of church-bells and make the Puerta del Sol, at certain hours of the day, like a street in Babylon the Great.

IV.

Chiton! A beautiful girl, with flaxen hair, blue eyes, and the form of a fairy in a midsummer night's dream, has just stepped out on the balcony beneath us! See how coquettishly she crosses her arms upon the balcony, thrusts her dainty little feet through the bars, and plays with her slipper! She is an Andalusian, from Malaga. Her brother is a bold dragoon, and wears a long sword; so beware! and "let not the creaking of shoes and the rustling of silks betray thy poor heart to woman." Her mother is a vulgar woman, "fat and forty;" eats garlic in her salad, and smokes cigars. But mind! that is a secret; I tell it to you in confidence.

V.

The following little ditty I translate from the Spanish. It is as delicate as a dew-drop.

She is a maid of artless grace,
Gentle in form, and fair of face.

Tell me, thou ancient mariner,
    That sailest on the sea,
If ship, or sail, or evening star
    Be half so fair as she!

Tell me, then gallant cavalier,
    Whose shining arms I see,
If steel, or sword, or battle-field
    Be half so fair as she!

Tell me, then swain, that guard'st thy flock
    Beneath the shadowy tree,
If flock, or vale, or mountain-ridge
    Be half so fair as she!

VI.

A miller has just passed by, covered with flour from head to foot, and perched upon the tip end of a little donkey, crying *"Arre borrico!"* and at every cry swinging a cudgel in his hand, and giving the ribs of the poor beast what in the vulgar dialect is called a *cachiporrazo*. I could not help laughing, though I felt provoked with the fellow for his cruelty. The truth is, I have great regard for a jackass. His meekness and patience and long-suffering are very amiable qualities, and, considering his situation, worthy of all praise. In Spain, a donkey plays as conspicuous a part as a priest or a village alcalde. There would be no getting along without him. And yet, who so beaten and abused as he?

VII.

Here comes a gay gallant, with white kid gloves, an eye-glass, a black cane with a white ivory pommel, and a little hat cocked pertly on one side of his head. He is an exquisite fop and a great lady's man. You will always find him on the

Prado at sunset, when the crowd and dust are thickest, ogling through his glass, flourishing his cane, and humming between his teeth some favorite air of the "Semiramis," or the "Barber of Seville." He is a great amateur, and patron of the Italian Opera,—beats time with his cane,—nods his head, and cries *Bravo!*—and fancies himself in love with the Prima Donna. The height of his ambition is to be thought the gay Lothario,—the gallant Don Cortejo of his little sphere. He is a poet withal, and daily besieges the heart of the cruel Doña Inez with sonnets and madrigals. She turns a deaf ear to his song, and is inexorable:—

Mas que no sea mas piadosa
A dos escudos en prosa,
No puede ser.

VIII.

What a contrast between this personage and the sallow, emaciated being who is now crossing the street! It is a barefooted Carmelite,—a monk of an austere order, wasted by midnight vigils and long penance. Abstinence is written on that pale cheek, and the bowed head and downcast eye are in accordance with the meek profession of a mendicant brotherhood.

What is this world to thee, thou man of penitence and prayer? What hast then to do with all this busy, turbulent scene about thee,—with all the noise and gayety and splendor of this thronged city? Nothing. The wide world gives thee nothing, save thy daily crust, thy crucifix, thy convent cell, thy pallet of straw! Pilgrim of heaven! thou hast no home on earth. Thou art journeying onward to "a house not made with hands," and, like the first apostles of thy faith, thou takest neither gold, nor silver, nor brass, nor scrip for thy journey. Thou hast shut thy heart to the endearments of earthly love,—thy shoulder beareth not the burden with thy fellow-man, in all this vast crowd thou hast no friends, no hopes, no sympathies. Thou standest aloof from man, and art thou nearer God? I know not. Thy motives, thy intentions, thy desires, are registered in heaven. I am thy fellow-man, and not thy judge.

"Who is the greater?" says the German moralist; "the wise man who lifts himself above the storms of time, and from aloof looks down upon them, and yet takes no part therein,—or he who, from the height of quiet and repose, throws himself boldly into the battle-tumult of the world? Glorious is it, when the eagle through the beating tempest flies into the bright blue heaven upward; but far more glorious, when, poising in the blue sky over the black storm-abyss, he plunges down ward to his aerie on the cliff, where cower his unfledged brood, and tremble."

IX.

Sultry grows the day, and breathless! The lately crowded street is silent and deserted,—hardly a footfall,—hardly here and there a solitary figure stealing along in the narrow strip of shade beneath the eaves! Silent, too, and deserted is the Puerta del Sol; so silent, that even at this distance the splashing of its fountain is distinctly audible,—so deserted, that not a living thing is visible there, save the outstretched and athletic form of a Galician water-carrier, who lies asleep upon the pavement in the cool shadow of the fountain! There is not air enough to stir the leaves of the jasmine upon the balcony, or break the thin column of smoke that issues from the cigar of Don Diego, master of the noble Spanish tongue, *y hombre de muchos dingolondangos*. He sits bolt upright between the window and the door, with the collar of his snuff-colored frock thrown back upon his shoulders, and his toes turned out like a dancing-master, poring over the "Diario de Madrid," to learn how high the thermometer rose yesterday, what patron saint has a festival to-day, and at what hour to-morrow the "King of Spain, Jerusalem, and the Canary Islands" will take his departure for the gardens of Aranjuez.

You have a proverb in your language, Don Diego, which says,—

Despues de comer
Ni un sobrescrito leer;—

after dinner read not even the superscription of a letter. I shall obey and indulge in the exquisite luxury of a *siesta*. I confess that I love this after dinner nap. If I have a gift, a vocation for anything, it is for sleeping; and from my heart I can say with honest Sancho, "Blessed be the man that first invented sleep!" In a sultry clime, too, where the noontide heat unmans you, and the cool, starry night seems made for anything but slumber, I am willing to barter an hour or two of intense daylight for an hour or two of tranquil, lovely, dewy night!

Therefore, Don Diego, *hasta la vista*!

X.

It is evening; the day is gone; fast gather and deepen the shades of twilight! In the words of a German allegory, "The babbling day has touched the hem of night's garment, and, weary and still, drops asleep in her bosom."

The city awakens from its slumber. The convent-bells ring solemnly and slow. The streets are thronged again. Once more I hear the shrill cry, the rattling wheel, the murmur of the crowd. The blast of a trumpet sounds from the Puerta del Sol,—then the tap of a drum; a mounted guard opens the way,—the crowd doff their hats, and the king sweeps by in a gilded coach drawn by six horses, and followed by a long train of uncouth, antiquated vehicles drawn by mules.

The living tide new sets towards the Prado, and the beautiful gardens of the Retiro. Beautiful are they at this magic hour! Beautiful, with the almond-tree in blossom, with the broad green leaves of the sycamore and the chestnut, with the fragrance of the orange and the lemon, with the beauty of a thousand flowers, with the soothing calm and the dewy freshness of evening!

XI.

I love to linger on the Prado till the crowd is gone and the night far advanced. There musing and alone I sit, and listen to the lulling fall of waters in their marble fountains, and watch the moon as it rises over the gardens of the Retiro, brighter than a northern sun. The beautiful scene lies half in shadow, half in light,—almost a fairyland. Occasionally the sound of a guitar, or a distant voice, breaks in upon my revery. Then the form of a monk, from the neighboring convent, sweeps by me like a shadow and disappears in the gloom of the leafy avenues; and far away from the streets of the city comes the voice of the watchman telling the midnight hour.

Lovely art thou, O Night, beneath the skies of Spain! Day, panting with heat, and laden with a thousand cares, toils onward like a beast of burden; but Night, calm, silent, holy Night, is a ministering angel that cools with its dewy breath the toil-heated brow, and, like the Roman sisterhood, stoops down to bathe the pilgrim's feet. How grateful is the starry twilight! How grateful the gentle radiance of the moon! How grateful the delicious coolness of "the omnipresent and deep-breathing air"! Lovely art thou, O Night, beneath the skies of Spain!

ANCIENT SPANISH BALLADS.

I love a ballad but even too well, if it be doleful matter merrily set down, or a very pleasant thing indeed, and sung lamentably.

WINTER'S TALE.

HOW universal is the love of poetry! Every nation has its popular songs, the offspring of a credulous simplicity and an unschooled fancy. The peasant of the North, as he sits by the evening fire, sings the traditionary ballad to his children,

Nor wants he gleeful tales, while round
The nut-brown bowl doth trot.

The peasant of the South, as he lies at noon in the shade of the sycamore, or sits by his door in the evening twilight, sings his amorous lay, and listlessly,

On hollow quills of oaten straw,
He pipeth melody.

The muleteer of Spain carols with the early lark, amid the stormy mountains of his native land. The vintager of Sicily has his evening hymn; the fisherman of Naples his boat-song; the gondolier of Venice his midnight serenade. The goatherd of Switzerland and the Tyrol,—the Carpathian boor,—the Scotch Highlander,—the English ploughboy, singing as he drives his team afield,—peasant, serf, slave,—all, all have their ballads and traditionary songs. Music is the universal language of mankind, poetry their universal pastime and delight.

The ancient ballads of Spain hold a prominent rank in her literary history. Their number is truly astonishing, and may well startle the most enthusiastic lover of popular song. The Romancero General[6] contains upwards of a

[6] Romancero General, en que se contiene todos los Romances que andan impresos. 4to. Madrid, 1604.

thousand; and though upon many of these may justly be bestowed the encomium which honest Izaak Walton pronounces upon the old English ballad of the Passionate Shepherd,—"old-fashioned poetry, but choicely good,"—yet, as a whole, they are, perhaps, more remarkable for their number than for their beauty. Every great historic event, every marvellous tradition, has its popular ballad. Don Roderick, Bernardo del Carpio, and the Cid Campeador are not more the heroes of ancient chronicle than of ancient song; and the imaginary champions of Christendom, the Twelve Peers of Charlemagne, have found an historian in the wandering ballad-singer no less authentic than the good Arch bishop Turpin.

Most of these ancient ballads had their origin during the dominion of the Moors in Spain. Many of them, doubtless, are nearly as old as the events they celebrate, though in their present form the greater part belong to the fourteenth century. The language in which they are now preserved indicates no higher antiquity, but who shall say how long they had been handed down by tradition, ere they were taken from the lips of the wandering minstrel, and recorded in a more permanent form?

The seven centuries of the Moorish sovereignty in Spain are the heroic ages of her history and her poetry. What the warrior achieved with his sword the minstrel published in his song. The character of those ages is seen in the character of their literature. History casts its shadow far into the land of song. Indeed, the most prominent characteristic of the ancient Spanish ballads is their warlike spirit. They shadow forth the majestic lineaments of the warlike ages, and through every line breathes a high and peculiar tone of chivalrous feeling. It is not the piping sound of peace, but a blast,—a loud, long blast from the war-horn—

> A trump with a stern breath,
> Which is cleped the trump of death.

And with this mingles the voice of lamentation, the requiem for the slain, with a melancholy sweetness:—

> Rio Verde, Rio Verde!
> Many a corpse is bathed in thee,

Both of Moors and eke of Christians,
Slain with swords most cruelly.

And thy pure and crystal waters
Dappled are with crimson gore;
For between the Moors and Christians
Long has been the fight and sore.

Dukes and counts fell bleeding near thee,
Lords of high renown were slain,
Perished many a brave hidalgo
Of the noblemen of Spain.

Another prominent characteristic of these ancient ballads is their energetic and beautiful simplicity. A great historic event is described in the fewest possible words; there is no ornament, no artifice. The poet's intention was to narrate, not to embellish. It is truly wonderful to observe what force and beauty and dramatic power are given to the old romances by this single circumstance. When Bernardo del Carpio leads forth his valiant Leonese against the host of Charlemagne, he animates their courage by alluding to their battles with the Moors, and exclaims, "Shall the lions that have bathed their paws in Libyan gore now crouch before the Frank?" When he enters the palace of the treacherous Alfonso, to upbraid him for a broken promise, and the king orders him to be arrested for contumely, he lays his hand upon his sword and cries, "Let no one stir! I am Bernardo; and my sword is not subject even to kings!" When the Count Alarcos prepares to put to death his own wife at the king's command, she submits patiently to her fate, asks time to say a prayer, and then exclaims, "Now bring me my infant boy, that I may give him suck, as my last farewell!" Is there in Homer an incident more touching, or more true to nature?

The ancient Spanish ballads naturally divide themselves into three classes: the Historic, the Romantic, and the Moorish. It must be confessed, however, that the line of demarcation between these three classes is not well defined; for many of the Moorish ballads are historic, and many others occupy a kind of debatable ground between the historic and the romantic. I have adopted this classification for the sake of its convenience, and shall now make a few hasty observations upon each class, and illustrate my remarks by specimens of the ballads.

The historic ballads are those which recount the noble deeds of the early heroes of Spain: of Bernardo del Carpio, the Cid, Martin Pelaez, Garcia Perez de Vargas, Alonzo de Aguilar, and many others whose names stand conspicuous in Spanish history. Indeed, these ballads may themselves be regarded in the light of historic documents; they are portraits of long-departed ages, and if at times their features are exaggerated and colored with too bold a contrast of light and shade, yet the free and spirited touches of a master's hand are recognized in all. They are instinct, too, with the spirit of Castilian pride, with the high and dauntless spirit of liberty that burned so fiercely of old in the heart of the brave hidalgo. Take, for example, the ballad of the Five Farthings. King Alfonso the Eighth, having exhausted his treasury in war, wishes to lay a tax of five farthings upon each of the Castilian hidalgos, in order to defray the expenses of a journey from Burgos to Cuenca. This proposition of the king was met with disdain by the noblemen who had been assembled on the occasion.

Don Nuno, Count of Lara,
In anger and in pride,
Forgot all reverence for the king,
And thus in wrath replied:—

"Our noble ancestors," quoth he,
"Ne'er such a tribute paid;
Nor shall the king receive of us
What they have once gainsaid.

"The base-born soul who deems it just
May here with thee remain;
But follow me, ye cavaliers,
Ye noblemen of Spain."

Forth followed they the noble Count,
They marched to Glera's plain;
Out of three thousand gallant knights
Did only three remain.

They tied the tribute to their spears,
They raised it in the air,

And they sent to tell their lord the king
    That his tax was ready there.

"He may send and take by force," said they,
    "This paltry sum of gold;
But the goodly gift of liberty
    Cannot be bought and sold."

The same gallant spirit breathes through all the historic ballads, but, perhaps, most fervently in those which relate to Bernardo del Carpio. How spirit-stirring are all the speeches which the ballad-writers have put into the mouth of this valiant hero! "Ours is the blood of the Goth," says he to King Alfonso; "sweet to us is liberty, and bondage odious!" "The king may give his castles to the Frank, but not his vassals; for kings themselves hold no dominion over the free will!" He and his followers would rather die freemen than live slaves! If these are the common watch words of liberty at the present day, they were no less so among the high-souled Spaniards of the eighth century.

One of the finest of the historic ballads is that which describes Bernardo's march to Roncesvalles. He sallies forth "with three thousand Leonese and more," to protect the glory and freedom of his native land. From all sides, the peasantry of the land flock to the hero's standard.

The peasant leaves his plough afield,
    The reaper leaves his hook,
And from his hand the shepherd-boy
    Lets fall the pastoral crook.

The young set up a shout of joy,
    The old forget their years,
The feeble man grows stout of heart,
    No more the craven fears.

All rush to Bernard's standard,
    And on liberty they call;
They cannot brook to wear the yoke,
    When threatened by the Gaul.

"Free were we born," 't is thus they cry,
"And willingly pay we
The duty that we owe our king,
By the divine decree.

"But God forbid that we obey
The laws of foreign knaves,
Tarnish the glory of our sires,
And make our children slaves.

"Our hearts have not so craven grown,
So bloodless all our veins,
So vigorless our brawny arms,
As to submit to chains.

"Has the audacious Frank, forsooth,
Subdued these seas and lands
Shall he a bloodless victory have?
No, not while we have hands.

"He shall learn that the gallant Leonese
Can bravely fight and fall,
But that they know not how to yield;
They are Castilians all.

"Was it for this the Roman power
Of old was made to yield
Unto Numantia's valiant hosts,
On many a bloody field?

"Shall the bold lions that have bathed
Their paws in Libyan gore,
Crouch basely to a feebler foe,
And dare the strife no more?

"Let the false king sell town and tower,
But not his vassals free;
For to subdue the free-born soul
No royal power hath he!"

These short specimens will suffice to show the spirit of the old heroic ballads of Spain the; Romances del Cid, and those that rehearse the gallant achievements of many other champions, brave and stalwart knights of old, I must leave unnoticed, and pass to another field of chivalry and song.

The next class of the ancient Spanish ballads is the Romantic, including those which relate to the Twelve Peers of Charlemagne and other imaginary heroes of the days of chivalry. There is an exaggeration in the prowess of these heroes of romance which is in accordance with the warmth of a Spanish imagination; and the ballads which celebrate their achievements still go from mouth to mouth among the peasantry of Spain, and are hawked about the streets by the blind ballad-monger.

Among the romantic ballads, those of the Twelve Peers stand preeminent, not so much for their poetic merit as for the fame of their heroes. In them are sung the valiant knights whose history is written more at large in the prose romances of chivalry,—Orlando, and Oliver, and Montesinos, and Durandarte, and the Marques de Mantua, and the other paladins, "*que en una mesa comian pan.*" These ballads are of different length and various degrees of merit. Of some a few lines only remain; they are evidently fragments of larger works; while others, on the contrary, aspire to the length and dignity of epic poems;—witness the ballads of the Conde de Irlos and the Marques de Mantua, each of which consists of nearly a thousand long and sonorous lines.

Among these ballads of the Twelve Peers there are many of great beauty; others possess little merit, and are wanting in vigor and conciseness. From the structure of the versification, I should rank them among the oldest of the Spanish ballads. They are all monorhythmic, with full consonant rhymes.

To the romantic ballads belong also a great number which recount the deeds of less celebrated heroes, but among them all none is so curious as that of Virgil. Like the old French romance-writers of the Middle Ages, the early Spanish poets introduced the Mantuan bard as a knight of chivalry. The ballad informs us that a certain king kept him imprisoned seven years, for what old Brantôme would call *outrecuydance* with a certain Doña Isabel. But being at mass on Sunday, the recollection of Virgil comes suddenly into his mind, when he ought to be attending to the priest; and, turning to his knights, he asks them what has become of Virgil. One of them replies, "Your Highness has him imprisoned in your dungeons;" to which the king makes answer with the greatest coolness, by telling them that the dinner is waiting, and that after they have dined they will pay Virgil a visit in his prison. Then up and spake the queen like a true heroine; quoth she, "I will not dine without him;" and straightway they all repaired to the prison, where they find the incarcerated knight engaged in the pleasant pastime of combing his hair and arranging his beard. He tells the king very coolly that on that very day he has been a prisoner seven years; to this the king replies, "Hush, hush, Virgil; it takes three more to make ten." "Sire," says Virgil, with the same philosophical composure, "if your Highness so ordains, I will pass my whole life here." "As a reward for your patience, you shall dine with me to-day," says the king. "My coat is torn," says Virgil; "I am not in trim to make a leg." But this difficulty is removed by the promise of a new suit from the king, and they go to dinner. Virgil delights both knights and damsels, but most of all Doña Isabel. The archbishop is called in; they are married forthwith, and the ballad closes like a scene in some old play: "He takes her by the hand, and leads her to the garden."

Such is this curious ballad.

I now turn to one of the most beautiful of these ancient Spanish poems;—it is the Romance del Conde Alarcos, a ballad full of interest and of touching pathos. The story is briefly this. The Count Alarcos, after being secretly betrothed to the Infanta Solisa, forsakes her and weds another lady. Many years afterward, the princess, sitting alone, as she was wont, and bemoaning her forsaken lot, resolves to tell the cause of her secret sorrow to the king her father; and, after confessing her clandestine love for Count Alarcos, demands the death of the Countess, to heal her wounded honor. Her story awakens the wrath of the king; he acknowledges the justness of her demand, seeks an interview with the Count, and sets the case before him in so strong a light, that finally he wrings from him a promise to put his wife to death with his own hand. The Count returns homeward a grief-stricken man, weeping the sad destiny of his wife, and saying within himself, "How shall I look upon her smile of joy, when she comes forth to meet me?" The Countess welcomes his return with affectionate tenderness, but he is heavy at heart and disconsolate. He sits down to supper with his children around him, but the food is untasted; he hides his face in his hands, and weeps. At length they retire to their chamber. In the language of Mr. Lockhart's translation,—

They came together to the bower, where they were used to rest,—
None with them but the little babe that was upon the breast:
The Count had barred the chamber-doors,—they ne'er were barred till
then:
"Unhappy lady," he began, "and I most lost of men!"

"Now speak not so, my noble lord, my husband, and my life!
Unhappy never can she be that is Alarcos' wife!"
"Alas! unhappy lady, 't is but little that you know;
For in that very word you've said is gathered all your woe.

"Long since I loved a lady,—long since I oaths did plight
To be that lady's husband, to love her day and night;
Her father is our lord the king,—to him the thing is known;
And now—that I the news should bring!—she claims me for her own.

"Alas! my love, alas! my life, the right is on their side;
Ere I had seen your face, sweet wife, she was betrothed my bride;
But—oh, that I should speak the word!—since in her place you lie,
It is the bidding of our lord that you this night must die."

"Are these the wages of my love, so lowly and so leal?
Oh, kill me not, thou noble Count, when at thy foot I kneel!
But send me to my father's house, where once I dwelt in glee;
There will I live a lone, chaste life, and rear my children three."

"It may not be,—mine oath is strong,—ere dawn of day you die."
"Oh, well 't is seen how all alone upon the earth am I!—
My father is an old, frail man; my mother's in her grave;
And dead is stout Don Garci,—alas! my brother brave!

"T was at this coward king's command they slew my brother dear,
And now I 'm helpless in the land!—It is not death I fear,
But loth, loth am I to depart, and leave my children so;—
Now let me lay them to my heart, and kiss them, ere I go."

"Kiss him that lies upon thy breast,—the rest thou mayst not see."
"I fain would say an Ave." "Then say it speedily."
She knelt her down upon her knee,—"O Lord, behold my case!
Judge not my deeds, but look on me in pity and great grace!"

When she had made her orison, up from her knees she rose:—
"Be kind, Alarcos, to our babes, and pray for my repose;
And now give me my boy once more, upon my breast to hold,
That he may drink one farewell drink before my breast be cold."

"Why would you waken the poor child? you see he is asleep;
Prepare, dear wife, there is no time, the dawn begins to peep."
"Now, hear me, Count Alarcos! I give thee pardon free:
I pardon thee for the love's sake wherewith I've loved thee;—

"But *they* have not my pardon,—the king and his proud daughter;
The curse of God be on them, for this unchristian slaughter!
I charge them with my dying breath, ere thirty days be gone,
To meet me in the realm of death, and at God's awful throne!"

The Count then strangles her with a scarf, and the ballad concludes with the fulfilment of the dying lady's prayer, in the death of the king and the Infanta within twenty days of her own.

Few, I think, will be disposed to question the beauty of this ancient ballad, though a refined and cultivated taste may revolt from the seemingly unnatural incident upon which it is founded. It must be recollected that this is a scene taken from a barbarous age, when the life of even the most cherished and beloved was held of little value in comparison with a chivalrous but false and exaggerated point of honor. It must be borne in mind, also, that, notwithstanding the boasted liberty of the Castilian hidalgos, and their frequent rebellions against the crown, a deep reverence for the divine right of kings, and a consequent disposition to obey the mandates of the throne, at almost any sacrifice, has always been one of the prominent traits of the Spanish character. When taken in connection with these circumstances, the story of this old ballad ceases to be so grossly improbable as it seems at first sight, and, indeed, becomes an illustration of national character. In all probability, the story of the Conde Alarcos had some foundation in fact.[7]

---

[7] This exaggerated reverence for the person and prerogatives of the king has furnished the groundwork of two of the best dramas in the Spanish language: *La Estrella de Sevilla*, by Lope de Vega, and *Del Rey abajo Ninguno*, by Francisco de Rojas.

The third class of the ancient Spanish ballads is the Moorish. Here we enter a new world, more gorgeous and more dazzling than that of Gothic chronicle and tradition. The stern spirits of Bernardo, the Cid, and Mudarra have passed away; the mail-clad forms of Guarinos, Orlando, and Durandarte are not here: the scene is changed; it is the bridal of Andalla, the bull-fight of Ganzul. The sunshine of Andalusia glances upon the marble halls of Granada, and green are the banks of the Xenil and the Darro. A band of Moorish knights gayly arrayed in gambesons of crimson silk, with scarfs of blue and jewelled tahalíes, sweep like the wind through the square of Vivarambla. They ride to the Tournament of Reeds; the Moorish maiden leans from the balcony; bright eyes glisten from many a lattice; and the victorious knight receives the prize of valor from the hand of her whose beauty is like the star-lit night. These are the Xarifas, the Celindas, and Lindaraxas,—the Andallas, Ganzules, and Abenzaydes of Moorish song.

Then comes the sound of the silver clarion, and the roll of the Moorish atabal, down from the snowy pass of the Sierra Nevada and across the gardens of the Vega. Alhama has fallen! woe is me, Alhama! The Christian is at the gates of Granada; the banner of the cross floats from the towers of the Alhambra! And these, too, are themes for the minstrel,—themes sung alike by Moor and Spaniard.

Among the Moorish ballads are included not only those which were originally composed in Arabic, but all that relate to the manners, customs, and history of the Moors in Spain. In most of them the influence of an Oriental taste is clearly visible; their spirit is more refined and effeminate than that of the historic and romantic ballads, in which no trace of such an influence is perceptible. The spirit of the Cid is stern, unbending, steel-clad; his hand grasps his sword Tizona; his heel wounds the flank of his steed Babieca;—

La mano aprieta á Tizona,
Y el talon fiere á Babieca.

But the spirit of Arbolan the Moor, though resolute in camps, is effeminate in courts; he is a diamond among scymitars, yet graceful in the dance;—

Diamante entre los alfanges,
Gracioso en baylar las zambras.

The ancient ballads are stamped with the character of their heroes. Abundant illustrations of this could be given, but it is not necessary.

Among the most spirited of the Moorish ballads are those which are interwoven in the History of the Civil Wars of Granada. The following, entitled "A very mournful Ballad on the Siege and Conquest of Alhama," is very beautiful; and such was the effect it produced upon the Moors, that it was forbidden, on pain of death, to sing it within the walls of Granada. The translation, which is executed with great skill and fidelity, is from the pen of Lord Byron.

The Moorish king rides up and down,
Through Granada's royal town;
From Elvira's gates to those
Of Bivarambla on he goes.
    Woe is me, Alhama!

Letters to the monarch tell
How Alhama's city fell;
In the fire the scroll he threw,
And the messenger he slew.
    Woe is me, Alhama!

He quits his mule, and mounts his horse,
And through the street directs his course;
Through the street of Zacatin
To the Alhambra spurring in.
    Woe is me, Alhama!

When the Alhambra's walls he gained,
On the moment he ordained
That the trumpet straight should sound
With the silver clarion round.
    Woe is me, Alhama!

And when the hollow drums of war
Beat the loud alarm afar,
That the Moors of town and plain
Might answer to the martial strain,—
    Woe is me, Alhama!

Then the Moors, by this aware
That bloody Mars recalled them there,
One by one, and two by two,
To a mighty squadron grew.
    Woe is me, Alhama!

Out then spake an aged Moor
In these words the king before:
"Wherefore call on us, O king?
What may mean this gathering?"
    Woe is me, Alhama!

"Friends! ye have, alas! to know
Of a most disastrous blow,—
That the Christians, stem and bold,
Have obtained Alhama's hold."
    Woe is me, Alhama!

Out then spake old Alfaqui,
With his heard so white to see:
"Good king! thou art justly served;
Good king! this thou hast deserved.
    Woe is me, Alhama!

"By thee were slain, in evil hour,
The Abencerrage, Granada's flower;
And strangers were received by thee
Of Córdova the chivalry.
    Woe is me, Alhama!

"And for this, O king! is sent
Ou thee a double chastisement;
Thee and thine, thy crown and realm,
One last wreck shall overwhelm.
    Woe is me, Alhama!

"He who holds no laws in awe,
He must perish by the law;
And Granada must be won,

And thyself with her undone."
Woe is me, Alhama!

Fire flashed from out the old Moor's eyes:
The monarch's wrath began to rise,
Because he answered, and because
He spake exceeding well of laws.
Woe is me, Alhama!

"There is no law to say such things
As may disgust the ear of kings!"
Thus, snorting with his choler, said
The Moorish king, and doomed him dead.
Woe is me, Alhama!

Such are the ancient ballads of Spain; poems which, like the Gothic cathedrals of the Middle Ages, have outlived the names of their builders. They are the handiwork of wandering, homeless minstrels, who for their daily bread thus "built the lofty rhyme," and whose names, like their dust and ashes, have long, long been wrapped in a shroud. "These poets," says an anonymous writer, "have left behind them no trace to which the imagination can attach itself; they have 'died and made no sign.' We pass from the infancy of Spanish poetry to the age of Charles, through a long vista of monuments without inscriptions, as the traveller approaches the noise and bustle of modern Rome through the lines of silent and unknown tombs that border the Appian Way."

Before closing this essay, I must allude to the unfavorable opinion which the learned Dr. Southey has expressed concerning the merit of these old Spanish ballads. In his preface to the Chronicle of the Cid, he says: "The heroic ballads of the Spaniards have been overrated in this country; they are infinitely and every way inferior to our own. There are some spirited ones in the Guerras Civiles de Granada, from which the rest have been estimated; but, excepting these, I know none of any value among the many hundreds which I have perused." On this field I am willing to do battle, though it be with a veteran knight who bears enchanted arms, and whose sword, like that of Martin Antolinez, "illumines all the field." That the old Spanish ballads may have been overrated, and that as a whole they are inferior to the English, I concede; that many of the hundred ballads of the Cid are wanting in interest, and that many of those of the Twelve Peers of France are languid, and drawn out beyond the patience of the most patient reader, I concede; I willingly confess, also, that among them all I have found none that can rival in graphic power the short but wonderful ballad of Sir Patrick Spence, wherein the mariner sees "the new moon with the old moon in her arm, or the more modern one of the Battle of Agincourt, by Michael Drayton, beginning,—

Fair stood the wind for France,
As we our sails advance,
Nor now to prove our chance
    Longer will tarry;
But putting to the main,
At Caux, the mouth of Seine,
With all his martial train,
    Landed King Harry.

All this I readily concede: but that the old Spanish ballads are infinitely and every way inferior to the English, and that among them all there are none of any value, save a few which celebrate the civil wars of Granada,—this I deny. The March of Bernardo del Carpio is hardly inferior to Chevy Chase; and the ballad of the Conde Alarcos, in simplicity and pathos, has hardly a peer in all English balladry,—it is superior to Edem 0' Gordon.

But a truce to criticism. Already, methinks, I hear the voice of a drowsy and prosaic herald proclaiming, in the language of Don Quixote to the puppet-player, "Make an end, Master Peter, for it grows toward supper-time, and I have some symptoms of hunger upon me."

THE VILLAGE OF EL PARDILLO

> When the lawyer is swallowed up with business, and the states man is preventing or contriving plots, then we sit on cowslip banks, hear the birds sing, and possess ourselves in as much quietness as these silent silver streams we now see glide so quietly by us.
>
> — IZAAK WALTON.

IN that delicious season when the coy and capricious maidenhood of spring is swelling into the warmer, riper, and more voluptuous womanhood of summer, I left Madrid for the village of El Pardillo. I had already seen enough of the villages of the North of Spain to know that for the most part they have few charms to entice one from the city; but I was curious to see the peasantry of the land in their native homes,—to see how far the shepherds of Castile resemble those who sigh and sing in the pastoral romances of Montemayor and Gaspar Gil Polo.

I love the city and its busy hum; I love that glad excitement of the crowd which makes the pulse beat quick, the freedom from restraint, the absence of those curious eyes and idle tongues which persecute one in villages and provincial towns. I love the country, too, in its season; and there is no scene over which my eye roves with more delight than the face of a summer landscape dimpled with soft sunny hollows, and smiling in all the freshness and luxuriance of June. There is no book in which I read sweeter lessons of virtue, or find the beauty of a quiet life more legibly recorded. My heart drinks in the tranquillity of the scene; and I never hear the sweet warble of a bird from its native wood, without a silent wish that such a cheerful voice and peaceful shade were mine. There is a beautiful moral feeling connected with everything in rural life, which is not dreamed of in the philosophy of the city. The voice of the brook and the language of the winds and woods are no poetic fiction. What an impressive lesson is there in the opening bud of spring! What an eloquent homily in the fall of the autumnal leaf! How well does the song of a passing bird represent the glad but transitory days of youth! and in the hollow tree and hooting owl what a melancholy image of the decay and imbecility of old age! In the beautiful language of an English poet,—

Your voiceless lips, O flowers, are living preachers,
Each cup a pulpit, every leaf a book,
Supplying to my fancy numerous teachers,
From loneliest nook.

'Neath cloistered boughs each floral bell that swingeth,
And tolls its perfume on the passing air,
Makes Sabbath in the fields, and ever ringeth
A call to prayer;

Not to the domes where crumbling arch and column
Attest the feebleness of mortal hand,
But to that fans most catholic and solemn
Which God hath planned;

To that cathedral, boundless as our wonder,
Whose quenchless lamps the sun and moon supply,—
Its choir the winds and waves, its organ thunder,
Its dome the sky.

There, amid solitude and shade, I wander
Through the green aisles, and, stretched upon the sod,
Awed by the silence, reverently ponder
The ways of God.

But the traveller who journeys through the northern provinces of Spain will look in vain for the charms of rural scenery in the villages he passes. Instead of trim cottages, and gardens, and the grateful shade of trees, he will see a cluster of stone hovels roofed with red tiles and basking in the hot sun, without a single tree to lend him shade or shelter; and instead of green meadows and woodlands vocal with the song of birds, he will find bleak and rugged mountains, and vast extended plains, that stretch away beyond his ken.

It was my good fortune, however, to find, not many leagues from the metropolis, a village which could boast the shadow of a few trees. El Pardillo is situated on the southern slope of the Guadarrama Mountains, just where the last broken spurs of the sierra stretch forward into the vast table land of New Castile. The village itself, like most other Castilian villages, is only a cluster of weather-stained and dilapidated houses, huddled together without beauty or regularity; but the scenery around it is picturesque,—a mingling of hill and dale, sprinkled with patches of cultivated land and clumps of forest-trees; and in the background the blue, vapory outline of the Guadarrama Mountains melting into the sky.

In this quiet place I sojourned for a season, accompanied by the publican Don Valentin and his fair daughter Florencia. We took up our abode in the cottage of a peasant named Lucas, an honest tiller of the soil, simple and good-natured; or, in the more emphatic language of Don Valentin, *"un hombre may infeliz, y sin malicia ninguna."* Not so his wife Matina; she was a Tartar, and so meddlesome withal, that poor Lucas skulked doggedly about his own premises, with his head down and his tail between his legs.

In this little village my occupations were few and simple. My morning's walk was to the Cross of Espalmado, a large wooden crucifix in the fields; the day was passed with books, or with any idle companion I was lucky enough to catch by the button, and bribe with a cigar into a long story, or a little village gossip; and I whiled away the evening in peeping round among the cottagers, studying the beautiful landscape that spread before me, and watching the occasional gathering of a storm about the blue peaks of the Guadarrama Mountains. My favorite haunt was a secluded spot in a little woodland valley, through which a crystal brook ran brawling along its pebbly channel. There, stretched in the shadow of a tree, I often passed the hours of noontide heat, now reading the magic numbers of Garcilaso, and anon listening to the song of the nightingale overhead; or watching the toil of a patient ant, as he rolled his stone, like Sisyphus, up hill, or the flight of a bee darting from flower to flower, and hiding "his murmurs in the rose."

Blame me not, thou studious moralist,—blame me not unheard for this idle dreaming; such moments are not wholly thrown away. In the language of Goethe, "I lie down in the grass near a falling brook, and close to the earth a thousand varieties of grasses become perceptible. When I listen to the hum of the little world between the stubble, and see the countless indescribable forms of insects, I feel the presence of the Almighty who has created us,—the breath of the All-benevolent who supports us in perpetual enjoyment."

The village church, too, was a spot around which I occasionally lingered of an evening, when in pensive or melancholy mood. And here, gentle reader, thy imagination will straightway conjure up a scene of ideal beauty,—a village church with decent white-washed walls, and modest spire just peeping forth from a clump of trees! No; I will not deceive thee;—the church of El Pardillo resembles not this picture of thy well-tutored fancy. It is a gloomy little edifice, standing upon the outskirts of the village, and built of dark and unhewn stone, with a spire like a sugar-loaf. There is no grass-plot in front, but a little esplanade beaten hard by the footsteps of the church-going peasantry. The tombstone of one of the patriarchs of the village serves as a doorstep, and a single solitary tree throws its friendly shade upon the portals of the little sanctuary.

One evening, as I loitered around this spot, the sound of an organ and the chant of youthful voices from within struck my ear; the church door was ajar, and I entered. There stood the priest, surrounded by a group of children, who were singing a hymn to the Virgin:—

Ave, Regina cœlorum,
Ave, Domina angelorum.

There is something exceedingly thrilling in the voices of children singing. Though their music be unskilful, yet it finds its way to the heart with wonderful celerity. Voices of cherubs are they, for they breathe of paradise; clear, liquid tones, that flow from pure lips and innocent hearts, like the sweetest notes of a flute, or the falling of water from a fountain! When the chant was finished, the priest opened a little book which he held in his hand, and began, with a voice as solemn as a funeral bell, to question this class of roguish catechumens, whom he was initiating into the mysterious doctrines of the mother church. Some of the questions and answers were so curious that I cannot refrain from repeating them here; and should any one doubt their authenticity, he will find them in the Spanish catechisms.

"In what consists the mystery of the Holy Trinity?"

"In one God, who is three persons; and three persons, who are but one God."

"But tell me, three human persons, are they not three men?"

"Yes, father."

"Then why are not three divine persons three Gods?"

"Because three human persons have three human natures; but the three divine persons have only one divine nature."

"Can you explain this by an example?"

"Yes, father; as a tree which has three branches is still but one tree, since all the three branches spring from one trunk, so the three divine persons are but one God, because they all have the same divine nature."

"Where were these three divine persons before the heavens and the earth were created?"

"In themselves."

"Which of them was made man?"

"The Son."

"And after the Son was made man, was he still God?"

"Yes, father; for in becoming man he did not cease to be God, any more than a man when he becomes a monk ceases to be a man."

"How was the Son of God made flesh?"

"He was born of the most holy Virgin Mary."

"And can we still call her a virgin?"

"Yes, father; for as a ray of the sun may pass through a pane of glass, and the glass remain unbroken, so the Virgin Mary, after the birth of her Son, was a pure and holy virgin as before."[8]

"Who died to save and redeem us?"

"The Son of God: as man, and not as God."

---

[8] This illustration was also made use of during the dark ages. Pierre de Corbiac, a Troubadour of the thirteenth century, thus introduces it in a poem entitled "Prayer to the Virgin":—

Domna, verges pue' e fina
And que fos l' enfantamens,
Et apres tot eissamens,
De vos trais sa carn humana
Jhesu-Christ nostre salvare;
Si com ses trenamens faire
Intra'l bel rais quan solelha
Per la fenestra veirina.

"How could he suffer and die as man only, being both God and man, and yet but one person?"

"As in a heated bar of iron upon which water is thrown, the heat only is affected and not the iron, so the Son of God suffered in his human nature and not in his divine."

"And when the spirit was separated from his most precious body, whither did the spirit go?"

"To limbo, to glorify the souls of the holy fathers."

"And the body?"

"It was carried to the grave."

"Did the divinity remain united with the spirit or with the body?"

"With both. As a soldier, when he unsheathes his sword, remains united both with the sword and the sheath, though they are separated from each other, so did the divinity remain united both with the spirit and the body of Christ, though the spirit was separated and removed from the body."

I did not quarrel with the priest for having been born and educated in a different faith from mine; but as I left the church and sauntered slowly homeward, I could not help asking myself, in a whisper, "Why perplex the spirit of a child with these metaphysical subtilties, these dark, mysterious speculations, which man in all his pride of intellect cannot fathom or explain?"

I must not forget, in this place, to make honorable mention of the little great men of El Pardillo. And first in order comes the priest. He was a short, portly man, serious in manner, and of grave and reverend presence, though at the same time there was a dash of the jolly-fat-friar about him; and on hearing a good joke or a sly innuendo, a smile would gleam in his eye, and play over his round face, like the light of a glowworm. His housekeeper was a brisk, smiling little woman, on the shady side of thirty, and a cousin of his to boot. Whenever she was mentioned, Don Valentin looked wise, as if this cousinship were apocryphal, but he said nothing,—not he; what right had he to be peeping into other people's business, when he had only one eye to look after his own withal? Next in rank to the dominie was the alcalde, justice of the peace and quorum; a most potent, grave, and reverend personage, with a long beak of a nose, and a pouch under his chin, like a pelican. He was a man of few words, but great in authority, and his importance was vastly increased in the village by a pair of double-barrelled spectacles, so contrived that, when bent over his desk and deeply buried in his musty papers, he could look up and see what was going on around him without moving his head, whereby he got the reputation of seeing twice as much as other people. There was the village surgeon, too, a tall man with a varnished hat and a starved dog; he had studied at the University of Salamanca, and was pompous and pedantic, ever and anon quoting some threadbare maxim from the Greek philosophers, and embellishing it with a commentary of his own. Then there was the gray-headed sacristan, who rang the church-bell, played on the organ, and was learned in tombstone lore; a politician, who talked me to death about taxes, liberty, and the days of the constitution; and a notary public, a poor man with a large family, who would make a paper cigar last half an hour, and who kept up his respectability in the village by keeping a horse.

Beneath the protecting shade of these great men full many an inhabitant of El Pardillo was born and buried. The village continued to flourish, a quiet, happy place, though all unknown to fame. The inhabitants were orderly and industrious, went regularly to mass and confession, kept every saint's day in the calendar, and devoutly hung Judas once a year in effigy. On Sundays and all other holidays, when mass was over, the time was devoted to sports and recreation; and the day passed off in social visiting, and athletic exercises, such as running, leaping, wrestling, pitching quoits, and heaving the bar. When evening came, the merry sound of the guitar summoned to the dance; then every nook and alley poured forth its youthful company,—light of heart and heel, and decked out in all the holiday finery of flowers, and ribbons, and crimson sashes. A group gathered before the cottage door; the signal was given, and away whirled the merry dancers to the wild music of voice and guitar, and the measured beat of castanet and tambourine.

I love these rural dances,—from my heart I love them. This world, at best, is so full of care and sorrow,—the life of a poor man is so stained with the sweat of his brow,—there is so much toil, and struggling, and anguish, and disappointment here below, that I gaze with delight on a scene where all these are laid aside and forgotten, and the heart of the toil-worn peasant seems to throw off its load, and to leap to the sound of music, when merrily,

Beneath soft eve's consenting star,
Fandango twirls his jocund castanet.

Not many miles from the village of El Pardillo stands the ruined castle of Villafranca, an ancient stronghold of the Moors of the fifteenth century. It is built upon the summit of a hill, of easy ascent upon one side, but precipitous and inaccessible on the other. The front presents a large, square tower, constituting the main part of the castle, on one side of which an arched gateway leads to a spacious court-yard within, surrounded by battlements. The corner towers are circular, with beetling turrets; and here and there, apart from the main body of the castle, stand several circular basements, whose towers have fallen and mouldered into dust. From the balcony in the square tower, the eye embraces the level landscape for leagues and leagues around; and beneath, in the depth of the valley, lies a beautiful grove, alive with the song of the nightingale. The whole castle is in ruin, and occupied only as a hunting-lodge, being inhabited by a solitary tenant, who has charge of the adjacent domain.

One holiday, when mass was said and the whole village was let loose to play, we made a pilgrimage to the ruins of this old Moorish alcázar. Our cavalcade was as motley as that of old,—the pilgrims "that toward Canterbury wolden ride;" for we had the priest, and the doctor of physic, and the man of laws, and a wife of Bath, and many more whom I must leave unsung. Merrily flew the hours and fast, and sitting after dinner in the gloomy hall of that old castle, many a tale was told, and many a legend and tradition of the past conjured up to satisfy the curiosity of the present.

Most of these tales were about the Moors who built the castle, and the treasures they had buried beneath it. Then the priest told the story of a lawyer who sold himself to the devil for a pot of money, and was burnt by the Holy Inquisition therefor. In his confession, he told how he had learned from a Jew the secret of raising the devil; how he went to the castle at midnight with a book which the Jew gave him, and, to make the charm sure, carried with him a loadstone, six nails from the coffin of a child of three years, six tapers of rosewax, made by a child of four years, the skin and blood of a young kid, an iron fork, with which the kid had been killed, a few hazel-rods, a flask of high-proof brandy, and some lignum-vitæ charcoal to make a fire. When he read in the book, the devil appeared in the shape of a man dressed in flesh-colored clothes, with long nails and large fiery eyes, and he signed an agreement with him written in blood, promising never to go to mass, and to give him his soul at the end of eight years in return for this, he was to have a million of dollars in good money, which the devil was to bring to him the next night; but when the next night came, and the lawyer had conjured from his book, instead of the devil, there appeared—who do you think?—the alcalde with half the village at his heels, and the poor lawyer was handed over to the Inquisition, and burnt for dealing in the black art.

I intended to repeat here some of the many tales that were told; but, upon reflection, they seem too frivolous, and must therefore give place to a more serious theme.

THE DEVOTIONAL POETRY OF SPAIN.

Heaven's dove, when highest he flies,
Flies with thy heavenly wings.

CRASHAW.

THERE is hardly a chapter in literary history more strongly marked with the peculiarities of national character than that which contains the moral and devotional poetry of Spain. It would naturally be expected that in this department of literature all the fervency and depth of national feeling would be exhibited. But still, as the spirit of morality and devotion is the same, wherever it exists,—as the enthusiasm of virtue and religion is everywhere essentially the same feeling, though modified in its degree and in its action by a variety of physical causes and local circumstances,—and as the subject of the didactic verse and the spiritual canticle cannot be materially changed by the change of nation and climate, it might at the first glance seem quite as natural to expect that the moral and devotional poetry of Christian countries would never be very strongly marked with national peculiarities. In other words, we should expect it to correspond to the warmth or coldness of national feeling, for it is the external and visible expression of this feeling; but not to the distinctions of national character, because, its nature and object being everywhere the same, these distinctions become swallowed up in one universal Christian character.

In moral poetry this is doubtless true. The great principles of Christian morality being eternal and invariable, the verse which embodies and represents them must, from this very circumstance, be the same in its spirit through all Christian lands. The same, however, is not necessarily true of devotional or religious poetry. There, the language of poetry is something more than the visible image of a devotional spirit. It is also an expression of religious faith, shadowing forth, with greater or less distinctness, its various creeds and doctrines. As these are different in different nations, the spirit that breathes in religious song, and the letter that gives utterance to the doctrine of faith, will not be universally the same. Thus, Catholic nations sing the praises of the Virgin Mary in language in which nations of the Protestant faith do not unite; and among Protestants themselves, the difference of interpretations, and the consequent belief or disbelief of certain doctrines, give a various spirit and expression to religious poetry. And yet, in all, the devotional feeling, the heavenward volition, is the same.

As far, then, as peculiarities of religious faith exercise an influence upon intellectual habits, and thus become a part of national character, so far will the devotional or religious poetry of a country exhibit the characteristic peculiarities resulting from this influence of faith and its assimilation with the national mind. Now Spain is by preëminence the Catholic land of Christendom. Most of her historic recollections are more or less intimately associated with the triumphs of the Christian faith; and many of her warriors—of her best and bravest—were martyrs in the holy cause, perishing in that war of centuries which was carried on within her own territories between the crescent of Mahomet and the cross of Christ. Indeed, the whole tissue of her history is interwoven with miraculous traditions. The intervention of her patron saint has saved her honor in more than one dangerous pass; and the war-shout of *"Santiago, y cierra España!"* has worked like a charm upon the wavering spirit of the soldier. A reliance on the guardian ministry of the saints pervades the whole people, and devotional offerings for signal preservation in times of danger and distress cover the consecrated walls of churches. An enthusiasm of religious feeling, and of external ritual observances, prevails throughout the land. But more particularly is the name of the Virgin honored and adored. *Ave Maria* is the salutation of peace at the friendly threshold, and the Godspeed to the wayfarer. It is the evening orison, when the toils of day are done; and at midnight it echoes along the solitary streets in the voice of the watchman's cry.

These and similar peculiarities of religious faith are breathing and moving through a large portion of the devotional poetry of Spain. It is not only instinct with religious feeling, but incorporated with "the substance of things not seen." Not only are the poet's lips touched with a coal from the altar, but his spirit is folded in the cloud of incense that rises before the shrines of the Virgin Mother and the glorious company of the saints and martyrs. His soul is not wholly swallowed up in the contemplation of the sublime attributes of the Eternal Mind; but, with its lamp trimmed and burning, it goeth out to meet the bridegroom, as if he were coming in a bodily presence.

The history of the devotional poetry of Spain commences with the legendary lore of Maestro Gonzalo de Berceo, a secular priest, whose life was passed in the cloisters of a Benedictine convent and amid the shadows of the thirteenth century. The name of Berceo stands foremost on the catalogue of Spanish poets, for the author of the poem of the Cid is unknown. The old patriarch of Spanish poetry has left a monument of his existence in upwards of thirteen thousand alexandrines, celebrating the lives and miracles of saints and the Virgin, as he found them written in the Latin chronicles and dusty legends of his monastery. In embodying these in rude verse in *roman paladino*, or the old Spanish romance tongue, intelligible to the common people, Fray Gonzalo seems to have passed his life. His writings are just such as we should expect from the pen of a monk of the thirteenth century. They are more ghostly than poetical, and throughout, unction holds the place of inspiration. Accordingly, they illustrate very fully the preceding remarks, and the more so, inasmuch as they are written with the most ample and childish credulity, and the utmost singleness of faith touching the events and miracles described.

The following extract is taken from one of Berceo's poems, entitled "Vida de San Millan." It is a description of the miraculous appearance of Santiago and San Millan, mounted on snow-white steeds, and fighting for the cause of Christendom, at the battle of Simancas in the *Campo de Tom*.

And when the kings were in the field,—their squadrons in array,—
With lance in rest they onward pressed to mingle in the fray;
But soon upon the Christians fell a terror of their foes,—
These were a numerous army,—a little handful those.

And while the Christian people stood in this uncertainty,
Upward to heaven they turned their eyes, and fixed their thoughts on high;
And there two figures they beheld, all beautiful and bright,
Even than the pure new-fallen snow their garments were more white.

They rode upon two horses more white than crystal sheen,
And arms they bore such as before no mortal man had seen;
The one, he held a crosier,—a pontiff's mitre wore;
The other held a crucifix,—such man ne'er saw before.

Their faces were angelical, celestial forms had they,—
And downward through the fields of air they urged their rapid way;
They looked upon the Moorish host with fierce and angry look,
And in their hands, with dire portent, their naked sabres shook.

The Christian host, beholding this, straightway take heart again;
They fall upon their bended knees, all resting on the plain,
And each one with his clenched fist to smite his breast begins,
And promises to God on high he will forsake his sins.

And when the heavenly knights drew near unto the battle-ground,
They dashed among the Moors and dealt unerring blows around;
Such deadly havoc there they made the foremost ranks along,
A panic terror spread unto the hindmost of the throng.

Together with these two good knights, the champions of the sky,
The Christians rallied and began to smite full sore and high;
The Moors raised up their voices and by the Koran swore
That in their lives such deadly fray they ne'er had seen before.

Down went the misbelievers,—fast sped the bloody fight,—
Some ghastly and dismembered lay, and some half dead with fright:
Full sorely they repented that to the field they came,
For they saw that from the battle they should retreat with shame.

Another thing befell them,—they dreamed not of such woes,—
The very arrows that the Moors shot from their twanging bows
Turned back against them in their flight and wounded them full sore,
And every blow they dealt the foe was paid in drops of gore.

* * *

Now he that bore the crosier, and the papal crown had on,
Was the glorified Apostle, the brother of Saint John;

And he that held the crucifix, and wore the monkish hood,
Was the holy San Millan of Cogolla's neighborhood.

Berceo's longest poem is entitled *Miraclos de Nuestra Señora*, "Miracles of Our Lady." It consists of nearly four thousand lines, and contains the description of twenty-five miracles. It is a complete homily on the homage and devotion due to the glorious Virgin, *Madre dc Jhu Xto*, Mother of Jesus Christ; but it is written in a low and vulgar style, strikingly at variance with the elevated character of the subject. Thus, in the twentieth miracle, we have the account of a monk who became intoxicated in a wine-cellar. Having lain on the floor till the vesper-bell aroused him, he staggered off towards the church in most melancholy plight. The Evil One besets him on the way, assuming the various shapes of a bull, a dog, and a lion; but from all these perils he is miraculously saved by the timely intervention of the Virgin, who finding him still too much intoxicated to make his way to bed, kindly takes him by the hand, leads him to his pallet, covers him with a blanket and a counterpane, smooths his pillow, and, after making the sign of the cross over him, tells him to rest quietly, for sleep will do him good.

To a certain class of minds there may be something interesting and even affecting in descriptions which represent the spirit of a departed saint as thus assuming a corporeal shape, in order to assist and console human nature even in its baser infirmities; but it ought also to be considered how much such descriptions tend to strip religion of its peculiar sanctity, to bring it down from its heavenly abode, not merely to dwell among men, but, like an imprisoned culprit, to be chained to the derelict of principle, manacled with the base desire and earthly passion, and forced to do the menial offices of a slave. In descriptions of this kind, as in the representations of our Saviour and of sainted spirits in human shape, execution must of necessity fall far short of the conception. The handiwork cannot equal the glorious archetype, which is visible only to the mental eye. Painting and sculpture are not adequate to the task of embodying in a permanent shape the glorious visions, the radiant forms, the glimpses of heaven, which fill the imagination when purified and exalted by devotion. The hand of man unconsciously inscribes upon all his works the sentence of imperfection, which the finger of the invisible hand wrote upon the wall of the Assyrian monarch. From this it would seem to be not only a natural but a necessary conclusion, that all the descriptions of poetry which borrow anything, either directly or indirectly, from these bodily and imperfect representations must par take of their imperfection, and assume a more earthly and material character than these which come glowing and burning from the more spiritualized perceptions of the internal sense.

It is very far from my intention to utter any sweeping denunciation against the divine arts of painting and sculpture, as employed in the exhibition of Scriptural scenes and personages. These I esteem meet ornaments for the house of God; though, as I have already said, their execution cannot equal the high conceptions of an ardent imagination, yet, whenever the hand of a master is visible,—when the marble almost moves before you, and the painting starts into life from the canvas,—the effect upon an enlightened mind will generally, if not universally, be to quicken its sensibilities and excite to more ardent devotion, by carrying the thoughts beyond the representations of bodily suffering to the contemplation of the intenser mental agony,—the moral sublimity exhibited by the martyr. The impressions produced, however, will not be the same in all minds; they will necessarily vary according to the prevailing temper and complexion of the mind which receives them. As there is no sound where there is no car to receive the impulses and vibrations of the air, so is there no moral impression,—no voice of instruction from all the works of nature and all the imitations of art,—unless there be within the soul itself a capacity for hearing the voice and receiving the moral impulse. The cause exists eternally and universally, but the effect is produced only when and where the cause has room to act, and just in proportion as it has room to act. Hence the various moral impressions, and the several degrees of the same moral impression, which an object may produce in different minds. These impressions will vary in kind and in degree according to the acuteness and the cultivation of the internal moral sense. And thus the representations spoken of above might exercise a very favorable influence upon an enlightened and well-regulated mind, and at the same time a very unfavorable influence upon an unenlightened and superstitious one. And the reason is obvious. An enlightened mind beholds all things in their just proportions, and receives from them the true impressions they are calculated to convey. It is not hoodwinked,—it is not shut up in a gloomy prison, till it thinks the walls of its own dungeon the limits of the universe, and the reach of its own chain the outer verge of all intelligence; but it walks abroad; the sunshine and the air pour in to enlighten and expand it; the various works of nature are its ministering angels; the glad recipient of light and wisdom, it develops new powers and acquires increased capacities, and thus, rendering itself less subject to error, assumes a nearer similitude to the Eternal Mind. But not so the dark and superstitious mind. It is filled with its own antique and mouldy furniture,—the moth-eaten tome, the gloomy tapestry, the dusty curtain. The straggling sunbeam from without streams through the stained window, and as it enters assumes the colors of the painted glass; while the half-extinguished fire within, now smouldering in its ashes, and now shooting forth a quivering flame, casts fantastic shadows through the chambers of the soul. Within the spirit sits, lost in its own abstractions. The voice of nature from without is hardly audible; her beauties are unseen, or seen only in shadowy forms, through a colored medium, and with a strained and distorted vision. The invigorating air does not enter that mysterious chamber; it visits not that lonely inmate, who, breathing only a close, exhausted atmosphere, exhibits in the languid frame and feverish pulse the marks of lingering, incurable disease. The picture is not too strongly sketched; such is the contrast between the free and the superstitious mind. Upon the latter, which has little power over its ideas,—to generalize them, to place them in their proper light and position, to reason upon, to discriminate, to judge them in detail, and thus to arrive at just conclusions; but, on the contrary, receives every crude and inadequate impression as it first presents itself, and treasures it up as an ultimate fact,—upon such a mind, representations of Scripture-scenes, like those mentioned above, exercise an unfavorable influence. Such a mind cannot rightly estimate, it cannot feel, the work of a master; and a miserable painting, or a still more miserable caricature carved in wood, will serve only the more to drag the spirit down to earth. Thus, in the unenlightened mind, these representations have a tendency to sensualize and desecrate the character of holy things. Being brought constantly before the eye, and represented in a real and palpable form to the external senses, they lose, by being made too familiar, that peculiar sanctity with which the mind naturally invests the unearthly and invisible.

It is curious to observe the influence of the circumstances just referred to upon the devotional poetry of Spain.[9]

[9] The following beautiful Latin hymn, written by Francisco Xavier, the friend and companion of Loyola, and from his zeal in the Eastern missions surnamed the Apostle of the Indies, would hardly have originated in any mind but that of one familiar with the representations of which I have spoken above.

O Deus! ego amo te:
Neo amo te, ut salves me,
Aut quia non amantes te
Æterno punis igne.

Tu, tu, mi Jesu, totum me
Amplexus es in cruce.
Tulisti clavos, lanceam,
Multamque ignominiam:
Innumeros dolores,
Sudores er angores,
Ac mortem: et hæc propter me
Ac pro me peccatore.

Cur igitur non amem te,
O Jesu amantissime?
Non ut in cœlo salves me,
Aut ne æternum damnes me,
Nec prœmii ullius spe:
Sed sicut tu amasti me,
Sic amo et amabo te:
Solum quia rex meus es,
Et solum quia Deus es.
Amen.

O God! My spirit loves but thee:
Not that in heaven its home may be,
Nor that the souls which love not thee
Shall groan in fire eternally.

But thou on the accursed tree
In mercy hast embraced me.
For me the cruel nails, the spear,

Sometimes it exhibits itself directly and fully, sometimes indirectly and incidentally, but always with sufficient clearness to indicate its origin. Sometimes it destroys the beauty of a poem by a miserable conceit; at other times it gives it the character of a beautiful allegory.[10]

The following sonnets will serve as illustrations. They are from the hand of the wonderful Lope de Vega:—

Shepherd! that with thine amorous sylvan song
Hast broken the slumber that encompassed me,

The ignominious scoff, didst bear,
Countless, unutterable woes,—
The bloody sweat,—death's pangs and throes,—
These thou didst bear, all these for me,
A sinner and estranged from thee.

And wherefore no affection show,
Jesus, to thee that lov'st me so?
Not that in heaven my home may be,
Not lest I die eternally,—
Nor from the hopes of joys above me:
But even as thou thyself didst love me,
So love I, and will ever love thee:
Solely because my King art thou,
My god forevermore as now.
Amen.

[10] I recollect but few instances of this kind of figurative poetry in our language. There is, however, one of most exquisite beauty and pathos, far surpassing anything I have seen of the kind in Spanish. It is a passage from Cowper.

I was a stricken deer, that left the herd
Long since: with many an arrow deep infixt
My panting side was charged, when I withdrew
To seek a tranquil death in distant shades.
There was I found by one who had himself
Been hurt by archers; in his side he bore,
And in his hands and feet, the cruel scars.
With gentle force soliciting the darts,
He drew them forth, and healed, and bade me live.

That madest thy crook from the accursed tree
On which thy powerful arms were stretched so long,—
Lead me to mercy's ever-flowing fountains,
For thou my shepherd, guard, and guide shalt be,
I will obey thy voice, and wait to see
Thy feet all beautiful upon the mountains.
Hear, Shepherd!—thou that for thy flock art dying,
Oh, wash away these scarlet sins, for thou
Rejoicest at the contrite sinner's vow.
Oh, wait!—to thee my weary soul is crying,—
Wait for me!—yet why ask it, when I see,
With feet nailed to the cross, thou art waiting still for me?

Lord, what am I, that with unceasing care
Thou didst seek after me,—that thou didst wait,
Wet with unhealthy dews before my gate,
And pass the gloomy nights of winter there?
O strange delusion!—that I did not greet
Thy blessed approach! and oh, to Heaven how lost,
If my ingratitude's unkindly frost
Hast chilled the bleeding wounds upon thy feet!
How oft my guardian angel gently cried,
"Soul, from thy casement look without and see
How he persists to knock and wait for thee!"
And oh, how often to that voice of sorrow,
"To-morrow we will open!" I replied;
And when the morrow came, I answered still, "To-morrow!"

The most remarkable portion of the devotional poetry of the Spaniards is to be found in their sacred dramas, their *Vidas de Santos* and *Autos Sacramentales.* These had their origin in the Mysteries and Moralities of the dark ages, and are indeed monstrous creations of the imagination. The *Vidas de Santos,* or Lives of Saints, are representations of their miracles, and of the wonderful traditions concerning them. The *Autos Sacramentales* have particular reference to the Eucharist and the ceremonies of the *Corpus Christi.* In these theatrical pieces are introduced upon the stage, not only angels and saints, but God, the Saviour, and the Virgin Mary; and, in strange juxtaposition with these, devils, peasants, and kings; in fine, they contain the strangest medley of characters, real and allegorical, which the imagination can conceive. As if this were not enough, in the midst of what was intended as a solemn, religious celebration, scenes of low buffoonery are often introduced.

The most remarkable of the sacred dramas which I have read is *La Devocion de la Cruz*, "The Devotion of the Cross," by Calderon; and it will serve as a specimen of that class of writing. The piece commences with a dialogue between Lisardo, the son of Curcio, a decayed nobleman, and Eusebio, the hero of the play and lover of Julia, Lisardo's sister. Though the father's extravagance has wasted his estates, Lisardo is deeply offended that Eusebio should aspire to an alliance with the family, and draws him into a secluded place in order to settle their dispute with the sword. Here the scene opens, and, in the course of the dialogue which precedes the combat, Eusebio relates that he was born at the foot of a cross, which stood in a rugged and desert part of these mountains; that the virtue of this cross preserved him from the wild beasts; that, being found by a peasant three days after his birth, he was carried to a neighboring village, and there received the name of Eusebio of the Cross; that, being thrown by his nurse into a well, he was heard to laugh, and was found floating upon the top of the water, with his hands placed upon his mouth in the form of a cross; that the house in which he dwelt being consumed by fire, he escaped unharmed amid the flames, and it was found to be Corpus Christi day; and, in fine, after relating many other similar miracles worked by the power of the cross, at whose foot he was born, he says that he bears its image miraculously stamped upon his breast. After this they fight, and Lisardo falls mortally wounded. In the next scene, Eusebio has an interview with Julia, at her father's house; they are interrupted, and Eusebio conceals himself; Curcio enters, and informs Julia that he has determined to send her that day to a convent, that she may take the veil, *"para ser de Cristo esposa."* While they are conversing, the dead body of Lisardo is brought in by peasants, and Eusebio is declared to be the murderer. The scene closes by the escape of Eusebio. The second act, or *jornada*, discovers Eusebio as the leader of a band of robbers. They fire upon a traveller, who proves to be a priest, named Alberto, and who is seeking a spot in those solitudes wherein to establish a hermitage. The shot is prevented from taking effect by a book which the pious old man carries in his bosom, and which he says is a "treatise on the true origin of the divine and heavenly tree, on which, dying with courage and fortitude, Christ triumphed over death; in fine, the book is called the 'Miracles of the Cross.'" They suffer the priest to depart unharmed, who in consequence promises Eusebio that he shall not die without confession, but that wherever he may be, if he but call upon his name, he will hasten to absolve him. In the meantime Julia retires to a convent, and Curcio goes with an armed force in pursuit of Eusebio, who has resolved to gain admittance to Julia's convent. He scales the walls of the convent by night, and silently gropes his way along the corridor. Julia is discovered sleeping in her cell, with a taper beside her. He is, however, deterred from executing his malicious designs by discovering upon her breast the form of a cross, similar to that which he bears upon his own, and "Heaven would not suffer him, though so great an offender, to lose his respect for the cross." To be brief, he leaps from the convent-walls and escapes to the mountains. Julia, counting her honor lost, having offended God, "*como á Dios, y como á esposa*", pursues him,—descends the ladder from the convent-wall, and, when she seeks to return to her cell, finds the ladder has been removed. In her despair, she accuses Heaven of having withdrawn its clemency, and vows to perform such deeds of wickedness as shall terrify both heaven and hell.

The third *jornada* transports the scene back to the mountains. Julia, disguised in man's apparel, with her face concealed, is brought to Eusebio by a party of the banditti. She challenges him to single combat, and he accepts the challenge, on condition that his antagonist shall declare who he is. Julia discovers herself, and relates several horrid murders she has committed since leaving the convent. Their interview is here interrupted by the entrance of banditti, who inform Eusebio that Curcio, with an armed force from all the neighboring villages, is approaching. The attack commences. Eusebio and Curcio meet, but a secret and mysterious sympathy prevents them from fighting, and a great number of peasants, coming in at this moment, rush upon Eusebio in a body, and he is thrown down a precipice. There Curcio discovers him, expiring with his numerous wounds. The *dénouement* of the piece commences. Curcio, moved by compassion, examines a wound in Eusebio's breast, discovers the mark of the cross, and thereby recognizes him to be his son. Eusebio expires, calling on the name of Alberto, who shortly after enters, as if lost in those mountains. A voice from the dead body of Eusebio calls his name. I shall here transcribe a part of the scene.

ALBERTO.

Homeward now from Rome returning,
In the deep and silent pauses
Of the night, upon this mountain
I again have lost my way!
This must be the very region
Where my life Eusebio gave me,
And I fear from his marauders
Danger threatens me to-day!

EUSEBIO.

Ho! Alberto!

ALBERTO.

What breath is it
Of a voice so full of terror,
That aloud my name repeating
Sounded then upon mine ear?

EUSEBIO.

Ho! Alberto!

ALBERTO.

It pronounces
Yet again my name; methought it
Came in this direction. Let me
Go still nearer.

GIL.

Santo Dios!
'T is Eusebio, and my terror
Of all terrors is the greatest!

EUSEBIO.

Ho! Alberto!

ALBERTO.

Nearer sounds it!
O thou voice that ridest swift
On the wind, my name repeating,
Who art thou?

EUSEBIO.

Eusebio am I.
Come, Alberto, hither hasten,
Hither, where I buried lie;
Come, and lift aside these branches;
Do not fear.

ALBERTO.

No fear have I.

GIL.

I have!

ALBERTO. (*uncovering Eusebio*).

Now thou art uncovered,
Tell me, in the name of God,
What thou wishest.

EUSEBIO.

In his name
'T was my Faith, Alberto, called thee,
So that ere my life be ended
Thou shouldst hear me in confession.
Long ago I should have died,
For remained untenanted
By the spirit this dead body;
But the mighty blow of death
Only robbed it of its motion,

Did not sever it asunder.
He rises.
Come where I may make confession
Of my sins, Alberto, for they
Or the atoms in the sun!
So much doth avail with Heaven
The Devotion of the Cross!

Eusebio then retires to confess himself to Alberto; and Curcio afterward relates that, when the venerable saint had given him absolution, his body again fell dead at his feet. Julia discovers herself, overwhelmed with the thoughts of her passion for Eusebio and her other crimes, and as Curcio, in a transport of indignation, endeavors to kill her, she seizes a cross which stands over Eusebio's grave, and with it ascends to heaven, while Alberto shouts, *"Gran milagro!"* and the curtain falls.

Thus far I have spoken of the devotional poetry of Spain as modified by the peculiarities of religious faith and practice. Considered apart from the dogmas of a creed, and as the expression of those pure and elevated feelings of religion which are not the prerogative of any one sect or denomination, but the common privilege of all, it possesses strong claims to our admiration and praise. I know of nothing in any modern tongue so beautiful as some of its finest passages. The thought springs heavenward from the soul,—the language comes burning from the lip. The imagination of the poet seems spiritualized; with nothing of earth, and all of heaven,—a heaven like that of his own native clime, without a cloud, or a vapor of earth, to obscure its brightness. His voice, speaking the harmonious accents of that noble tongue, seems to flow from the lips of an angel,—melodious to the ear and to the internal sense,—breathing those

Effectual whispers, whose still voice
The soul itself more feels than hears.

The following sonnets of Francisco de Aldana, a writer remarkable for the beauty of his conceptions and the harmony of his verse, are illustrations of this remark. In what glowing language he describes the aspirations of the soul for its paternal heaven, its celestial home! how beautifully he portrays in a few lines the strong desire, the ardent longing, of the exiled and imprisoned spirit to wing its flight away and be at rest! The strain bears our thoughts upward with it; it transports us to the heavenly country; it whispers to the soul,—Higher, immortal spirit! higher!

> Clear fount of light! my native land on high,
> Bright with a glory that shall never fade!
> Mansion of truth! without a veil or shade,
> Thy holy quiet meets the spirit's eye.
> There dwells the soul in its ethereal essence,
> Gasping no longer for life's feeble breath;
> But, sentinelled in heaven, its glorious presence
> With pitying eye beholds, yet fears not death.
> Beloved country! banished from thy shore,
> A stranger in this prison-house of clay,
> The exiled spirit weeps and sighs for thee!
> Heavenward the bright perfections I adore
> Direct, and the sure promise cheers the way,
> That whither love aspires, there shall my dwelling be.
> O Lord! that seest from you starry height
> Centred in one the future and the past,
> Fashioned in thine own image, see how fast
> The world obscures in me what once was bright!
> Eternal Sun! the warmth which thou hast given
> To cheer life's flowery April fast decays;
> Yet in the hoary winter of my days,
> Forever green shall be my trust in Heaven.
> Celestial King! Oh, let thy presence pass
> Before my spirit, and an image fair
> Shall meet that look of mercy from on high,
> As the reflected image in a glass
> Doth meet the look of him who seeks it there,
> And owes its being to the gazer's eye.

The prevailing characteristics of Spanish devotional poetry are warmth of imagination and depth and sincerity of feeling. The conception is always striking and original, and, when not degraded by dogmas and the poor, puerile conceits arising from them, beautiful and sublime. This results from the frame and temperament of the mind, and is a general characteristic of the Spanish poets, not only in this department of song, but in all others. The very ardor of imagination which, exercised upon minor themes, leads them into extravagance and hyperbole, when left to act in a higher and wider sphere conducts them nearer and nearer to perfection. When imagination spreads its wings in the bright regions of devotional song,—in the pure empyrean,—judgment should direct its course, but there is no danger of its soaring too high. The heavenly land still lies beyond its utmost flight. There are heights it cannot reach; there are fields of air which tire its wing; there is a splendor which dazzles its vision;—for there is a glory "which eye hath not seen, nor ear heard, nor hath it entered into the heart of man to conceive."

But perhaps the greatest charm of the devotional poets of Spain is their sincerity. Most of them were ecclesiastics,—men who had in sober truth renounced the realities of this life for the hopes and promises of another. We are not to suppose that all who take holy orders are saints; but we should be still further from believing that all are hypocrites. It would be even more absurd to suppose that none are sincere in their professions than that all are. Besides, with whatever feelings a man may enter the monastic life, there is something in its discipline and privations which has a tendency to wean the mind from earth, and to fix it upon heaven. Doubtless many have seemingly renounced the world from motives of worldly aggrandizement, and others have renounced it because it has renounced them. The former have carried with them to the cloister their earthly ambition, and the latter their dark misanthropy; and though many have daily kissed the cross and yet grown hoary in iniquity, and shrived their souls that they might sin more gayly on,—yet solitude works miracles in the heart, and many who enter the cloister from worldly motives find it a school wherein the soul may be trained to more holy purposes and desires. There is not half the corruption and hypocrisy within the convent's walls that the church bears the shame of hiding there. Hermits may be holy men, though knaves have sometimes been hermits. Were they all hypocrites, who of old for their souls' sake exposed their naked bodies to the burning sun of Syria? Where they, who wandered houseless in the solitudes of Engaddi? Where they, who dwelt beneath the palm-trees by the Red Sea? Oh, no! They were ignorant, they were deluded, they were fanatic, but they were not hypocrites; if there be any sincerity in human actions, they were not hypocrites. During the Middle Ages, there was corruption in the church,—

foul, shameful corruption; and now also hypocrisy may scourge itself in feigned repentance and ambition hide its face beneath a hood; yet all is not therefore rottenness that wears a cowl. Many a pure spirit, through a heavenly-mindedness, and an ardent though mistaken zeal, has fled from the temptation of the world to seek in solitude and self-communion a closer walk with God. And not in vain. They have found the peace they sought. They have felt, indeed, what many profess to feel, but do not feel,—that they are strangers and sojourners here, travellers who are bound for their home in a far country. It is this feeling which I speak of as giving a peculiar charm to the devotional poetry of Spain. Compare its spirit with the spirit which its authors have exhibited in their lives. They speak of having given up the world, and it is no poetical hyperbole; they speak of longing to be free from the weakness of the flesh, that they may commence their conversation in heaven, and we feel that they had already begun it in lives of penitence, meditation, and prayer.

THE PILGRIM'S BREVIARY.

> If thou vouchsafe to read this treatise, it shall seem no otherwise to thee than the way to an ordinary traveler,—sometimes fair, sometimes foul; here champaign, there enclosed; barren in one place, better soyle in another; by woods, groves, hills, dales, plains, I shall lead thee.
>
> BURTON'S ANATOMIE OF MELANCHOLY.

THE glittering spires and cupolas of Madrid have sunk behind me. Again and again I have turned to take a parting look, till at length the last trace of the city has disappeared, and I gaze only upon the sky above it.

And now the sultry day is passed; the freshening twilight falls, and the moon and the evening star are in the sky. This river is the Xarama. This noble avenue of trees leads to Aranjuez. Already its lamps begin to twinkle in the distance. The hoofs of our weary mules clatter upon the wooden bridge; the public square opens before us; yonder, in the moonlight, gleam the walls of the royal palace; and near it, with a rushing sound, fall the waters of the Tagus.

We have now entered the vast and melancholy plains of La Mancha,—a land to which the genius of Cervantes has given a vulgo-classic fame. Here are the windmills, as of old; every village has its Master Nicholas,—every venta its Maritornes. Wondrous strong are the spells of fiction! A few years pass away, and history becomes romance, and romance history. To the peasantry of Spain, Don Quixote and his squire are historic personages; and woe betide the luckless wight who unwarily takes the name of Dulcinea upon his lips within a league of El Toboso! The traveler, too, yields himself to the delusion, and as he traverses the arid plants of La Mancha, pauses with willing credulity to trace the footsteps of the mad Hildalgo, with his "velvet breeches on a holiday, and slippers of the same." The high-road from Aranjuez to Córdova crosses and recrosses the knight-errant's path. Between Manzanares and Valdepeñas stands the inn where he was dubbed a knight; to the northward, the spot where he encountered the windmills; to the westward, the inn where he made the balsam of Fierabras, the scenes of his adventures with the fulling-mills, and his tournament with the barber; and to the south-ward, the Sierra Morena, where he did penance, like the knights of olden time.

For my own part, I confess that there are seasons when I am willing to be the dupe of my imagination; and if this harmless folly but lends its wings to a dull-paced hour, I am even ready to believe a fairy tale.

On the fourth day of our journey we dined at Manzanares, in an old and somber-looking inn, which, I think, some centuries back, must have been the dwelling of a grandee. A wide gateway admitted us into the inn-yard, which was a paved court, in the centre of the edifice, surrounded by a colonnade, and open to the sky above. Beneath this colonnade we were shaved by the village barber, a supple, smooth-faced Figaro, with a brazen laver and a gray montera cap. There, too, we dined in the open air, with bread as white as snow, and the rich red wine of Valdepeñas; and there, in the listlessness of after-dinner, smoked the sleep-inviting cigar, while in the court-yard before us the muleteers danced a fandango with the maids of the inn, to such music as three blind musicians could draw from a violin, a guitar, and a clarinet. When this scene was over, and the blind men had groped their way out of the yard, I fell into a delicious slumber, from which I was soon awakened by music of another kind. It was a clear, youthful voice, singing a national song to the sound of a guitar. I opened my eyes, and near me stood a tall, graceful figure, leaning against one of the pillars of the colonnade, in the attitude of a serenader. His dress was that of a Spanish student. He wore a black gown and cassock, a pair of shoes made of an ex-pair of boots, and a hat in the shape of a half-moon, with the handle of a wooden spoon sticking out on one side like a cockade. When he had finished his song, we invited him to the remnant of a Vich sausage, a bottle of Valdepeñas, bread at his own discretion, and a pure Havana cigar. The stranger made a leg, and accepted these signs of good company with the easy air of a man who is accustomed to earn his livelihood by hook or by crook; and as the wine was of that stark and generous kind which readily "ascends one into the brain," our gentleman with the half-moon hat grew garrulous and full of anecdote, and soon told us his own story, beginning with his birth and parentage, like the people in Gil Blas.

"I am the son of a barber," quoth he; "and first saw the light some twenty years ago, in the great city of Madrid. At a very early age, I was taught to do something for myself, and began my career of gain by carrying a slow-match in the Prado, for the gentlemen to light their cigars with, and catching the wax that dropped from the friars' tapers at funerals and other religious processions.

"At school I was noisy and unruly, and was finally expelled for hooking the master's son with a pair of ox-horns, which I had tied to my head, in order to personate the bull in a mock bullfight. Soon after this my father died, and I went to live with my maternal uncle, a curate in Fuencarral. He was a man of learning, and resolved that I should be like him. He set his heart upon making a physician of me, and to this end taught me Latin and Greek.

"In due time I was sent to the University of Alcalá. Here a new world opened before me. What novelty,—what variety,—what excitement! But, alas! three months were hardly gone, when news came that my worthy uncle had passed to a better world. I was now left to shift for myself. I was penniless, and lived as I could, not as I would. I became a *sopista*, a soup-eater,—a knight of the wooden spoon. I see you do not understand me. In other words, then, I became one of that respectable body of charity scholars who go armed with their wooden spoons to eat the allowance of eleemosynary soup which is daily served out to them at the gate of the convents. I had no longer house nor home. But necessity is the mother of invention. I became a hanger-on of those who were more fortunate than myself; studied in other people's books, slept in other people's beds, and breakfasted at other people's expense. This course of life has been demoralizing, but it has quickened my wits to a wonderful degree.

"Did you ever read the life of the Gran Tacaño, by Quevedo? In the first book you have a faithful picture of life in a Spanish University. What was true in his day is true in ours. O Alcalá! Alcalá! if your walls had tongues as well as ears, what tales could they repeat! what midnight frolics! what madcap revelries! what scenes of merriment and mischief! How merry is a student's life, and yet how changeable! Alternate feasting and fasting,—alternate Lent and Carnival,—alternate want and extravagance! Care given to the winds, no thought beyond the passing hour; yesterday, forgotten,—to-morrow, a word in an unknown tongue!

"Did you ever hear of raising the dead? not literally,—but such as the student raised, when he dug for the soul of the licentiate Pedro Garcias, at the fountain between Peñafiel and Salamanca,—money? No? Well, it is done after this wise. Gambling, you know, is our great national vice; and then gamblers are so dishonest! Now, our game is to cheat the cheater. We go at night to some noted gaming-house,—five or six of us in a body. We stand around the table, watch those that are at play, and occasionally put in a trifle ourselves to avoid suspicion. At length the favorable moment arrives. Some eager player ventures a large stake. I stand behind his chair. He wins. As quick as thought, I stretch my arm over his shoulder and seize the glittering prize, saying very coolly, 'I have won at last.' My gentleman turns round in a passion, and I meet his indignant glance with a look of surprise. He storms, and I expostulate; he menaces,—I heed his menaces no more than the buzzing of a fly that has burnt his wings in my lamp. He calls the whole table to witness; but the whole table is busy, each with his own gain or loss, and there stand my comrades, all loudly asserting that the stake was mine. What can he do? there was a mistake; he swallows the affront as best he may, and we bear away the booty. This we call raising the dead. You say it is disgraceful,—dishonest. Our maxim is, that all is fair among sharpers; *Baylar al son que se toca*,—Dance to any tune that is fiddled. Besides, as I said before, poverty is demoralizing. One loses the nice distinctions of right and wrong, of *meum* and *tuum*.

"Thus merrily pass the hours of term-time. When the summer vacations come round, I sling my guitar over my shoulder, and with a light heart, and a lighter pocket, scour the country, like a strolling piper or a mendicant friar. Like the industrious ant, in summer I provide for winter; for in vacation we have time for reflection, and make the great discovery that there is a portion of time called the future. I pick up a trifle here and a trifle there, in all the towns and villages through which I pass, and before the end of my tour I find myself quite rich—for the son of a barber. This we call the *vida tunantesca*,—a rag-tag-and-bobtail sort of life. And yet the vocation is as honest as that of a begging Franciscan. Why not?

"And now, gentlemen, having dined at your expense, with your leave I will put this loaf of bread and the remains of this excellent Vich sausage into my pocket, and, thanking you for your kind hospitality, bid you a good afternoon. God be with you, gentlemen!"

In general, the aspect of La Mancha is desolate and sad. Around you lies a parched and sunburnt plain, which, like the ocean, has no limits but the sky; and straight before you, for many a weary league, runs the dusty and level road, without the shade of a single tree. The villages you pass through are poverty-stricken and half-depopulated, and the squalid inhabitants wear a look of misery that makes the heart ache. Every league or two, the ruins of a post-house, or a roofless cottage with shattered windows and blackened walls, tells a sad tale of the last war. It was there that a little band of peasantry made a desperate stand against the French, and perished by the bullet, the sword, or the bayonet. The lapse of many years has not changed the scene, nor repaired the battered wall; and at almost every step the traveller may pause and exclaim:—

Here was the camp, the watch-flame, and the host;
Here the bold peasant stormed the dragon's nest.

From Valdepeñas southward the country wears a more lively and picturesque aspect. The landscape breaks into hill and valley, covered with vineyards and olive-fields; and before you rise the dark ridges of the Sierra Morena, lifting their sullen fronts into a heaven all gladness and sun shine. Erelong you enter the wild mountain-pass of Despeña-Perros. A sudden turn in the road brings you to a stone column, surmounted by an iron cross, marking the boundary line between La Mancha and Andalusia. Upon one side of this column is carved a sorry-looking face, not unlike the death's-heads on the tombstones of a country church-yard. Over it is written this inscription: "EL VERDADERO RETRATO DE LA SANTA CARA DEL DIOS DE XAEN,"—The true portrait of the holy countenance of the God of Xaen! I was so much struck with this strange superscription that I stopped to copy it.

"Do you really believe that this is what it pretends to be?" said I to a muleteer, who was watching my movements.

"I don't know," replied he, shrugging his brawny shoulders; "they say it is."

"Who says it is?"

"The priest,—the Padre Cura."

"I supposed so. And how was this portrait taken?"

He could not tell. The Padre Cura knew all about it.

When I joined my companions, who were a little in advance of me with the carriage, I got the mystery explained. The Catholic Church boasts of three portraits of our Saviour, miraculously preserved upon the folds of a handkerchief, with which St. Veronica wiped the sweat from his brow, on the day of the crucifixion. One of these is at Toledo, another in the kingdom of Xaen, and the third at Rome.

The impression which this monument of superstition made upon my mind was soon effaced by the magnificent scene which now burst upon me. The road winds up the mountain-side with gradual ascent; wild, shapeless, gigantic crags overhang it upon the right, and upon the left the wary foot starts back from the brink of a fearful chasm hundreds of feet in depth. Its sides are black with ragged pines, and rocks that have toppled down from above; and at the bottom, scarcely visible, wind the silvery waters of a little stream, a tributary of the Guadalquivir. The road skirts the ravine for miles,—now climbing the barren rock, and now sliding gently downward into shadowy hollows, and crossing some rustic bridge thrown over a wild mountain-brook.

At length the scene changed. We stood upon the southern slope of the Sierra, and looked down upon the broad, luxuriant valleys of Andalusia, bathed in the gorgeous splendor of a southern sunset. The landscape had already assumed the "burnished livery" of autumn; but the air I breathed was the soft and balmy breath of spring,—the eternal spring of Andalusia.

If ever you should be fortunate enough to visit this part of Spain, stop for the night at the village of La Carolina. It is indeed a model for all villages, with its broad streets, its neat, white houses, its spacious market-place surrounded with a colonnade, and its public walk ornamented with fountains and set out with luxuriant trees. I doubt whether all Spain can show a village more beautiful than this.

The approach to Córdova from the east is enchanting. The sun was just rising as we crossed the Guadalquivir and drew near to the city; and, alighting from the carriage, I pursued my way on foot, the better to enjoy the scene and the pure morning air. The dew still glistened on every leaf and spray, for the burning sun had not yet climbed the tall hedge-row of wild figs and aloes which skirts the roadside. The highway wound along through gardens, orchards, and vineyards, and here and there above me towered the glorious palm in all its leafy magnificence. On my right, a swelling mountain-ridge, covered with verdure and sprinkled with little white hermitages, looked forth towards the rising sun; and on the left, in a long, graceful curve, swept the bright waters of the Guadalquivir, pursuing their silent journey through a verdant reach of soft lowland landscape. There, amid all the luxuriance of this sunny clime, arises the ancient city of Córdova, though stripped, alas! of its former magnificence. All that reminds you of the past is the crumbling wall of the city, and a Saracen mosque, now changed to a Christian cathedral. The stranger, who is familiar with the history of the Moorish dominion in Spain, pauses with a sigh, and asks himself, Is this the imperial city of Alhakam the Just, and Abdoulrahman the Magnificent?

This, then, is Seville, that "pleasant city, famous for oranges and women." After all I have heard of its beauty, I am disappointed in finding it less beautiful than my imagination had painted it. The wise saw,—

Quien no ha visto Sevilla,
No ha visto maravilla,"—

He who has not seen Seville has seen no marvel,—is an Andalusian gasconade. This, however, is the judgment of a traveller weary and wayworn with a journey of twelve successive days in a carriage drawn by mules; and I am well aware how much our opinions of men and things are colored by these trivial ills. A sad spirit is like a rainy day; its mists and shadows darken the brightest sky, and clothe the fairest landscape in gloom.

I am, likewise, a disappointed man in another respect. I have come all the way from Madrid to Seville without being robbed! And this, too, when I journeyed at a snail's pace, and had bought a watch large enough for the clock of a village church, for the express purpose of having it violently torn from me by a fierce-whiskered highwayman, with his blunderbuss and his *"Boca abajo, ladrones!"* If I print this in a book, I am undone. What! travel in Spain and not be robbed! To be sure, I came very near it more than once. Almost every village we passed through had its tale to tell of atrocities committed in the neighborhood. In one place, the stage coach had been stopped and plundered; in another, a man had been murdered and thrown into the river; here and there a rude wooden cross and a shapeless pile of stones marked the spot where some unwary traveller had met his fate; and at night, seated around the blazing hearth of the inn kitchen, my fellow-travellers would converse in a mysterious undertone of the dangers we were to pass through on the morrow. But the morrow came and went, and, alas! neither *salteador*, nor *ratero* moved a finger. At one place, we were a day too late; at another, a day too early.

I am now at the *Fonda de los Americanos*. My chamber-door opens upon a gallery, beneath which is a little court paved with marble, having a fountain in the centre. As I write, I can just distinguish the tinkling of its tiny jet, falling into the circular basin with a murmur so gentle that it scarcely breaks the silence of the night. At day dawn I start for Cadiz, promising myself a pleasant sail down the Guadalquivir. All I shall be able to say of Seville is what I have written above,—that it is "a pleasant city, famous for oranges and women."

I am at length in Cadiz. I came across the bay yesterday morning in an open boat from Santa Maria, and have established myself in very pleasant rooms, which look out upon the *Plaza de San Antonio*, the public square of the city. The morning sun awakes me, and at evening the sea-breeze comes in at my window. At night the square is lighted by lamps suspended from the trees, and thronged with a brilliant crowd of the young and gay.

Cadiz is beautiful almost beyond imagination. The cities of our dreams are not more enchanting. It lies like a delicate sea-shell upon the brink of the ocean, so wondrous fair that it seems not formed for man. In sooth, the Paphian queen, born of the feathery sea-foam, dwells here. It is the city of beauty and of love.

The women of Cadiz are world-renowned for their loveliness. Surely earth has none more dazzling than a daughter of that bright, burning clime. What a faultless figure! what a dainty foot! what dignity! what matchless grace!

> What eyes, what lips, what everything about her!
> How like a swan she swims her pace, and bears
> Her silver breasts!

The Gaditana is not ignorant of her charms. She knows full well the necromancy of a smile. You see it in the flourish of her fan,—a magic wand, whose spell is powerful; you see it in her steady gaze, the elastic step,

> The veil,
> Thrown back a moment with the glancing hand,
> While the o'erpowering eye, that turns you pale,
> Flashes into the heart.

When I am grown old and gray, and sit by the fireside wrapped in flannels, if, in a listless moment, recalling what is now the present, but will then be the distant and almost forgotten past, I turn over the leaves of this journal till my watery eye falls upon the page I have just written, I shall smile at the enthusiasm with which I have sketched this portrait. And where will then be the bright forms that now glance before me, like the heavenly creations of a dream? All gone,—all gone! Or, if perchance a few still linger upon earth, they will be bowed with age and sorrow, saying their paternosters with a tremulous voice.

Old age is a Pharisee; for he makes broad his phylacteries, and wears them upon his brow, in scribed with prayer, but in the "crooked autograph" of a palsied hand. "I see with pain," says Madame de Pompadour, "that there is nothing durable upon earth. We bring into the world a fair face, and lo! in less than thirty years it is covered with wrinkles; after which a woman is no longer good for anything."

Were I to translate these sombre reflections into choice Castilian, and read them to the bright-eyed maiden who is now leaning over the balcony opposite, she would laugh, and laughing say, *"Cuando el demonio es viejo, se mete frayle."*

The devotion paid at the shrine of the Virgin is one of the most prominent and characteristic features of the Catholic religion. In Spain it is one of its most attractive features. In the southern provinces, in Granada and in Andalusia, which the inhabitants call *"La tierra de María Santísima,"*—the land of the most holy Mary,—this adoration is ardent and enthusiastic. There is one of its outward observances which struck me as peculiarly beautiful and impressive. I refer to the Ave Maria, an evening service of the Virgin. Just as the evening twilight commences, the bell tolls to prayer. In a moment, throughout the crowded city, the hum of business is hushed, the thronged streets are still; the gay multitudes that crowd the public walks stand motionless; the angry dispute ceases; the laugh of merriment dies away; life seems for a moment to be arrested in its career, and to stand still. The multitude uncover their heads, and, with the sign of the cross, whisper their evening prayer to the Virgin. Then the bells ring a merrier peal; the crowds move again in the streets, and the rush and turmoil of business recommence. I have always listened with feelings of solemn pleasure to the bell that sounded forth the Ave Maria. As it announced the close of day, it seemed also to call the soul from its worldly occupations to repose and devotion. There is something beautiful in thus measuring the march of time. The hour, too, naturally brings the heart into unison with the feelings and sentiments of devotion. The close of the day, the shadows of evening, the calm of twilight, inspire a feeling of tranquillity; and though I may differ from the Catholic in regard to the object of his supplication, yet it seems to me a beautiful and appropriate solemnity, that, at the close of each daily epoch of life,—which, if it have not been fruitful in incidents to ourselves, has, nevertheless, been so to many of the great human family,—the voice of a whole people, and of the whole world, should go up to heaven in praise, and supplication, and thankfulness.

The Moorish king rides up and down
Through Granada's royal town;
From Elvira's gates to those
Of Bivarambla on he goes.
Woe is me, Alhama!

Thus commences one of the fine old Spanish ballads, commemorating the downfall of the city of Alhama, where we have stopped to rest our horses on their fatiguing march from Velez-Málaga to Granada. Alhama was one of the last strong holds of the Moslem power in Spain. Its fall opened the way for the Christian army across the Sierra Nevada, and spread consternation and despair through the city of Granada. The description in the old ballad is highly graphic and beautiful; and its beauty is well preserved in the spirited English translation by Lord Byron.

As we crossed the Sierra Nevada, the snowy mountains that look down upon the luxuriant Vega of Granada, we overtook a solitary rider, who was singing a wild national song, to cheer the loneliness of his journey. He was an athletic man, and rode a spirited horse of the Arab breed. A black bearskin jacket covered his broad shoulders, and around his waist was wound the crimson *faja*, so universally worn by the Spanish peasantry. His velvet breeches reached below his knee, just meeting a pair of leather gaiters of elegant workmanship. A gay silken handkerchief was tied round his head, and over this he wore the little round Andalusian hat, decked out with a profusion of tassels of silk and bugles of silver. The steed he mounted was dressed no less gayly than his rider. There was a silver star upon his forehead, and a bright-colored woollen tassel between his ears; a blanket striped with blue and red covered the saddle, and even the Moorish stirrups were ornamented with brass studs.

This personage was a *contrabandista*,—a smuggler between Granada and the seaport of Velez-Málaga. The song he sung was one of the popular ballads of the country.

Worn with speed is my good steed,
And I march me hurried, worried;
Onward! caballito mio,
With the white star in thy forehead!
Onward! for here comes the Ronda,
And I hear their rifles crack!
Ay, jaleo! Ay, ay, jaleo!
Ay, jaleo! they cross our track![11]

The air to which these words are sung is wild and high, and the prolonged and mournful cadence gives it the sound of a funeral wail, or a cry for help.

---

[11] I here transcribe the original of which this is a single stanza. Its only merit is simplicity, and a certain grace which belongs to its provincial phraseology, and which would be lost in a translation.

Yo que soy contrabandista,
Y campo por mi respeto,
Á todos los desafio,
Porque á naide tengo mieo.
¡Ay, jaleo! ¡Muchachas, jaleo!
¿Quien me compra jilo negro?

Mi caballo eatá cansao,
Y yo me marcho corriendo.
¡Anda, caballito mio,
Caballo mio careto!
¡Anda, que viene la ronda,
Y se mueve el tiroteo!
¡Ay, jaleo! ¡Ay, ay, jaleo!
¡Ay, jaleo, que nos cortan!
Sácane de aqueste aprieto.

Mi caballo ya no corre,
Ya mi caballo paró.
Todo para en este mundo,
Tembien he do parar yo.
¡Ay, jaleo! ¡Muchachas, jaleo!
¿Quien me compra jilo negro?

To have its full effect upon the mind, it should be heard by night, in some wild mountain-pass, and from a distance. Then the harsh tones come softened to the ear, and, in unison with the hour and the scene, produce a pleasing melancholy.

The contrabandista accompanied us to Granada. The sun had already set when we entered the Vega,—those luxuriant meadows which stretch away to the south and west of the city, league after league of rich, unbroken verdure. It was Saturday night; and, as the' gathering twilight fell around us, and one by one the lamps of the city twinkled in the distance, suddenly kindling here and there, as the stars start to their places in the evening sky, a loud peal of bells rang forth its glad welcome to the day of rest, over the meadows to the distant hills, "swinging slow, with solemn roar."

Is this reality and not a dream? Am I indeed in Granada? Am I indeed within the walls of that earthly paradise of the Moorish kings? How my spirit is stirred within me! How my heart is lifted up! How my thoughts are rapt away in the visions of other days!

Ave, Maria purissima! It is midnight. The bell has tolled the hour from the watch-tower of the Alhambra, and the silent street echoes only to the watchman's cry, *Ave, Maria purissima!* I am alone in my chamber,—sleepless,— spellbound by the genius of the place, entranced by the beauty of the starlit night. As I gaze from my window, a sudden radiance brightens in the east. It is the moon, rising behind the Alhambra. I can faintly discern the dusky and indistinct outline of a massive tower, standing amid the uncertain twilight, like a gigantic shadow. It changes with the rising moon, as a palace in the clouds, and other towers and battlements arise,—every moment more distinct, more palpable, till now they stand between me and the sky, with a sharp outline, distant, and yet so near that I seem to sit within their shadow.

Majestic spirit of the night, I recognize thee! Thou hast conjured up this glorious vision for thy votary. Thou hast baptized me with thy baptism. Thou hast nourished my soul with fervent thoughts and holy aspirations and ardent longings after the beautiful and the true. Majestic spirit of the past, I recognize thee! Thou hast bid the shadow go back for me upon the dial-plate of time. Thou hast taught me to read in thee the present and the future,—a revelation of man's destiny on earth. Thou hast taught me to see in thee the principle that unfolds itself from century to century in the progress of our race,—the germ in whose bosom lie unfolded the bud, the leaf, the tree. Generations perish, like the leaves of the forest, passing away when their mission is completed; but at each succeeding spring, broader and higher spreads the human mind unto its perfect stature, unto the fulfilment of its destiny, unto the perfection of its nature. And in these high revelations, thou hast taught me more,—thou hast taught me to feel that I, too, weak, humble, and unknown, feeble of purpose and irresolute of good, have something to accomplish upon earth,—like the falling leaf, like the passing wind, like the drop of rain. O glorious thought! that lifts me above the power of time and chance, and tells me that I cannot pass away, and leave no mark of my existence. I may not know the purpose of my being,—the end for which an all-wise Providence created me as I am, and placed me where I am; but I do know—for in such things faith is knowledge that my being has a purpose in the omniscience of my Creator, and that all my actions tend to the completion, to the full accomplishment of that purpose. Is this fatality? No. I feel that I am free, though an infinite and invisible power overrules me. Man proposes, and God disposes. This is one of the many mysteries in our being which human reason cannot find out by searching.

Yonder towers, that stand so huge and massive in the midnight air, the work of human hands that have long since forgotten their cunning in the grave, and once the home of human beings immortal as ourselves, and filled like us with hopes and fears, and powers of good and ill,—are lasting memorials of their builders; inanimate material forms, yet living with the impress of a creative mind. These are landmarks of other times. Thus from the distant past the history of the human race is telegraphed from generation to generation, through the present to all succeeding ages. These are manifestations of the human mind at a remote period of its history, and among a people who came from another clime,—the children of the desert. Their mission is accomplished, and they are gone; yet leaving behind them a thousand records of themselves and of their ministry, not as yet fully manifest, but "seen through a glass darkly," dimly shadowed forth in the language, and character, and manners, and history of the nation, that was by turns the conquered and the conquering. The Goth sat at the Arab's feet; and athwart the cloud and storm of war, streamed the light of Oriental learning upon the Western world,—

As when the autumnal sun,
Through travelling rain and mist,
Shines on the evening hills.

This morning I visited the Alhambra; an enchanted palace, whose exquisite beauty baffles the power of language to describe. Its outlines may be drawn,—its halls and galleries, its court-yards and its fountains, numbered; but what skilful limner shall portray in words its curious architecture, the grotesque ornaments, the quaint devices, the rich tracery of the walls, the ceilings inlaid with pearl and tortoise-shell? what language paint the magic hues of light and shade, the shimmer of the sunbeam as it falls upon the marble pavement, and the brilliant panels inlaid with many-colored stones? Vague recollections fill my mind,—images dazzling but undefined, like the memory of a gorgeous dream. They crowd my brain confusedly, but they will not stay; they change and mingle, like the tremulous sunshine on the wave, till imagination itself is dazzled,—bewildered,—overpowered!

What most arrests the stranger's foot within the walls of the Alhambra is the refinement of luxury which he sees at every step. He lingers in the deserted bath; he pauses to gaze upon the now vacant saloon, where, stretched upon his gilded couch, the effeminate monarch of the East was wooed to sleep by softly-breathing music. What more delightful than this secluded garden, green with the leaf of the myrtle and the orange, and freshened with the gush of fountains, beside whose basin the nightingale still wooes the blushing rose? What more fanciful, more exquisite, more like a creation of Oriental magic, than the lofty tower of the Tocador,—its airy sculpture resembling the fretwork of wintry frost, and its windows overlooking the romantic valley of the Darro; and the city, with its gardens, domes, and spires, far, far below? Cool through this lattice comes the summer wind from the icy summits of the Sierra Nevada. Softly in yonder fountain falls the crystal water, dripping from its marble vase with never-ceasing sound. On every side comes up the fragrance of a thousand flowers, the murmur of in numerable leaves and overhead is a sky where not a vapor floats,—as soft, and blue, and radiant as the eye of childhood!

Such is the Alhambra of Granada; a fortress, a palace, an earthly paradise,—a ruin, wonderful in its fallen greatness!

THE JOURNEY INTO ITALY.

What I catch is at present only sketch-ways, as it were; but I prepare myself betimes for the Italian journey.

GOETHE'S *Faust.*

ON the afternoon of the 15th of December, in the year of grace one thousand eight hundred and twenty-seven, I left Marseilles for Genoa, taking the sea-shore road through Toulon, Draguignan, and Nice. This journey is written in my memory with a sunbeam. We were a company whom chance had thrown together,—different in ages, humors, and pursuits,—and yet so merrily the days went by, in sunshine, wind, or rain, that methinks some lucky star must have ruled the hour that brought us five so auspiciously together. But where is now that merry company? One sleeps in his youthful grave; two sit in their fatherland, and "coin their brain for their daily bread;" and the others,—where are they? If still among the living, I beg them to remember in their prayers the humble historian of their journey into Italy.

At Toulon we took a private carriage in order to pursue our journey more leisurely and more at ease. I well remember the strange, outlandish vehicle, and our vetturino Joseph, with his *blouse*, his short-stemmed pipe, his limping gait, his comical phiz, and the lowland dialect his mother taught him at Avignon. Every scene, every incident of the journey is now before me as if written in a book. The sunny landscapes of the Var,—the peasant girls, with their broad-brimmed hats of straw,—the inn at Draguignan, with its painting of a lady on horseback, underwritten in French and English, "*Une jeune dame á la promenade,*—A young ladi taking a walk,"—the mouldering arches of the Roman aqueducts at Fréjus, standing in the dim twilight of morning like shadowy apparitions of the past, the wooded bridge across the Var, the glorious amphitheatre of hills that half encircle Nice, the midnight scene at the village inn of Monaco, the mountain-road overhanging the sea at a dizzy height, and its long, dark passages cut through the solid rock, the tumbling mountain-torrent, and a fortress perched on a jutting spur of the Alps; these, and a thousand varied scenes and landscapes of this journey, rise before me, as if still visible to the eye of sense, and not to that of memory only. And yet I will not venture upon a minute description of them. I have not colors bright enough for such landscapes; and besides, even the most determined lovers of the picturesque grow weary of long descriptions; though, as the French guide book says of these scenes, *"Tout cela fait sans doute un spectacle admirable!"*

On the tenth day of our journey, we reached Genoa, the city of palaces,—the superb city. The writer of an old book, called "Time's Storehouse," thus poetically describes its situation: "This cittie is most proudly built upon the seacoast and the downefall of the Appenines, at the foot of a mountaine; even as if she were descended downe the mount, and come to repose herselfe uppon a plaine."

It was Christmas eve,—a glorious night! I stood at midnight on the wide terrace of our hotel, which overlooks the sea, and, gazing on the tiny and crisping waves that broke in pearly light beneath the moon, sent back my wandering thoughts far over the sea, to a distant home. The jangling music of church-bells aroused me from my dream. It was the sound of jubilee at the approaching festival of the Nativity, and summoned alike the pious devotee, the curious stranger, and the gallant lover to the church of the Annunziata.

I descended from the terrace, and, groping my way through one of the dark and narrow lanes which intersect the city in all directions, soon found myself in the Strada Nuova. The long line of palaces lay half in shadow, half in light, stretching before me in magical perspective, like the long vapory opening of a cloud in the summer sky. Following the various groups that were passing onward towards the public square, I entered the church, where midnight mass was to be chanted. A dazzling blaze of light from the high altar shone upon the red marble columns which support the roof, and fell with a solemn effect upon the kneeling crowd that filled the body of the church. All beyond was in darkness; and from that darkness at intervals burst forth the deep voice of the organ and the chanting of the choir, filling the soul with solemnity and awe. And yet, among that prostrate crowd, how many had been drawn thither by unworthy motives,—motives even more unworthy than mere idle curiosity! How many sinful purposes arose in souls unpurified, and mocked at the bended knee! How many a heart beat wild with earthly passion, while the unconscious lip repeated the accustomed prayer! Immortal spirit! canst thou so heedlessly resist the imploring voice that calls thee from thine errors and pollutions? Is not the long day long enough, is not the wide world wide enough, has not society frivolity enough for thee, that thou shouldst seek out this midnight hour, this holy place, this solemn sacrifice, to add irreverence to thy folly?

In the shadow of a column stood a young man wrapped in a cloak, earnestly conversing in a low whisper with a female figure, so veiled as to hide her face from the eyes of all but her companion. At length they separated. The young man continued leaning against the column, and the girl, gliding silently along the dimly lighted aisle, mingled with the crowd, and threw herself upon her knees. Beware, poor girl, thought I, lest thy gentle nature prove thy undoing! Perhaps, alas, thou art already undone! And I almost heard the evil spirit whisper, as in the Faust, "How different was it with thee, Margaret, when, still full of innocence, thou camest to the altar here,—out of the well-worn little book lispedst prayers, half child-sport, half God in the heart! Margaret, where is thy head? What crime in thy heart!"

The city of Genoa is magnificent in parts, but not as a whole. The houses are high, and the streets in general so narrow that in many of them you may almost step across from side to side. They are built to receive the cool sea-breeze, and shut out the burning sun. Only three of them—if my memory serves me—are wide enough to admit the passage of carriages; and these three form but one continuous street,—the street of palaces. They are the Strada Nuova, the Strada Novissima, and the Strada Balbi, which connect the Piazza Amorosa with the Piazza dell' Annunziata. These palaces, the Doria, the Durazzo, the Ducal Palace, and others of less magnificence,—with their vast halls, their marble staircases, vestibules, and terraces, and the aspect of splendor and munificence they wear,—have given this commercial city the title of Genoa the Superb. And, as if to humble her pride, some envious rival among the Italian cities has launched at her a biting sarcasm in the well-known proverb, *"Mare senza pesce, uomini senza fede, e donne senza vergogna,"*—A sea without fish, men without faith, and women without shame!

The road from Genoa to Lucca strongly resembles that from Nice to Genoa. It runs along the seaboard, now dipping to the water's edge, and now climbing the zigzag mountain-pass, with toppling crags, and yawning chasms, and verdant terraces of vines and olive-trees. Many a sublime and many a picturesque landscape catches the traveller's eye, now almost weary with gazing; and still brightly painted upon my mind lies a calm evening scene on the borders of the Gulf of Spezia, with its broad sheet of crystal water,—the blue-tinted hills that form its oval basin, the crimson sky above, and its bright reflection,—

Where it lay
Deep bosomed in the still and quiet bay,
The sea reflecting all that glowed above,
Till a new sky, softer but not so gay,
Arched in its bosom, trembled like a dove.

Pisa, the melancholy city, with its Leaning Tower, its Campo Santo, its bronze-gated cathedral, and its gloomy palaces,—Florence the Fair, with its magnificent Duomo, its gallery of ancient art, its gardens, its gay society, and its delightful environs,—Fiesole, Camaldoli, Vallombrosa, and the luxuriant Val d'Arno;—these have been so often and so beautifully described by others, that I need not repeat the twice-told tale.

At Florence I took lodgings in a house which looks upon the Piazza Novella. In front of my windows was the venerable church of Santa Maria Novella, in whose gloomy aisles Boccaccio has placed the opening scene of his Decamerone. There, when the plague was raging in the city, one Tuesday morning, after mass, "the seven ladies, young and fair," held counsel together, and resolved to leave the infected city and flee to their rural villas in the environs, where they might "hear the birds sing, and see the green hills, and the plains, and the fields covered with grain and undulating like the sea, and trees of Species manifold."

In the Florentine museum is a representation in wax of some of the appalling scenes of the plague which desolated this city about the middle of the fourteenth century, and which Boccaccio has described with such simplicity and power in the introduction of his Decamerone. It is the work of a Sicilian artist, by the name of Zumbo. He must have been a man of the most gloomy and saturnine imagination, and more akin to the worm than most of us, thus to have revelled night and day in the hideous mysteries of death, corruption, and the charnel-house. It is strange how this representation haunts one. It is like a dream of the sepulchre, with its loathsome corses, with "the blackening, the swelling, the bursting of the trunk—the worm, the rat, and the tarantula at work." You breathe more freely as you step out into the open air again; and when the bright sunshine and the crowded busy streets next meet your eye, you are ready to ask, Is this indeed a representation of reality? Can this pure air have been laden with pestilence? Can this gay city have ever been a city of the plague?

The work of the Sicilian artist is admirable as a piece of art—the description of the Florentine prose-poet equally admirable as a piece of eloquence. "How many vast palaces," he exclaims, "how many beautiful houses, how many noble dwellings, aforetime filled with lords and ladies and trains of servants, were now untenanted even by the lowest menial! How many memorable families, how many ample heritages, how many renowned possessions, were left without an heir! How many valiant men, how many beautiful women, how many gentle youths, breakfasted in the morning with their relatives, companions, and friends, and, when the evening came, supped with their ancestors in the other world!"

I met with an odd character at Florence, a complete humorist. He was an Englishman of some forty years of age, with a round, good-humored countenance, and a nose that wore the livery of good company. He was making the grand tour through France and Italy, and home again by the way of the Tyrol and the Rhine. He travelled post, with a double-barrelled gun, two pairs of pistols, and a violin without a bow. He had been in Rome without seeing St. Peter's,—he did not care about it; he had seen St. Paul's in London. He had been in Naples without visiting Pompeii, because "they told him it was hardly worth seeing,—nothing but a parcel of dark streets and old walls." The principal object he seemed to have in view was to complete the grand tour.

I afterward met with his counterpart in a countryman of my own, who made it a point to see everything which was mentioned in the guide-books, and boasted how much he could accomplish in a day. He would despatch a city in an incredibly short space of time. A Roman aqueduct, a Gothic cathedral, two or three modern churches, and an ancient ruin or so, were only a breakfast for him. Nothing came amiss; not a stone was left unturned.

A city was like a Chinese picture to him,—it had no perspective. Every object seemed of equal magnitude and importance. He saw them all; they were all wonderful.

"Life is short, and art is long," says Hippocrates; yet spare me from thus travelling with the speed of thought, and trotting, from daylight until dark, at the heels of a cicerone, with an umbrella in one hand, and a guide-book and plan of the city in the other.

I copied the following singular inscription from a tombstone in the Protestant cemetery at Leghorn. It is the epitaph of a lady, written by herself, and engraven upon her tomb at her own request.

> Under this stone lies the victim of sorrow.
> Fly, wandering stranger, from her mouldering dust,
> Lest the rude wind, conveying a particle thereof unto thee,
> Should communicate that venom melancholy
> That has destroyed the strongest frame and liveliest spirit.
> With joy of heart has she resigned her breath,
> A living martyr to sensibility!

How inferior in true pathos is this inscription to one in the cemetery of Bologna:—

> Lucrezia Picini
> Implora eterna pace.

Lucretia Picini implores eternal peace!

From Florence to Rome I travelled with a vetturino, by the way of Siena. We were six days upon the road, and, like Peter Rugg in the storybook, were followed constantly by clouds and rain. At times, the sun, not all forgetful of the world, peeped from beneath his cowl of mist, and kissed the swarthy face of his beloved land; and then, like an anchorite, withdrew again from earth, and gave himself to heaven. Day after day the mist and the rain were my fellow-travellers; and as I sat wrapped in the thick folds of my Spanish cloak, and looked out upon the misty landscape and the leaden sky, I was continually saying to myself, "Can this be Italy?" and smiling at the untravelled credulity of those who, amid the storms of a northern winter, give way to the illusions of fancy, and dream of Italy as a sunny land, where no wintry tempest beats, and where, even in January, the pale invalid may go about without his umbrella, or his India-rubber walk-in-the-waters.

Notwithstanding all this, with the help of a good constitution and a thick pair of boots, I contrived to see all that was to be seen upon the road. I walked down the long hillside at San Lorenzo, and along the border of the Lake of Bolsena, which, veiled in the driving mist, stretched like an inland sea beyond my ken; and through the sacred forest of oak, held in superstitious reverence by the peasant, and inviolate from his axe. I passed a night at Montefiascone, renowned for a delicate Muscat wine, which bears the name of Est, and made a midnight pilgrimage to the tomb of the Bishop John Defoucris, who died a martyr to his love of this wine of Montefiascone.

Propter nimium Est, Est, Est,
Dominus meus mortuus est.

A marble slab in the pavement, worn by the footsteps of pilgrims like myself, covers the dominie's ashes. There is a rude figure carved upon it, at whose feet I traced out the cabalistic words, "Est, Est, Est." The remainder of the inscription was illegible by the flickering light of the sexton's lantern.

At Baccano I first caught sight of the dome of Saint Peter's. We had entered the desolate Campagna; we passed the tomb of Nero, we approached the Eternal City; but no sound of active life, no thronging crowds, no hum of busy men, announced that we were near the gates of Rome. All was silence, solitude, and desolation.

ROME IN MIDSUMMER.

> She who tamed the world seemed to tame herself at last, and, falling under her own weight, grew to be a prey to Time, who with his iron teeth commas all bodies at last, making all things, both animate and inanimate, which have their being under that changeling, the moon, to be subject unto corruption and desolation. — HOWELL'S SIGNORIE OF VENICE.

THE masks and mummeries of Carnival are over; the imposing ceremonies of Holy Week have become a tale of the times of old; the illumination of St. Peter's and the Girandola are no longer the theme of gentle and simple; and finally, the barbarians of the North have retreated from the gates of Rome, and left the Eternal City silent and deserted. The cicerone stands at the corner of the street with his hands in his pockets; the artist has shut himself up in his studio to muse upon antiquity; and the idle facchino lounges in the market-place, and plays at *mora* by the fountain. Midsummer has come, and you may now hire a palace for what, a few weeks ago, would hardly have paid your night's lodging in its garret.

I am still lingering in Rome,—a student, not an artist,—and have taken lodgings in the Piazza Navona, the very heart of the city, and one of the largest and most magnificent squares of modern Rome. It occupies the site of the ancient amphitheatre of Alexander Severus, and the churches, palaces, and shops that now surround it are built upon the old foundations of the amphitheatre. At each extremity of the square stands a fountain; the one with a simple jet of crystal water, the other with a triton holding a dolphin by the tail. In the centre rises a nobler work of art—a fountain with a marble basin more than two hundred feet in circumference. From the midst uprises a huge rock pierced with grottoes, wherein sit a rampant seahorse and a lion couchant. On the sides of the rock are four colossal statues, representing the four principal rivers of the world; and from its summit, forty feet from the basin below, shoots up an obelisk of red granite, covered with hieroglyphics, and fifty feet in height,—a relic of the amphitheatre of Caracalla.

In this quarter of the city I have domiciliated myself, in a family of whose many kindnesses I shall always retain the most lively and grateful remembrance. My mornings are spent in visiting the wonders of Rome, in studying the miracles of ancient and modern art, or in reading at the public libraries. We breakfast at noon, and dine at eight in the evening. After dinner comes the conversazione, enlivened with music, and the meeting of travellers, artists, and literary men from every quarter of the globe. At midnight, when the crowd is gone, I retire to my chamber, and, poring over the gloomy pages of Dante, or "Bandello's laughing tale," protract my nightly vigil till the morning star is in the sky.

Our windows look out upon the square, which circumstance is a source of infinite enjoyment to me. Directly in front, with its fantastic belfries and swelling dome, rises the church of St. Agnes; and sitting by the open window, I note the busy scene below, enjoy the cool air of morning and evening, and even feel the freshness of the fountain, as its waters leap in mimic cascades down the sides of the rock.

The Piazza Navona is the chief market-place of Rome; and on market-days is filled with a noisy crowd of the Roman populace, and the peasantry from the neighboring villages of Albano and Frascati. At such times the square presents an animated and curious scene. The gayly-decked stalls, the piles of fruits and vegetables, the pyramids of flowers, the various costumes of the peasantry, the constant movement of the vast, fluctuating crowd, and the deafening clamor of their discordant voices, that rise louder than the roar of the loud ocean,—all this is better than a play to me, and gives me amusement when naught else has power to amuse.

Every Saturday afternoon in the sultry month of August, this spacious square is converted into a lake, by stopping the conduit-pipes which carry off the water of the fountains. Vehicles of every description, axle-deep, drive to and fro across the mimic lake; a dense crowd gathers around its margin, and a thousand tricks excite the loud laughter of the idle populace. Here is a fellow groping with a stick after his seafaring hat there another splashing in the water in pursuit of a mischievous spaniel, who is swimming away with his shoe; while from a neighboring balcony a noisy burst of military music fills the air, and gives fresh animation to the scene of mirth. This is one of the popular festivals of midsummer in Rome, and the merriest of them all. It is a kind of carnival unmasked, and many a popular bard, many a *Poeta di dozzina*, invokes this day the plebeian Muse of the market-place to sing in high-sounding rhyme, *"Il Lago di Piazza Navona."*

I have before me one of these sublime effusions. It describes the square, the crowd, the rattling carriages, the lake, the fountain, raised by "the superhuman genius of Bernini," the lion, the sea-horse, and the triton grasping the dolphin's tail. "Half the grand square," thus sings the poet, "where Rome with food is satiate, was changed into a lake, around whose margin stood the Roman people, pleased with soft idleness and merry holiday, like birds upon the margin of a limpid brook. Up and down drove car and chariot, and the women trembled for fear of the deep water; though merry were the young, and well I ween, had they been borne away to unknown shores by the bull that bore away Europa, they would neither have wept nor screamed!"

On the eastern slope of the Janiculum, now called, from its yellow sands, Montorio or the Golden Mountain, stands the fountain of Acqua Paola, the largest and most abundant of the Roman fountains. It is a small Ionic temple, with six columns of reddish granite in front, a spacious hall and chambers within, and a garden with a terrace in the rear. Beneath the pavement, a torrent of water from the ancient aqueducts of Trajan, and from the lakes of Bracciano and Martignano, leaps forth in three beautiful cascades, and from the overflowing basin rushes down the hillside to turn the busy wheels of a dozen mills.

The key of this little fairy palace is in our hands, and as often as once a week we pass the day there, amid the odor of its flowers, the rushing sound of its waters, and the enchantments of poetry and music. How pleasantly the sultry hours steal by! Cool comes the summer wind from the Tiber's month at Ostia. Above us is a sky without a cloud; beneath us the magnificent panorama of Rome and the Campagna, bounded by the Abruzzi and the sea. Glorious scene! one glance at thee would move the dullest soul,—one glance can melt the painter and the poet into tears!

In the immediate neighborhood of the fountain are many objects worthy of the stranger's notice. A bowshot down the hillside towards the city stands the convent of San Pietro in Montorio; and in the cloister of this convent is a small, round Doric temple, built upon the Spot which an ancient tradition points out as the scene of St. Peter's martyrdom. In the opposite direction the road leads you over the shoulder of the hill, and out through the city-gate to gardens and villas beyond. Passing beneath a lofty arch of Trajan's aqueduct, an ornamented gateway on the left admits you to the Villa Pamfili-Doria, built on the western declivity of the hill. This is the largest and most magnificent of the numerous villas that crowd the immediate environs of Rome. Its spacious terraces, its marble statues, its woodlands and green alleys, its lake and waterfalls and fountains, give it an air of courtly splendor and of rural beauty, which realizes the bean ideal of a suburban villa.

This is our favorite resort, when we have passed the day at the fountain, and the afternoon shadows begin to fall. There we sit on the broad marble steps of the terrace, gaze upon the varied land scape stretching to the misty sea, or ramble beneath the leafy dome of the woodland and along the mar gin of the lake,

And drop a pebble to see it sink
Down in those depths so calm and cool.

Oh, did we but know when we are happy! Could the restless, feverish, ambitious heart be still, but for a moment still, and yield itself, without one farther-aspiring throb, to its enjoyment,—then were I happy,—yes, thrice happy! But no; this fluttering, struggling, and imprisoned spirit beats the bars of its golden cage,—disdains the silken fetter; it will not close its eye and fold its wings; as if time were not swift enough, its swifter thoughts outstrip his rapid flight, and on ward, onward do they wing their way to the distant mountains, to the fleeting clouds of the future; and yet I know that erelong, weary, and wayworn, and disappointed, they shall return to nestle in the bosom of the past!

This day, also, I have passed at Acqua Paola. From the garden terrace I watched the setting sun, as, wrapped in golden vapor, he passed to other climes. A friend from my native land was with me, and as we spake of home, a liquid star stood trembling like a tear upon the closing eyelid of the day. Which of us wrote these lines with a pencil upon the cover of Julia's Corinna?

Bright star! whose soft, familiar ray,
    In colder climes and gloomier skies,
I've watched so oft when closing day

Had tinged the west with crimson dyes;
Perhaps to-night some friend I love,
Beyond the deep, the distant sea,
Will gaze upon thy path above,
And give one lingering thought to me.

TORQUATI TASSO OSSA HIC JACENT—Here lie the bones of Torquato Tasso—is the simple inscription upon the poet's tomb, in the church of St. Onofrio. Many a pilgrimage is made to this grave. Many a hard from distant lands comes to visit the spot, and, as he paces the secluded cloisters of the convent where the poet died, and where his ashes rest, muses on the sad vicissitudes of his life, and breathes a prayer for the peace of his soul. He sleeps midway between his cradle at Sorrento and his dungeon at Ferrara.

The monastery of St. Onofrio stands on the Janiculum, overlooking the Tiber and the city of Rome; and in the distance rise the towers of the Roman Capitol, where, after long years of sickness, sorrow, and imprisonment, the laurel crown was prepared for the great epic poet of Italy. The chamber in which Tasso died is still shown to the curious traveller, and the tree in the garden, under whose shade he loved to sit. The feelings of the dying man, as he reposed in this retirement, are not the vague conjectures of poetic revery. He has himself recorded them in a letter which he wrote to his friend Antonio Constantini, a few days only before his dissolution. These are his melancholy words:—

"What will my friend Antonio say, when he hears the death of Tasso? Erelong, I think, the news will reach him, for I feel that the end of my life is near, being able to find no remedy for this wearisome indisposition which is superadded to my customary infirmities, and by which, as by a rapid torrent, I see myself swept away, without a hand to save. It is no longer time to speak of my unyielding destiny, not to say the ingratitude of the world, which has longed even for the victory of driving me a beggar to my grave; while I thought that the glory which, in spite of those who will it not, this age shall receive from my writings was not to leave me thus without reward. I have come to this monastery of St. Onofrio, not only because the air is commended by physicians as more salubrions than in any other part of Rome, but that I may, as it were, commence, in this high place, and in the conversation of these devout fathers, my conversation in heaven. Pray God for me; and be assured that as I have loved and honored you in this present life, so in that other and more real life will I do for you all that belongs to charity unfeigned and true. And to the divine mercy I commend both you and myself."

The modern Romans are a very devout people. The Princess Doria washes the pilgrims' feet in Holy Week; every evening, foul or fair, the whole year round, there is a rosary sung before an image of the Virgin, within a stone's throw of my window; and the young ladies write letters to St. Louis Gonzaga, who in all paintings and sculpture is represented as young and angelically beautiful. I saw a large pile of these letters a few weeks ago in Gonzaga's chapel, at the church of St. Ignatius. They were lying at the foot of the altar, prettily written on smooth paper, and tied with silken ribands of various colors. Leaning over the marble balustrade, I read the following superscription upon one of them: "*All' Angelico Giovane S. Luigi Gonzaga, Paradiso,*—To the angelic youth St. Louis Gonzaga, Paradise." A soldier, with a musket, kept guard over this treasure, and I had the audacity to ask him at what hour the mail went out; for which heretical impertinence he cocked his moustache at me with the most savage look imaginable, as much as to say, "Get thee gone:"—

Andate,
Niente pigliate,
E mai ritornate.

The modern Romans are likewise strongly given to amusements of every description. *Panem et circenses,* says the Latin satirist, when chiding the degraded propensities of his countrymen; *Panem et circenses,*—they are content with bread and the sports of the circus. The same may be said at the present day. Even in this hot weather, when the shops are shut at noon, and the fat priests waddle about the streets with fans in their hands, the people crowd to the Mausoleum of Augustus, to be choked with the smoke of fireworks, and see deformed and humpback dwarfs tumbled into the dirt by the masked horns of young bullocks. What a refined amusement for the inhabitants of "pompous and holy Rome"!

The Sirocco prevails to-day,—a hot wind from the burning sands of Africa, that bathes its wings in the sea, and comes laden with fogs and vapors to the shores of Italy. It is oppressive and dispiriting, and quite unmans one, like the dog-days of the North. There is a scrap of an old English song running in my mind, in which the poet calls it a cool wind; though ten to one I misquote.

When the cool Sirocco blows,
And daws and pies and rocks and crows
Sit and curse the wintry snows,
Then give me ale!

I should think that stark English beer might have a potent charm against the powers of the foul fiend that rides this steaming, reeking wind. A flask of Montefiascone, or a bottle of Lacryma Christi does very well.

Beggars all,—beggars all! The Papal city is full of them, and they hold you by the button through the whole calendar of saints. You cannot choose but hear. I met an old woman yesterday, who pierced my car with this alluring petition:—

"Ah signore! Qualche piccola cosa, per carità! Vi diró la buona ventura! C'è una bella signorina, che vi ama molto! Per il Sacro Sacramento! Per la Madonna!"

Which being interpreted, is, "Ah, sir, a trifle, for charity's sake! I will tell your fortune for you! There is a beautiful young lady who loves you well! For the Holy Sacrament,—for the Madonna's sake!"

Who could resist such an appeal?

I made a laughable mistake this morning in giving alms. A man stood on the shady side of the street with his hat in his hand, and as I passed he gave me a piteous look, though he said nothing. He had such a woe-begone face, and such a threadbare coat, that I at once took him for one of those mendicants who bear the title of *poveri vergognosi*,—bashful beggars; persons whom pinching want compels to receive the stranger's charity, though pride restrains them from asking it. Moved with compassion, I threw into the hat the little I had to give; when, instead of thanking me with a blessing, my man with the threadbare coat showered upon me the most sonorous maledictions of his native tongue, and, emptying his greasy hat upon the pavement, drew it down over his ears with both hands, and stalked away with all the dignity of a Roman senator in the best days of the republic,—to the infinite amusement of a green-grocer, who stood at his shop-door bursting with laughter. No time was given me for an apology; but I resolved to be for the future more discriminating in my charities, and not to take for a beggar every poor gentleman who chose to stand in the shade with his hat in his hand on a hot summer's day.

There is an old fellow who hawks pious legends and the lives of saints through the streets of Rome, with a sharp, cracked voice, that knows no pause nor division in the sentences it utters. I just heard him cry at a breath:—

"*La Vita di San Giuseppe quel fidel servitor di Dio santo e maraviglioso mezzo bajocco,*— The Life of St. Joseph that faithful servant of God holy and wonderful ha'penny!"

This is the way with some people; everything helter-skelter,—heads and tails,—prices current and the lives of saints!

It has been a rainy day,—a day of gloom. The church-bells never rang in my ears with so melancholy a sound, and this afternoon I saw a mournful scene, which still haunts my imagination. It was the funeral of a monk. I was drawn to the window by the solemn chant, as the procession came from a neighboring street and crossed the square. First came a long train of priests, clad in black, and bearing in their hands large waxen tapers, which flared in every gust of wind, and were now and then extinguished by the rain. The bier followed, home on the shoulders of four barefooted Carmelites; and upon it, ghastly and grim, lay the body of the dead monk, clad in his long gray kirtle, with the twisted cord about his waist. Not even a shroud was thrown over him. His head and feet were bare, and his hands were placed upon his bosom, palm to palm, in the attitude of prayer. His face was emaciated, and of a livid hue; his eyes unclosed; and at every movement of the bier, his head nodded to and fro, with an earthly and hideous aspect. Behind walked the monastic brotherhood, a long and melancholy procession, with their cowls thrown back, and their eyes cast upon the ground; and last of all came a man with a rough, unpainted coffin upon his shoulders, closing the funeral train.

Many of the priests, monks, monsignori, and cardinals of Rome have a bad reputation, even after deducting a tithe or so from the tales of gossip. To some of them may be applied the rhyming Latin distich, written for the monks of old:—

O Monachi,
Vestri stomachi
Sunt amphora Bacchi;
Vos estis,
Deus est testis,
Turpissima pestis.

The graphic description which Thomson gives in his "Castle of Indolence" would readily find an impersonation among the Roman priesthood:—

Full oft by holy feet our ground was trod,—
Of clerks good plenty here you mote espy;—
A little, round, fat, oily man of God
Was one I chiefly marked among the fry;
He had a roguish twinkle in his eye,
Which shone all glittering with ungodly dew,
When a tight damsel chanced to trippen by;
But when observed, he shrunk into his mew,
And straight would recollect his piety anew.

Yonder across the square goes a *Minente* of Trastevere, a fellow who boasts the blood of the old Romans in his veins. He is a plebeian exquisite of the western bank of the Tiber, with a swarthy face and the step of an emperor. He wears a slouched hat, and blue velvet jacket and breeches, and has enormous silver buckles in his shoes. As he marches along, he sings a ditty in his own vulgar dialect:—

Uno, due, e tre,
E lo Papa non è Re.

Now he stops to talk with a woman with a pan of coals in her hand. What violent gestures! what expressive attitudes! Head, hands, and feet are all in motion,—not a muscle is still! It must be some interesting subject that excites him so much, and gives such energy to his gestures and his language. No; he only wants to light his pipe!

It is now past midnight. The moon is full and bright, and the shadows lie so dark and massive in the street that they seem a part of the walls that cast them. I have just returned from the Coliseum, whose ruins are so marvellously beautiful by moonlight. No stranger at Rome omits this midnight visit for though there is something unpleasant in having one's admiration forestalled, and being as it were romantic aforethought, yet the charm is so powerful, the scene so surpassingly beautiful and sublime,—the hour, the silence, and the colossal ruin have such a mastery over the soul,—that you are disarmed when most upon your guard, and betrayed into an enthusiasm which perhaps you had silently resolved you would not feel.

On my way to the Coliseum, I crossed the Capitoline Hill, and descended into the Roman Forum by the broad staircase that leads to the triumphal arch of Septimius Severus. Close upon my right hand stood the three remaining columns of the Temple of the Thunderer, and the beautiful Ionic portico of the Temple of Concord,—their base in shadow, and the bright moonbeam striking aslant upon the broken entablature above. Before me rose the Phocian Column, an isolated shaft, like a thin vapor hanging in the air scarce visible; and far to the left, the ruins of the Temple of Antonio and Faustina, and the three colossal arches of the Temple of Peace,—dim, shadowy, indistinct,—seemed to melt away and mingle with the sky. I crossed the Forum to the foot of the Palatine, and, ascending the Via Sacra, passed beneath the Arch of Titus. From this point, I saw below me the gigantic outline of the Coliseum, like a cloud resting upon the earth. As I descended the hillside, it grew more broad and high,—more definite in its form, and yet more grand in its dimensions,—till, from the vale in which it stands encompassed by three of the Seven Hills of Rome,—the Palatine, the Cœlian, and the Esquiline,—the majestic ruin in all its solitary grandeur "swelled vast to heaven."

A single sentinel was pacing to and fro beneath the arched gateway which leads to the interior, and his measured footsteps were the only sound that broke the breathless silence of the night. What a contrast with the scene which that same midnight hour presented, when, in Domitian's time, the eager populace began to gather at the gates, impatient for the morning sports! Nor was the contrast within less striking. Silence, and the quiet moonbeams, and the broad, deep shadows of the ruined wall! Where were the senators of Rome, her matrons, and her virgins? where the ferocious populace that rent the air with shouts, when, in the hundred holidays that marked the dedication of this imperial slaughter-house, five thousand wild beasts from the Libyan deserts and the forests of Anatolia made the arena sick with blood? Where were the Christian martyrs, that died with prayers upon their lips, amid the jeers and imprecations of their fellow-men? where the barbarian gladiators, brought forth to the festival of blood, and "butchered to make a Roman holiday"? The awful silence answered, "They are mine!" The dust beneath me answered, "They are mine!"

I crossed to the opposite extremity of the amphitheatre. A lamp was burning in the little chapel, which has been formed from what was once a den for the wild beasts of the Roman festivals. Upon the steps sat the old beadsman, the only tenant of the Coliseum, who guides the stranger by night through the long galleries of this vast pile of ruins. I followed him up a narrow wooden staircase, and entered one of the long and majestic corridors, which in ancient times ran entirely round the amphitheatre. Huge columns of solid mason-work, that seem the labor of Titans, support the flattened arches above; and though the iron clamps are gone, which once fastened the hewn stones together, yet the columns stand majestic and unbroken, amid the ruin around them, and seem to defy "the iron tooth of time." Through the arches at the right, I could faintly discern the ruins of the baths of Titus on the Esquiline; and from the left, through every chink and cranny of the wall, poured in the brilliant light of the full moon, casting gigantic shadows through the long arcades. At length I came to an open space, where the arches above had crumbled away, leaving the pavement an unroofed terrace high in air. From this point, I could see the whole interior of the amphitheatre spread out beneath me, with such a soft and indefinite outline that it seemed less an earthly reality than a reflection in the bosom of a lake. The figures of several persons below were just perceptible, mingling grotesquely with their foreshortened shadows. The sound of their voices reached me in a whisper, and the cross that stands in the centre of the arena looked like a dagger thrust into the sand. I did not conjure up the past, for the past had already become identified with the present. It was before me in one of its visible and most majestic forms. The arbitrary distinctions of time, years, ages, centuries, were annihilated. I was a citizen of Rome! This was the amphitheatre of Flavius Vespasian! Mighty is the spirit of the past, amid the ruins of the Eternal City!

THE VILLAGE OF LA RICCIA.

Egressum magnâ me excepit Aricia Româ,
Hospitio modico.

HORACE.

I PASSED the month of September at the village of La Riccia, which stands upon the western declivity of the Albanian hills, looking towards Rome. Its situation is one of the most beautiful which Italy can boast. Like a mural crown, it encircles the brow of a romantic hill; woodlands of the most luxuriant foliage whisper around it; above rise the rugged summits of the Abruzzi, and beneath lies the level floor of the Campagna, blotted with ruined tombs, and marked with broken but magnificent aqueducts that point the way to Rome. The whole region is classic ground. The Appian Way leads you from the gate of Rome to the gate of La Riccia. On one hand you have the Alban Lake, on the other the Lake of Nemi; and the sylvan retreats around were once the dwellings of Hippolytus and the nymph Egeria.

The town itself, however, is mean and dirty. The only inhabitable part is near the northern gate, where the two streets of the village meet. There, face to face, upon a square terrace, paved with large, flat stones, stand the Chigi palace and the village church with a dome and portico. There, too, stands the village inn, with its beds of cool, elastic maize-husks, its little dormitories, six feet square, and its spacious saloon, upon whose walls the melancholy story of Hippolytus is told in gorgeous frescoes. And there, too, at the union of the streets, just peeping through the gateway, rises the wedge shaped Casa Antonini, within whose dusty chambers I passed the month of my *villeggiatura*, in company with two much-esteemed friends from the Old Dominion,—a fair daughter of that generous clime, and her husband, an artist, an enthusiast, and a man of "infinite jest."

My daily occupations in this delightful spot were such as an idle man usually whiles away his time withal in such a rural residence. I read Italian poetry, strolled in the Chigi park, rambled about the wooded environs of the village, took an airing on a jackass, threw stones into the Alban Lake, and, being seized at intervals with the artist-mania, that came upon me like an intermittent fever, sketched—or thought I did—the trunk of a hollow tree, or the spire of a distant church, or a fountain in the shade.

At such seasons, the mind is "tickled with a straw," and magnifies each trivial circumstance into an event of some importance. I recollect one morning, as I sat at breakfast in the village coffee-house, a large and beautiful spaniel came into the room, and placing his head upon my knee looked up into my face with a most piteous look, poor dog! as much as to say that he had not breakfasted. I gave him a morsel of bread, which he swallowed without so much as moving his long silken ears; and keeping his soft, beautiful eyes still fixed upon mine, he thumped upon the floor with his bushy tail, as if knocking for the waiter. He was a very beautiful animal, and so gentle and affectionate in his manner, that I asked the waiter who his owner was.

"He has none now," said the boy.

"What!" said I, "so fine a dog without a master?"

"Ah, sir, he used to belong to Gasparoni, the famous robber of the Abruzzi mountains, who murdered so many people, and was caught at last and sent to the galleys for life. There's his portrait on the wall."

It hung directly in front of me; a coarse print, representing the dark, stern countenance of that sinful man, a face that wore an expression of savage ferocity and coarse sensuality. I had heard his story told in the village—the accustomed tale of outrage, violence, and murder. And is it possible, thought I, that this man of blood could have chosen so kind and gentle a companion? What a rebuke must he have met in those large, meek eyes, when he patted his favorite on the head, and dappled his long ears with blood! Heaven seems in mercy to have ordained that none—no, not even the most depraved—should be left entirely to his evil nature, without one patient monitor,—a wife,—a daughter,—a fawning, meek-eyed dog, whose silent, supplicating look may rebuke the man of sin! If this mute, playful creature, that licks the stranger's hand, were gifted with the power of articulate speech, how many a tale of midnight storm, and mountain-pass, and lonely glen, would—but these reflections are commonplace!

On another occasion, I saw an overladen ass fall on the steep and slippery pavement of the street. He made violent but useless efforts to get upon his feet again, and his brutal driver—more brutal than the suffering beast of burden—beat him unmercifully with his heavy whip. Barbarian! is it not enough that you have laid upon your uncomplaining servant a burden greater than he can bear? Must you scourge this unresisting slave, because his strength has failed him in your hard service? Does not that imploring look disarm you? Does not—and here was another theme for commonplace reflection!

Again. A little band of pilgrims, clad in white, with staves and scallop-shells and sandal shoon, have just passed through the village gate, wending their toilsome way to the holy shrine of Loretto. They wind along the brow of the hill with slow and solemn pace,—just as they ought to do, to agree with my notion of a pilgrimage, drawn from novels. And now they disappear behind the hill; and bark! they are singing a mournful hymn, like Christian and Hopeful on their way to the Delectable Mountains. How strange it seems to me, that I should ever behold a scene like this! a pilgrimage to Loretto. Here was another outline for the imagination to fill up.

But my chief delight was in sauntering along the many woodland walks, which diverge in every direction from the gates of La Riccia. One of these plunges down the steep declivity of the hill, and, threading its way through a most romantic valley, leads to the shapeless tomb of the Horatii and the pleasant village of Albano. Another conducts you over swelling uplands and through wooded hollows to Genzano and the sequestered Lake of Nemi, which lies in its deep crater, like the waters of a well, "all coiled into itself and round, as sleeps the snake." A third, and the most beautiful of all, runs in an undulating line along the crest of the last and lowest ridge of the Albanian Hills, and leads to the borders of the Alban Lake. In parts it hides itself in thick-leaved hollows, in parts climbs the open hillside and overlooks the Campagna. Then it winds along the brim of the deep, oval basin of the lake, to the village of Castel Gandolfo, and thence onward to Marino, Grotta Ferrata, and Frascati.

That part of the road which looks down upon the lake passes through a magnificent gallery of thick embowering trees, whose dense and luxuriant foliage completely shuts out the noonday sun, forming

A greensward wagon-way, that, like
Cathedral aisle, completely roofed with branches,

Runs through the gloomy wood from top to bottom,
And has at either end a Gothic door
Wide open.

This long sylvan arcade is called the *Galleria-di-sopra*, to distinguish it from the *Galleria-di-sotto*, a similar, though less beautiful avenue, leading from Castel Gandolfo to Albano, under the brow of the hill. In this upper gallery, and almost hidden amid its old and leafy trees, stands a Capuchin convent, with a little esplanade in front, from which the eye enjoys a beautiful view of the lake and the swelling hills beyond. It is a lovely spot,—so lonely, cool, and still, and was my favorite and most frequented haunt.

Another pathway conducts you round the southern shore of the Alban Lake, and, after passing the site of the ancient Alba Longa and the convent of Palazzuolo, turns off to the right through a luxuriant forest, and climbs the rugged precipice of Rocca di Papa. Behind this village swells the rounded peak of Monte Cavo, the highest pinnacle of the Albanian Hills, rising three thousand feet above the level of the sea. Upon its summit once stood a temple of Jupiter, and the Triumphal Way, by which the Roman conquerors ascended once a year in solemn procession to offer sacrifices, still leads you up the side of the hill. But a convent has been built upon the ruins of the ancient temple, and the disciples of Loyola are now the only conquerors that tread the pavement of the Triumphal Way.

The view from the windows of the convent is vast and magnificent. Directly beneath you, the sight plunges headlong into a gulf of dark-green foliage,—the Alban Lake seems so near that you can almost drop a pebble into it,—and Nemi, embosomed in a green and cup-like valley, lies like a dew-drop in the hollow of a leaf. All around you, upon every swell of the landscape, the white walls of rural towns and villages peep from their leafy coverts,—Genzano, La Riccia, Castel Gandolfo, and Albano; and beyond spreads the flat and desolate Campagna, with Rome in its centre and seamed by the silver thread of the Tiber, that at Ostia, "with a pleasant stream, whirling in rapid eddies, and yellow with much sand, rushes forward into the sea." The scene of half the Æneid is spread beneath you like a map, and it would need volumes to describe each point that arrests the eye in this magnificent panorama.

As I stood leaning over the balcony of the convent, giving myself up to those reflections which the scene inspired, one of the brotherhood came from a neighboring cell, and entered into conversation with me. He was an old man, with a hoary head and a trembling hand; yet his voice was musical and soft, and his eye still beamed with the enthusiasm of youth.

"How wonderful," said he, "is the scene before us I have been an inmate of these walls for thirty years, and yet this prospect is as beautiful to my eye as when I gazed upon it for the first time. Not a day passes that I do not come to this window to behold and to admire. My heart is still alive to the beauties of the scene, and to all the classic associations it inspires."

"You have never, then, been whipped by an angel for reading Cicero and Plautus, as St. Jerome was?"

"No," said the monk, with a smile. "From my youth up I have been a disciple of Chrysostom, who often slept with the comedies of Aristophanes beneath his pillow; and yet I confess that the classic associations of Roman history and fable are not the most thrilling which this scene awakens in my mind. Yonder is the bridge from which Constantine beheld the miraculous cross of fire in the sky, and I can never forget that this convent is built upon the ruins of a pagan temple. The town of Ostia, which lies before us on the sea-shore, is renowned as the spot where the Trojan fugitive first landed on the coast of Italy. But other associations than this have made the spot holy in my sight. Marcus Minutius Felix, a Roman lawyer, who flourished in the third century, a convert to our blessed faith, and one of the purest writers of the Latin Church, here places the scene of his 'Octavius.' This work has probably never fallen into your hands, for you are too young to have pushed your studies into the dusty tomes of the early Christian fathers."

I replied that I had never so much as heard the book mentioned before; and the monk continued:—

"It is a dialogue upon the vanity of pagan idolatry and the truth of the Christian religion, between Cæcilius, a heathen, and Octavius, a Christian. The style is rich, flowing, and poetical; and if the author handles his weapons with less power than a Tertullian, yet he exhibits equal adroit ness and more grace. He has rather the studied elegance of the Roman lawyer than the bold spirit of a Christian martyr. But the volume is a treasure to me in my solitary hours, and I love to sit here upon the balcony, and con its poetic language and sweet imagery. You shall see the volume; I carry it in my bosom."

With these words, the monk drew from the folds of his gown a small volume, bound in parchment, and clasped with silver; and, turning over its well-worn leaves, continued:—

"In the introduction, the author describes himself as walking upon the seashore at Ostia, in company with his friends Octavius and Cæcilius. Observe in what beautiful language he describes the scene."

Here he read to me the following passage, which I transcribe, not from memory, but from the book itself:—

"It was vacation-time, and that gave me aloose from my business at the bar; for it was the season after the summer's heat, when autumn promised fair, and put on the face of temperate. We set out, therefore, in the morning early, and as we were walking upon the seashore, and a kindly breeze fanned and refreshed our limbs, and the yielding sand softly submitted to our feet and made it delicious travelling, Cæcilius on a sudden espied the statue of Serapis, and, according to the vulgar mode of superstition, raised his hand to his mouth, and paid his adoration in kisses. Upon which, Octavius, addressing himself to me, said, 'It is not well done, my brother Marcus, thus to leave your inseparable companion in the depth of vulgar darkness, and to suffer him, in so clear a day, to stumble upon stones—stones, indeed, of figure, and anointed with oil, and crowned—but stones, however, still they are; for you cannot but be sensible that your permitting so foul an error in your friend redounds no less to your disgrace than his.' This discourse of his held us through half the city, and now we began to find ourselves upon the free and open shore. There the gently washing waves had spread the extremest sands into the order of an artificial walk; and as the sea always expresses some roughness in his looks, even when the winds are still, although he did not roll in foam and angry surges to the shore, yet were we much delighted, as we walked upon the edges of the water, to see the crisping, frizzly waves glide in snaky folds, one while playing against our feet, and then again retiring and lost in the devouring ocean. Softly then, and calmly as the sea about us, we travelled on, and kept upon the brim of the gently declining shore, beguiling the way with our stories."

Here the sound of the convent-bell interrupted the reading of the monk, and, closing the volume, he replaced it in his bosom, and bade me farewell, with a parting injunction to read the "Octavius" of Minutius Felix as soon as I should return to Rome.

During the summer months, La Riccia is a favorite resort of foreign artists who are pursuing their studies in the churches and galleries of Rome. Tired of copying the works of art, they go forth to copy the works of nature; and you will find them perched on their camp-stools at every picturesque point of view, with white umbrellas to shield them from the sun, and paint-boxes upon their knees, sketching with busy hands the smiling features of the landscape. The peasantry, too, are fine models for their study. The women of Genzano are noted for their beauty, and almost every village in the neighborhood has something peculiar in its costume.

The sultry day was closing, and I had reached, in my accustomed evening's walk, the woodland gallery that looks down upon the Alban Lake. The setting sun seemed to melt away in the sky, dissolving into a golden rain, that bathed the whole Campagna with unearthly splendor, while Rome in the distance, half-hidden, half-revealed, lay floating like a mote in the broad and misty sunbeam. The woodland walk before me seemed roofed with gold and emerald, and at intervals across its leafy arches shot the level rays of the sun, kindling, as they passed, like the burning shaft of Acestes. Beneath me the lake slept quietly. A blue, smoky vapor floated around its overhanging cliffs; the tapering cone of Monte Cavo hung reflected in the water; a little boat skimmed along its glassy surface, and I could even hear the sound of the laboring oar, so motionless and silent was the air around me.

I soon reached the convent of Castel Gandolfo. Upon one of the stone benches of the esplanade sat a monk with a book in his hand. He saluted me, as I approached, and some trivial remarks upon the scene before us led us into conversation. I observed by his accent that he was not a native of Italy, though he spoke Italian with great fluency. In this opinion I was confirmed by his saying that he should soon bid farewell to Italy and return to his native lakes and mountains in the north of Ireland. I then said to him in English,—

"How strange, that an Irishman and an Anglo-American should be conversing together in Italian upon the shores of Lake Albano!"

"It is strange," said he, with a smile; "though stranger things have happened. But I owe the pleasure of this meeting to a circumstance which changes that pleasure into pain. I have Men detained here many weeks beyond the time I had fixed for my departure by the illness of a friend, who lies at the point of death within the walls of this convent."

"Is he, too, a Capuchin friar like yourself?"

"He is. We came together from our native land, some six years ago, to study at the Jesuit College in Rome. This summer we were to have returned home again, but I shall now make the journey alone."

"Is there, then, no hope of his recovery?"

"None whatever," answered the monk, shaking his head. "He has been brought to this convent from Rome, for the benefit of a purer air, but it is only to die, and be buried near the borders of this beautiful lake. He is a victim of consumption. But come with me to his cell. He will feel it a kindness to have you visit him. Such a mark of sympathy in a stranger will be grateful to him in this foreign land, where friends are so few."

We entered the chapel together, and, ascending a flight of steps beside the altar, passed into the cloisters of the convent. Another flight of steps led us to the dormitories above, in one of which the sick man lay. Here my guide left me for a moment, and softly entered a neighboring cell. He soon returned and beckoned me to come in. The room was dark and hot, for the window-shutters had been closed to keep out the rays of the sun, that in the after part of the day fell unobstructed upon the western wall of the convent. In one corner of the little room, upon a pallet of straw, lay the sick man, with his face towards the wall. As I entered, he raised himself upon his elbow, and, stretching out his hand to me, said, in a faint voice, "I am glad to see you. It is kind in you to make me this visit."

Then speaking to his friend, he begged him to open the shutters and let in the light and air; and as the bright sunbeam through the wreathing vapors of evening played upon the wall and ceiling, he said, with a sigh, "How beautiful is an Italian sunset! Its splendor is all around us, as if we stood in the horizon itself and could touch the sky. And yet, to a sick man's feeble and dis tempered sight, it has a wan and sickly hue. He turns away with an aching heart from the splendor he cannot enjoy. The cool air seems the only friendly thing that is left for him."

As he spake, a deeper shade of sadness stole over his pale countenance, sallow and attenuated by long illness. But it soon passed off; and as the conversation changed to other topics, he grew cheerful again. He spoke of his return to his native land with childish delight. This hope had not deserted him. It seemed never to have entered his mind that even this consolation would be denied him,—that death would thwart even these fond anticipations.

"I shall soon be well enough," said he, "to undertake the journey; and, oh, with what delight shall I turn my back upon the Apennines! We shall cross the Alps into Switzerland, then go down the Rhine to England, and soon, soon we shall see the shores of the Emerald Isle, and once more embrace father, mother, sisters! By my profession, I have renounced the world, but not those holy emotions of love which are one of the highest attributes of the soul, and which, though sown in corruption here, shall hereafter be raised in incorruption. No; even he that died for us upon the cross, in the last hour, in the unutterable agony of death, was mindful of his mother; as if to teach us that this holy love should be our last worldly thought, the last point of earth from which the soul should take its flight for heaven."

He ceased to speak. His eyes were fastened upon the sky with a fixed and steady gaze, though all unconsciously, for his thoughts were far away amid the scenes of his distant home. As I left his cell, he seemed sinking to sleep, and hardly noticed my departure. The gloom of twilight had already filled the cloisters; the monks were chanting their evening hymn in the chapel; and one unbroken shadow spread through the long cathedral aisle of forest-trees which led me homeward. There, in the silence of the hour, and amid the almost sepulchral gloom of the woodland scene, I tried to impress upon my careless heart the serious and affecting lesson I had learned.

I saw the sick monk no more, but a day or two afterward I heard in the village that he had de parted,—not for an earthly, but for a heavenly home.

NOTE-BOOK.

Once more among the old, gigantic hills,
With vapors clouded o'er,
The vales of Lombardy grow dim behind,
And rocks ascend before.
They beckon me,—the giants,—from afar,
They wing my footsteps on;
Their helms of ice, their plumage of the pine,
Their cuirasses of stone.

OEHLENSCHLÄGER.

THE glorious autumn closed. From the Abruzzi Mountains came the Zampognari, playing their rustic bagpipes beneath the images of the Virgin in the streets of Rome, and hailing with rude minstrelsy the approach of merry Christmas. The shops were full of dolls and playthings for the Bifana, who enacts in Italy the same merry interlude for children that Santa Claus does in the North; and travellers from colder climes began to fly southward, like sun-seeking swallows.

I left Rome for Venice, crossing the Apennines by the wild gorge of the Strettura, in a drenching rain. At Fano we struck into the sands of the Adriatic, and followed the sea-shore northward to Rimini, where in the market-place stands a pedestal of stone, from which, as an officious cicerone informed me, "Julius Cæsar preached to his army, before crossing the Rubicon." Other principal points in my journey were Bologna, with its Campo Santo, its gloomy arcades, and its sausages; Ferrara, with its ducal palace and the dungeon of Tasso; Padua the Learned, with its sombre and scholastic air, and its inhabitants "apt for pike or pen."

I first saw Venice by moonlight, as we skimmed by the island of St. George in a felucca, and entered the Grand Canal. A thousand lamps glittered from the square of St. Mark, and along the water's edge. Above rose the cloudy shapes of spires, domes, and palaces, emerging from the sea; and occasionally the twinkling lamp of a gondola darted across the water like a shooting star, and suddenly disappeared, as if quenched in the wave. There was something so unearthly in the scene,—so visionary and fairy-like,—that I almost expected to see the city float away like a cloud, and dissolve into thin air. Howell, in his "Signorie of Venice," says, "It is the water, wherein she lies like a swan's nest, that doth both fence and feed her." Again: "She swims in wealth and wantonness, as well as she doth in the waters she melts in softness and sensuality, as much as any other whatsoever." And still farther: "Her streets are so neat and evenly paved, that in the dead of winter one may walk up and down in a pair of satin pantables and crimson silk stockings, and not be dirtied." And the old Italian proverb says,—

> Venegia, Venegia,
> Chi non ti vede non ti pregia;
> Ma chi t' ha troppo veduto
> Ti dispregia!

Venice, Venice, who sees thee not doth not prize thee; but who hath too much seen thee doth despise thee!

Should you ever want a gondolier at Venice to sing you a passage from Tasso by moonlight, inquire for Toni Toscan. He has a voice like a raven. I sketched his portrait in my note-book; and he wrote beneath it this inscription:—

> Poeta Natural che Venizian,
> Ch' el so nome xe un tal Toni Toscan.

The road from Venice to Trieste traverses a vast tract of level land, with the Friulian Mountains on the left, and the Adriatic on the right. You pass through long avenues of trees, and the road stretches in unbroken perspective before and behind. Trieste is a busy, commercial city, with wide streets intersecting each other at right angles. It is a mart for all nations. Greeks, Turks, Italians, Germans, French, and English meet you at every corner and in every coffee-house, and the ever-changing variety of national countenance and costume affords an amusing and instructive study for a traveller.

Trieste to Vienna. Daybreak among the Carnic Alps. Above and around me huge snow-covered pinnacles, shapeless masses in the pale starlight,—till touched by the morning sunbeam, as by Ithuriel's spear, they assume their natural forms and dimensions. A long, winding valley beneath, sheeted with spotless snow. At my side a yawning and rent chasm; a mountain brook, seen now and then through the chinks of its icy bridge, black and treacherous, and tinkling along its frozen channel with a sound like a distant clanking of chains.

Magnificent highland scenery between Grätz and Vienna in the Steiermark. The wild mountain-pass from Meerzuschlag to Schottwien. A castle built like an eagle's nest upon the top of a perpendicular crag. A little hamlet at the base of the mountain. A covered wagon, drawn by twenty-one horses, slowly toiling up the slippery, zigzag road. A snowstorm. Reached Vienna at midnight.

On the southern bank of the Danube, about sixteen miles above Vienna, stands the ancient castle of Greifenstein, where—if the tale be true, though many doubt, and some deny it—Richard the Lion-heart of England was imprisoned, when returning from the third crusade. It is built upon the summit of a steep and rocky hill, that rises just far enough from the river's brink to leave a foothold for the highway. At the base of the hill stands the village of Greifenstein, from which a winding pathway leads you to the old castle. You pass through an arched gate into a narrow courtyard, and thence onward to a large, square tower. Near the doorway, and deeply cut into the solid rock, upon which the castle stands, is the form of a human hand, so perfect that your own lies in it as in a mould. And hence the name of Greifenstein. In the square tower is Richard's prison, completely isolated from the rest of the castle. A wooden staircase leads up on the outside to a light balcony, running entirely round the tower, not far below its turrets. From this balcony you enter the prison,—a small, square chamber, lighted by two Gothic windows. The walls of the tower are some five feet thick; and in the pavement is a trap-door, opening into a dismal vault,—a vast dungeon, which occupies all the lower part of the tower, quite down to its rocky foundations, and which formerly had no entrance but the trap-door above. In one corner of the chamber stands a large cage of oaken timber, in which the royal prisoner is said to have been shut up—the grossest lie that ever cheated the gaping curiosity of a traveller.

The balcony commands some fine and picturesque views. Beneath you winds the lordly Danube, spreading its dark waters over a wide tract of meadow-land, and forming numerous little islands; and all around the landscape is bounded by forest-covered hills, topped by the mouldering turrets of a feudal castle or the tapering spire of a village church. The spot is well worth visiting, though German antiquaries say that Richard was not imprisoned there; this story being at best a bold conjecture of what is possible, though not probable.

From Vienna I passed northward, visiting Prague, Dresden, and Leipsic, and then folding my wings for a season in the scholastic shades of Göttingen. Thence I passed through Cassel to Frankfort-on-the-Maine; and thence to Mayence, where I took the steamboat down the Rhine. These several journeys I shall not describe, for as many several reasons. First,—but no matter,—I prefer thus to stride across the earth like the Saturnian in Micromegas, making but one step from the Adriatic to the German Ocean. I leave untold the wonders of the wondrous Rhine, a fascinating theme. Not even the beauties of the Vautsburg and the Bingenloch shall detain me. I hasten, like the blue waters of that romantic river, to lose myself in the sands of Holland.

The Pilgrim's Salutation

Ye who have traced the Pilgrim to the scene
Which is his last, if in your memories dwell
A thought which once was his, if on ye swell
A single recollection, not in vain
He wore his sandal-shoon and scallop-shell.
CHILDE HAROLD.

THESE, fair dames and courteous gentlemen, are some of the scenes and musings of my pilgrimage, when I journeyed away from my kith and kin into the land of Outre-Mer. And yet, amid these scenes and musings,—amid all the novelties of the Old World, and the quick succession of images that were continually calling my thoughts away, there were always fond regrets and longings after the land of my birth lurking in the secret corners of my heart. When I stood by the sea-shore and listened to the melancholy and familiar roar of its waves, it seemed but a step from the threshold of a foreign land to the fireside of home; and when I watched the out-bound sail, fading over the water's edge and losing itself in the blue mists of the sea, my heart went with it, and I turned away fancy sick with the blessings of home and the endearments of domestic love.

I know not how,—but in you land of roses
My heart was heavy still;
I startled at the warm nightingale,
The zephyr on the hill.

They said the stars shone with a softer gleam:
It seemed not so to me!
In vain a scene of beauty beamed around,—
My thoughts were o'er the sea.

At times I would sit at midnight in the solitude of my chamber, and give way to the recollection of distant friends. How delightful it is thus to strengthen within us the golden threads that unite our sympathies with the past,—to fill up, as it were, the blanks of existence with the images of those we love! How sweet are these dreams of home in a foreign land! How calmly across life's stormy sea blooms that little world of affection, like those Hesperian isles where eternal summer reigns, and the olive blossoms all the year round, and honey distils from the hollow oak! Truly, the love of home is interwoven with all that is pure, and deep, and lasting in earthly affection. Let us wander where we may, the heart looks back with secret longing to the paternal roof. There the scattered rays of affection concentrate. Time may enfeeble them, distance overshadow them, and the storms of life obstruct them for a season; but they will at length break through the cloud and storm, and glow, and burn, and brighten around the peaceful threshold of home.

And now, farewell! The storm is over, and through the parting clouds the radiant sunshine breaks upon my path. God's blessing upon you for your hospitality. I fear I have but poorly repaid it by these tales of my pilgrimage, and I bear your kindness meekly, for I come not like Theudas of old, "boasting myself to be somebody."

Farewell! My prayer is that I be not among you as the stranger at the court of Busiris; that your God-speed be not a thrust that kills.

The Pilgrim's benison upon this honorable company. *Pax vobiscum!*

Colophon

Heart, take thine ease,—
Men hard to please
Thou haply mightst offend.
Though some speak ill
Of thee, some will
Say better;—there's an end.

HEYLIN.

MY pilgrimage is ended. I have come home to rest; and, recording the time past, I have fulfilled these things, and written them in this book, as it would come into my mind,—for the most part, when the duties of the day were over, and the world around me was hushed in sleep. The pen wherewith I write most easily is a feather stolen from the sable wing of night. Even now, as I record these parting words, it is long past midnight. The morning watches have begun. And as I write, the melancholy thought intrudes upon me,—To what end is all this toil? Of what avail these midnight vigils? Dost thou covet fame? Vain dreamer! A few brief days, and what will the busy world know of thee? Alas! this little book is but a bubble on the stream; and although it may catch the sunshine for a moment, yet it will soon float down the swift-rushing current, and be seen no more!

DRIFT-WOOD

So must I likewise take some time to view
What I have done, ere I proceed anew.
Perhaps I may have cause to interline,
To alter, or to add; the work is mine,
And I may manage it as I see best.

QUARLES.

In 1852 Mr. Longfellow projected a volume to contain his scattered prose papers, contributed to magazines and reviews. He proposed to call the book *Drift-Wood*, and went so far as to have some of it set up. He abandoned the project, however, and renewed it in part only when, in 1857, his prose-works were published in the Blue and Gold edition. In that collection he had a division entitled *Drift-Wood*, which differed from that which he finally sanctioned by not including *Ancient French Romances*, and by including papers on *Dante* and the *Divina Commedia*. The article on *Ancient French Romances* was printed in the first number, January, 1833, of *The Select Journal of Foreign Periodical Literature*, published in Boston by Charles Bowen, and edited by two Cambridge men, Professor Andrews Norton and Mr. Charles Folsom. The article in its original form was a letter to M. de Monmerqué, prefixed to "Li Romans de Berte aus Grans Piés," and reprinted in Férussac's *Bulletin Universel*. The notes given in the Appendix were contributed by the translator.

ANCIENT FRENCH ROMANCES.

From the French of Paulin Paris.

THE very name of Queen Bertha carries us back to the remotest period of the good old times. Many an ancient romance records the praises of her unspotted virtue; and, if we may rely upon the testimony of a song-writer of the nineteenth century, it was she who founded the monastery of Saints-Avelle, dedicated to Our Lady of the Woods. I know not whether you have ever observed, among the statues that look down upon us from the portals of our Gothic churches, the figure known throughout France by the name of *la Reine Pédauque*, Queen Goose-Foot. She is the heroine of our romance; and, be it said with all the veracity of an historian, for this opprobrious surname she must thank her own feet, whose vast dimensions are revealed to us by the indiscretion of the statuary. During her lifetime she was surnamed Bertha of the Great Feet; after her death, she was neither more nor less than Bertha of the Goose Feet. So true is it that the origin of the custom of flattering the great while living, and reviling them when dead, is lost in the night of ages. The story of Queen Pédauque reminds me of poor Midas; perhaps the ears of the Phrygian monarch, who fell a victim to the malevolence of his barber, were in truth only somewhat long.

This statue of Queen Pédauque has long exercised the imagination of the antiquaries. They have successively imagined it to be Clotilde, wife of Clovis, Brunehault, and Frédégonde. The Abbé Lebœuf, however, supposes it to be the Queen of Sheba; though it is no easy matter to devise why the Abbé Lebœuf, generally so very considerate, should thus have felt himself obliged to call in question the beauty of the Oriental princess and the practised taste of Solomon, the wisest of men. He remarks, in his learned dissertation, that the Masorites, who were great admirers of the hands of the Queen of Sheba, have maintained the most scrupulous silence in regard to her feet:—there is, however, a vast distance between the silence of Biblical commentators and the conjecture he allows himself.

Now both the historians and the poets, who make mention of Queen Bertha, affirm that she had large feet; and this is the first point of analogy between her and the celebrated statue. Moreover, the inhabitants of Toulouse, according to the author of the "Contes d'Eutrapel," are in the habit of swearing by the distaff of Queen Pédauque,—*par la guenouille de la reine Pédaugue;* while we speak proverbially of the time when Bertha span, *du temps que Berthe filait;* and the Italians say, in nearly the same signification, "The days when Bertha span have gone by,"—*Non è più il tempo che Berta filava*. After all this, and especially after the direct testimony of the poem which I now present you, how can any one doubt the perfect identity of Bertha of the

Great Feet, and the Queen of the Goose Feet? I entertain a high respect for the Abbé Lebœuf, but a higher for the truth; and I cannot refrain from expressing my opinion, that he would have done better to look to the court of Pepin-le-Bref for the model of the statue which he saw at the church of Saint-Bénigne in Dijon, at the cathedral of Nevers, at the priory of Saint-Pourçain, and at the abbey of Nesle.

Bertha, the wife of Pepin, has been often named by the most respectable historians. She died in 783, and until the revolution of 1793 her tomb was still to be seen in the vaults of Saint-Denis. It bore this beautiful inscription: *Berta mater Caroli Magni*.

Eginhart speaks of the respectful deference which the hero of the West generally paid to the virtues of his mother. All historians coincide in regard to the time of her coronation and her death; but in regard to the name of her father, some difference of opinion prevails. According to the Annals of Metz, she was the daughter of Caribert, Count of Laon; but unfortunately for this hypothesis, the city of Laon was not at that time governed by a Count. Some trace her origin to the court of Constantinople, and others to the kingdom of Germany. You will perceive that our poet has embraced this last opinion. In the romance, Flores, king of Hungary, is father of Bertha of the Great Feet. This Flores himself and his wife Blanchefleurs are the hero and heroine of another celebrated poem of the Middle Ages, and their adventures, badly enough analyzed in one of the numbers of the *Bibliothèque des Romans*, seem to have been put into rhyme before those of Queen Bertha their daughter.

Thus it appears that Bertha can boast her statuaries as well as her poets; but whilst the former have given to her countenance a marked and striking character, the latter, by recording her touching misfortunes, have only followed the beaten path, and added another delicate flower to that poetic wreath which was woven in the heroic ages of our history. The poem of Bertha is one of the series of *Romances of the Twelve Peers*. It belongs to the number of those great epic compositions whose origin is incontestably linked to the cradle of the modern languages, and whose subjects are always borrowed from our old national traditions.

Until the present day, both critics and antiquaries have neglected to examine these singular creations of the human mind. Even those who have been wise enough to avail themselves of them in the composition of their learned works have gone no farther than to make such extracts as would throw light upon the subjects of heraldry or philology, hardly bestowing a passing glance upon those questions of manners and literature which they might suggest, enlighten, and perhaps resolve. It is strange that the press should have been so busy in giving to the world the *Fabliaux*, which lay buried in our vast libraries, and yet should never have preserved from the most unmerited oblivion a single one of these ancient epics! If by a catastrophe, improbable, yet not impossible, the Royal Cabinet of Manuscripts should be destroyed, nothing of our old heroic poetry would remain but a few shreds scattered here and there through the *Glossary* of Ducange and the *History of Lorraine* by Dom Calmet. Such a loss would indeed be immense and irreparable to those who wish, even at this distant period, to study the manners and customs of our ancestors.

Perhaps, then, I may justly claim some right to the thanks of the friends of letters for this attempt to preserve and perpetuate the *Romances of the Twelve Peers of France*. I now commence the series of these publications with *Berte aus Grans Piés*. In selecting this poem of the minstrel-king Adenès, I have been guided by the consideration, that, in order to gain readers for our ancient poets, it would be necessary to commence, not with the most beautiful, but with the shortest and the least incumbered with philological difficulties. And again, the romance of Bertha, however inferior it may be to some of the longer romances of the twelfth century, as, for example, *Raoul de Cambrai*, *Guillaume au Court Nez*, or *Garin de Loherain*, nevertheless possesses the most lively interest for readers of the present age. Besides, as its subject is drawn from the close of the reign of Pepin-le-Bref, it has the advantage of commencing that series of historic paintings, of which the eighth and ninth centuries are the frame.

And now I will venture a few reflections upon the structure of all these great works which I would willingly call our French Epics, had it not been decided, since the days of Ronsard, Chapelain, and Voltaire, that the French have no genius for epic poetry, and had not the word Epic, which always recalls the Iliad of Homer, been of late so much abused. But in thus submitting my opinions to your judgment, I feel myself bound to advance nothing either incorrect or imaginary. Besides, I am well aware that at length we have become quite weary of those long and admirable theories, to which nothing is wanting but proof. All mine will be found in the works concerning which I now write to you, and which I intend to publish in succession, if leisure and the favor of the public permit.

Independently of sacred subjects, the early French poets or *Trouvères* of the Middle Ages possessed three distinct sources of inspiration the traditions of classic antiquity, of the Britons, and of the French. All the chief compositions in the vulgar tongue, down to the thirteenth century, may be traced back to one of these three sources.

To the first belong the numerous poems of Alexander the Great, Philip of Macedon, Æneas, the valiant Hector, Jason, and Theseus. But this class of traditions has lost all its value, through our study of the elements of ancient history. In proportion as we have been farther removed from antiquity, we have become better acquainted with it. The writers of the Middle Ages were all more or less the dupes of the simplicity of their own times they could never comprehend the distinction between the fictions of the poets of the historic ages and the narratives of prose-writers. And hence, blending the most marvellous tales with the more authentic events of history, they have made of the records of antiquity a confused picture, totally destitute of every kind of perspective. We can derive no possible advantage, then, from their undiscriminating imitations; and their simple credulity, exercised alike towards Ovid and Cornelius Nepos, soon becomes insupportable.

The traditions of the Britons, however, are full of lively interest. The romances of the Round Table, which have sprung from these traditions, refer us back to a glorious epoch in the history of Albion; an epoch of which, by some strange fatality, no distinct account has been transmitted to us. All that we can be said to know is, that in the fifth century, whilst Clovis was laying the foundation of the French empire, the Britons, more successful than the Gauls, repulsed the hordes of Picts, Angles, and Saxons who menaced them on all sides. Arthur was then their king. A century later, having fallen a prey to those fierce barbarians, the Britons cherished the memory of a hero, whose name represented all that a noble-minded people esteems most dear on earth,—religion and liberty. Songs of departed glory are the privilege of a conquered people, and prophetic hopes are a consolation seldom wanting to the oppressed. Thus sprang up and multiplied those marvellous tales, which recorded the glory of Arthur, and in which the recollection of former victories was joined to the promise of victories yet to come. Not far from the twelfth century, a priest collected various traditions, and wrought them up into those religious forms in which his zeal prompted him to embody them. This collection, originally written in Latin, was afterwards translated into the vulgar tongue in prose during the reign of Henry the Second, father of Richard Cœur de Lion. Erelong it reappeared in a poetic dress in all the modern languages of Europe. Even at the present day the old prose translation would be a work full of pleasant reading.

Still we cannot hope to trace the footsteps of history in these romances of the Round Table; for the primitive story is lost amid the multitude of episodes and embellishments. Excepting the name of the hero, whose deeds they celebrate, there is nothing—I do not say Celtic, for that would be too indefinite—nothing Armoric about them. The heroic valor of King Arthur is displayed throughout, but it is directed against giants, wild beasts, or the adversaries of persecuted beauty, and not against the oppressors of his country. His steed is barbed with iron, and we recognize the gallant warrior's shield by its golden crowns in a field of blue, but his good sword Excalibur seems rather the handiwork of a skilful Norman artisan, than of an ancient blacksmith of Armorica. Let us not, then, seek in these old romances the history of ages anterior to the Roman, Saxon, or even Norman conquest; it would be a loss of time and labor. But if we desire only piquant adventures of love and gallantry, fierce sabre-blows, and terrible encounters of Pagans and Christians, we shall find enough to repay the study of this ancient lore particularly if we take care to peruse the oldest prose translations.

We now come to the old romances, which have their source in our national traditions. These are the true standard of our ancient poetry; for surely you would not pretend that it could claim a very elevated rank in the history of the human mind, if it could boast no other masterpieces than such epics as the *Alexandréide or Perceval*; such dramas as the *Mystère de Saint Christophe*, or even the curious and simple pastoral of *Robin et Marion*, for whose publication we are indebted to you; and, in fine, such satires as our coarse and vulgar *Fabliaux*, which (as one of our most profound and erudite scholars has remarked) are generally full of such insipid marvels. Not having sufficiently compared the various productions of the Middle Ages, we have hitherto been in the habit of passing judgment upon them, if I may use the phrase, in the lump, and with a sweeping expression of unlimited praise or censure. Those who have been disheartened by the *Romance of the Rose*,[12] or the *Tales of Barbazan*,[13] can discover nothing in our ancient literature but a confused mass of coarse and tedious fictions. To others, whom a more superficial study of the classics has rendered more indulgent in their opinions, these same productions appear in a far different light, possessing a grace, a charm, a simplicity, that no language can describe; nay, the very sight of a manuscript blotted with ink of the fourteenth century is enough to excite their enthusiasm. Midway between these two contending parties, and on the field which you have trodden before them, all judicious critics will hereafter pitch their tents. True, it is painful thus to annoy the doughty champions of the ancient Muse of France; but the love of the Middle Ages bears an enchanter's wand, and leads its votaries blindfold; and I fear, that if, like them, we should proclaim the merit of so many productions, composed by ignorant mountebanks to amuse the populace, we should give occasion for the belief that we are incapable of appreciating the full value of those great poems, which were destined to charm the most brilliant assemblies, and grace the most magnificent festivals.

The same remark is true of the Middle Ages as of our own and of every age. If the state of society is shadowed forth in its literature, then this literature must necessarily represent two distinct and strongly marked characters: one,

---

[12] Cs est li Rommanz de la Roze
Ou l'art d'amota est tote enclose.

The "Romance of the Rose" is an allegorical poem of no inconsiderable fame. It was commenced about the middle of the thirteenth century by Guillaume de Lorris, and completed nearly a half century later by Jean de Meun. The bitter sarcasms against the corruption and hypocrisy of the priesthood contained in this Romaunt drew upon it and its authors the anathemas of the clergy. A certain Gerson, then Chancellor of Paris, writes thus of Meun and his book: "There is one Johannes Meldinensis, who wrote a book called 'The Romaunt of the Rose'; which book, if I only had, and that there were no more in the world, if I might have five hundred pound for the same, I would rather burn it than take the money." About the middle of the fourteenth century the "Romance of the Rose" was translated into English by Chaucer, under the title of "The Romaunt of the Rose; or the Art of Love; wherein is showed the helpes and furtherances, an also the lets and impediments that lovers have in their suits."

[13] Fabliaux et Contes des Poètes François des XI, XII., XIII., XIV. et XV. Siècles, tirés des Meilleurs Auteurs; publiés par Barbazan. 4 vols. 8vo.

of the castle and the court; another, of the middle classes and the populace;—the former, elegant, harmonious, and delicate the latter, rude, grotesque, and vulgar. Each of these classes has its own peculiar merits; but our manuscripts, by presenting them to us united, sometimes in the same volume, and always upon the same shelves of our libraries, have led us insensibly into the habit of confounding the manners of the court with those of the city. Hence great prejudices have arisen against the purity of some of our most estimable writers, and against the refinement of society in those ages in which they were admired. Hence, too, all the difficulties which later historians have encountered, when, before classifying their authorities, they have sought to examine anew the manners and customs of an age.

But the desire of proving that even in the twelfth century there was a refined and polished class in society would lead me too far from my original design, and I will therefore resist the temptation. I would only ask those whom the love of a native land they do know has too strongly prejudiced against that other and earlier native land they do not know, to cast their eyes for a moment upon some noble monument of Gothic architecture; for example, upon the cathedral of Rheims. When they have contemplated this "Pantheon of our glory," as a writer of our own day has appropriately called it, let them ask themselves whether those ages which conceived the de sign and completed the construction of that noble edifice, ignorant as they were of Homer, Cicero, and Quinctilian, must not have possessed a native literature worthy, in some degree, of such a stupendous style of architecture. What! Villehardouin, Joinville, Philip Augustus, and Saint Louis ignorant of all other poetry but the burlesque proverbs of Maroon, the superstitious reveries of Gautier de Coinsy, and the indecent profanities of such writers as Rutebeuf and Jean de Condé! Were it true it would not be probable, and, in such a case, we must say that Gothic architecture is an effect without a cause,—*prolem sine matre creatam.*

But it is not true. We possessed in former times great epic poems, which, for four centuries, constituted the principal study of our fathers. And during that period all Europe,—Germany, England, Spain, and Italy,—having nothing of the kind to boast of, either in their historic recollections or in their historic records, disputed with each other the secondary glory of translating and imitating them.

Even amid the darkness of the ninth and tenth centuries, the French still preserved the recollection of an epoch of great national glory. Under Charlemagne, they had spread their conquests from the Oder to the Ebro, from the Baltic to the Sicilian sea. Mussulmans and Pagans, Saxons, Lombards, Bavarians, and Batavians,—all had submitted to the yoke of France, all had trembled at the power of Charles the Great. Emperor of the West, King of France and Germany, restorer of the arts and sciences, wise lawgiver, great converter of infidels,—how many titles to the recollection and gratitude of posterity! Add to this, that long before his day the Franks were in the habit of treasuring up in their memory the exploits of their ancestors; that Charlemagne himself, during his reign, caused all the heroic ballads, which celebrated the glory of the nation, to be collected together; and, in fine, that the weakness of his successors, the misfortunes of the times, and the invasions of the Normans must have increased the national respect and veneration for the illustrious dead,—and you will be forced to confess that, if no poetic monuments of the ninth century remained, we ought rather to conjecture that they had been lost than that they had never existed.

As to the contemporaneous history of those times, it offers us, if I may so speak, only the outline of this imposing colossus. Read the Annals of the Abbey of Fulde and those of Metz, Paul the Deacon, the continuator of Frédégaire, and even Eginhart himself, and you will there find registered, in the rapid style of an itinerary, the multiplied conquests of the French. The Bavarians, the Lombards, the Gascons revolt; Charles goes forth to subdue the Bavarians, the Lombards, and the Gascons. Witikind rebels ten times, and ten times Charles passes the Rhine and routs the insurgent army and there the history ends. Nevertheless, the Emperor had his generals, his companions in glory, his rivals in genius; but in all history we find not a whisper of their services,—hardly are their names mentioned. It has been left to the popular ballads, barren as they are of all historic authority, to transmit to posterity the proofs of their ancient renown.

But although these ancient *Chansons de Geste*, or historic ballads, fill up the chasms of true history, and clothe with flesh the meagre skeleton of old contemporaneous chroniclers, yet you must not therefore conclude that I am prepared to maintain the truth of their narratives. Far from it. Truth does not reign supreme on earth; and these romances, after all, are only the expression of public opinion, separated by an interval of many generations from that whose memory they transmit to us. But to supply the want of historians, each great epoch in national history inspires the song of bards; and when the learned and the wise neglect to prepare the history of events which they themselves have witnessed, the people prepare their national songs; their sonorous voice, prompted by childish credulity and a free and unlimited admiration, echoes alone through succeeding ages, and kindles the imagination, the feelings, the enthusiasm of the children, by proclaiming the glory of the fathers. Thus Homer sang two centuries after the Trojan war; and thus arose, two or three centuries after the death of Charlemagne, all those great poems called the *Romances of the Twelve Peers.*

And now let us suppose for a moment, that, after the lapse of two centuries, the mirror of history should reflect nothing of the reign of Napoleon, but the majestic figure of the conqueror himself, and a chronological list of his victories and defeats. Then the exploits of his marshals and the deeds of his high dignitaries would excite the suspicion and the scepticism of the historian; but then, too, would songs and popular ballads proclaim loudly, not the final treason of Murat, but his chivalrous gallantry; they would repeat the pretended death of Cambronne, and the odious crimes with which the people so blindly charge M. de Raguse. Nor would a Roland and a Ganelon suffice; around the new Charlemagne would be grouped another warlike Almoner, another prudent Duke Naimes. Such, were history silent, would be outlines of the poetic tale; and our children would easily supply the coloring.

To return to the *Romances of the Twelve Peers.* They recommend themselves equally to the admiration of the poet, and to the attention of the antiquary. Whilst the former will be astonished at the unity of the plots, the connection of the episodes, the interest of the stories, and the originality of the descriptions they contain, the latter will find new light thrown by them upon the ancient topography of France, upon the date of many venerable structures, and upon the history of an infinite number of cities, fiefs, chateaux, and seigniories. When these singular productions shall appear in the broad daylight of the press, then shall we see France enveloped in a bright poetic glory, new and unexpected. And, on the other hand, what an ample field will than be laid open for new doubts concerning our ancient jurisprudence, our ancient political constitution, and the nature of the feudal system, so complicated in modern theory, but so natural in its origin and so simple in its form! In the writings of our old romancers, the feudal system is embodied; it moves, acts, speaks, battles; now with the monarch at its head, it is present at the tilts and tournaments, and now it discusses the affairs of state; now it suffer penalties, and now cries aloud for vengeance. I assert, then, without fear of contradiction, that, in order to become thoroughly acquainted with the history of the Middle Ages,—I do not mean the bare history of facts, but of the manners and customs which render those facts probable,—we must study it in the pages of old romance; and this is the reason why the history of France is yet unwritten.

Hitherto the fate of these great works has been a singular one. I have already remarked that for the space of four hundred years, that is from the eleventh to the fifteenth century, they constituted almost the only literature of our ancestors. Immediately afterward foreign nations took possession of them; first the Germans, and next the Italians; and it would seem that, in thus relinquishing them to our neighbors, we have had some scruples as to the propriety of retaining even so much as the memory of them. Thus by slow degrees they have quite disappeared from our literature. The renown, however, of the enchanting fictions of Pulci and Ariosto gave birth to a few lifeless and paltry imitations; only one point was forgotten, and that was to have recourse to the old Gallic originals. But, alas! what was ancient France, her history, her manners, and her literature, to a class of writers who only dreamed of reviving once more the ages of Rome and Athens, and who, in their strange hallucination, hoped to persuade the people to suppress all rhyme in their songs, and to supply its place by dactyls and anapests.

This exclusive love of classic antiquity acquired new force during the whole of the seventeenth century: so that no one thought of contradicting Boileau, when he so carelessly called Villon

> The first who, in those rude, unpolished times,
> Cleared the dark mystery of our ancient rhymes.

In the eighteenth century a kind of conservative instinct seemed to bring our men of letters back to the productions of the Middle Ages; but by their anxiety to remove all philological difficulties from the old romances, they have retarded the time when these poems shall be as universally read among us as the *Romanceros* are in Spain, and Dante and Boccaccio in Italy. The imitations of Tressan and Caylus had their day; but as these productions were tricked out to suit the fashion of the age, they disappeared with the fashion which gave them birth.

But the moment seems at length to have arrived when these ancient poems shall be raised from the dead. A desire to know more of the earliest monuments of modern literature is at length manifesting itself among us; and before the expiration of ten years it is probable that the most important of these works will have emerged, so to speak, into the perpetual light of the press.

One word concerning the metre of these poems. They were written to be sung; and this is one point of resemblance observable between the old Greek rhapsodies and the heroic ballads of France. Doubtless the music of these poems was solemn and monotonous, like that of our devotional chants, or those village songs, whose final notes mark the recommencement of the tune. The ancient ballad of "Count Orri" is a piece of this kind; and so also is the burlesque description of the death of Malbrouk, if you suppress the refrain.[14] This kind of music strikes the ear agreeably, though its cadence is monotonous; in proof of which I appeal to all our recollections of childhood.

In these old romances, as in the song to which I have just alluded, the verse is monorhythmic, and the metre either pentameter or Alexandrine. As these poems were written to be sung, it is evident that the pause or rest would naturally come after the fourth syllable in pentameter lines, and after the sixth in Alexandrines.[15] Nor is this all. This necessary rest in the middle of the line gave the poet an opportunity of introducing at the close of the hemistich an unaccented syllable, as at the end of the feminine rhymes of the present day.

---

[14] Though this song is certainly well enough known, yet it may be necessary to quote a few lines in proof of my assertion. It will be seen that the measure is *Alexandrine,* and the verse *monorythmic.*

Madame à sa tour monte,—si haut qu'el peut monter,
Elle aperçoit son page—de noir tout habillé.
"Beau page, mon beau page—quel' nouvelle a ortés?"
"La nouvell' que j'aporte,—vos beaux yeux vont pleurer;
Monsieur Malbrough est mort,—est mort et enterré," etc.

[15] To this rest, which was absolutely essential to the musical accompaniment, we can trace back the use of the hemistich, which is still preserved by the French, through all other modern nations have abandoned it.

After an attentive examination of our ancient literature, it is impossible to doubt for a moment, that the old monorhythmic romances were set to music, and accompanied by a viol, harp, or guitar; and yet this seems hitherto to have escaped observation. In the olden time no one was esteemed a good minstrel, whose memory was not stored with a great number of historic ballads, like those of *Roncesvalles, Garin de Loherain*, and *Gerars de Roussillon*. It is not to be supposed that any one of these poems was ever recited entire; but as the greater part of them contained various descriptions of battles, hunting adventures, and marriages,—scenes of the court, the council, and the castle,—the audience chose those stanzas and episodes which best suited their taste. And this is the reason why each stanza contains in itself a distinct and complete narrative, and also why the closing lines of each stanza are in substance repeated at the commencement of that which immediately succeeds.

In the poem of *Gerars de Nevers* I find the following curious passage. Gerars, betrayed by his mistress and stripped of his earldom of Nevers by the Duke of Metz, determines to revisit his ancient domains. To avoid detection and arrest, he is obliged to assume the guise of a minstrel.

Then Gerars donned a garment old,
And round his neck a viol hung,
For cunningly he played and sung. ...
Steed he had none; so he was fain
To trudge on foot o'er hill and plain,
Till Nevers' gate he stood before.
There merry burghers full a score,
Staring, exclaimed in pleasant mood:
"This minstrel cometh for little good;
I ween, if he singeth all day long,
No one will listen to his song."

In spite of these unfavorable prognostics, Gerars presents himself before the castle of the Duke of Metz.

Whilst at the door he thus did wait,
A knight came through the courtyard gate,
Who bade the minstrel enter straight,

And led him to the crowded hall,
That he might play before them all.
The minstrel then full soon began,
In gesture like an aged man,
But with clear voice and music gay,
The song of Guillaume au Cornez.
Great was the court in the hall of Loön,
The tables were full of fowl and venison,
On flesh and fish they feasted every one;
But Guillaume of these viands tasted none,
Brown crusts ate he, and water drank alone.
When had feasted every noble baron,
The cloths were removed by squire and scallion.
Count Guillaume then with the king did thus reason:
"What thinketh now," quoth he, "the gallant Charlon?"[16]
Will he aid me against the prowess of Mahon"
Quoth Loéis, "We will take council thereon,
To-morrow in the morning shalt thou conne,
If aught by us in this matter can be done."
Guillaume heard this,—black was he as carbon,
He louted low, and seized a baton,
And said to the king, "Of your fief will I none,
I will not keep so much as a spur's iron;
Your friend and vassal I cease to be anon;
But come you shall, whether you will or non."
Thus full four verses sang the knight,
For their great solace and delight.

Observe the expression "full four verses," which very evidently means four stanzas or couplets.

Thus, then, we may consider the fact as well established, that the old romances were sung; and that hence there was a good reason for dividing them into monorhyme stanzas.

And thus, too, we discover the reason why these romances were called chansons, or songs, and why they generally commenced with some such expressions as the following:—

---

[16] Charlemagne.

Good song, my lords, will it please you to hear?...
Listen, lordlings, to a merry song. ...
Historic song, and of marvellous renown. ...

We shall no longer look for the famous *Chanson de Roland* or *de Roncevaux* in some forgotten page of our ancient manuscripts; nor shall we longer insist upon its having the brevity, the form, and even the accustomed burden of the modern ballad. We shall now be content with a reference to the manuscripts entitled *Li Romans*, or *La Chansons de Roncevals*, which can be easily found in the Royal Library; and after having read them, we shall no longer believe that this precious monument of our national traditions and literature has forever perished.

It is because we have not already done this, that we have always interpreted so incorrectly the pas sage in the romance of the *Brut*,[17] where the author, after enumerating the army of William the Conqueror, adds:—

Taillefer, who sung full well, I wot,
Mounted on steed that was swift of foot,
Went forth before the armed train

---

[17] The original of this romance was an ancient chronicle entitled *Bruty Brenhined*, or Brutus of Brittany, written in the old Armoric dialect, and first brought into England at the commencement of the twelfth century by Walter or Gualter, Archdeacon of Oxford. It was given by him to Geoffrey of Monmouth, a Benedictine monk, who translated it into Latin prose. Afterwards, by the order of Henry II. of England, it was translated into French verse by Robert Wace, under the title of *Le Brut d'Engleterre*. From this romance originated the Romances of King Arthur and the Round Table. The following quaint notice of this old chronicle is from the pen of an English writer of the sixteenth century.

"Among our owne ancient chronicles, John of Wethamsted, Abbot of S. Alban, holdeth the whole narration of *Brute* to be rather poeticall, than historicall, which me thinkes, is agreable to reason. ... The first that ever broached it was *Geffry of Monmoth* aboute foure hundred yeares agoe, during the raigne of Henry the Second, who, publishing the Brittish story in Latine, pretended to have taken it out of ancient monuments written in the Brittish tongue: but this booke, as scone as it peeped forth into the light, was sharply censured both by Giraldus Cambrensis, and William of Newberry who lived at the same time, the former tearming it no better than *Fabulosam historiam*, a fabulous history, and the latter, *Ridiculo figmenta*, ridiculous fictions, and it now stands branded with a blacke cole among the bookes prohibited by the Church of Rome."—*An Apologie of the Power and Providence of God in the Government of the World*, p. 8.

Singing of Roland and Charlemain,
Of Oliver and the brave vassals,
Who died at the pass of Roncesvals.

We formerly thought, with the Duc de la Vallière, that some short ballad was here spoken of; and M. de Châteaubriand was the first to suspect the truth, when he said, "This ballad must still exist somewhere in the romance of 'Oliver,' which was formerly preserved in the Royal Library." The whole truth is that the Chanson de Roncevaux exists nowhere but in the *Chanson de Roncevaux*.

Hitherto, by way of excuse for not reading these old romances, it has been fashionable to load them with all kinds of censure. It may not be amiss to examine some of the charges brought against them.

It has been said that they contain nothing but ridiculous and incredible adventures; that these adventures are all founded upon a pretended journey of Charlemagne to Jerusalem; and that they are a copy or a paraphrase of that absurd and insipid history of Charlemagne attributed to the Archbishop Turpin. Consequently their date is fixed no earlier than the close of the twelfth or the commencement of the thirteenth century. But these opinions will not bear a very rigid scrutiny.

Those who urge the improbability of the adventures contained in these writings confound together two classes of works, which have no kind of connection,—that is to say, the old traditions of Brittany, and the ancient heroic ballads of France. The former, indeed, founded upon the marvels of the Saint Graal,[18] contain nothing but strange and miraculous adventures; but the *Romances of the Twelve Peers* contain a continued narrative, the more probable in its detail, inasmuch as these romances belong to a period of greater antiquity. The impossible forms no part of their plan, and Lucan is not more sparing of the marvellous than the first poets who sang the praises of Roland and Guillaume au Cornez. Nay, if any one should compare the details of the

[18] The *Saint Graal* was the dish in which Joseph of Arimathea is said to have caught the blood which flowed from the Saviour's wounds, when he embalmed the body. According to the traditions of old romance, he afterwards carried it to Great Britain, where he made use of it in converting the inhabitants to Christianity,—or, as it is expressed in the Romance of Tristan, "*pour la terr susdite peupler de bonne gent.*" It figures in all the romances of the Round Table.

lives of our ancient kings, as they are described in the Chronicle of Saint-Denis, and in our oldest romances, he would soon be persuaded that the latter have incontestably the advantage in point of probability.

The second charge is equally ill-founded. I am well aware that the antiquarians of the last century discovered a legend describing the journey of Charlemagne to the Holy Land; I am equally well aware that in addition to this there exists a very ancient romance, whose subject is the conquest of a part of the Grecian empire by Charlemagne, and his pilgrimage to Jerusalem. But it is very unfair to conclude from this, that all the romances of the Twelve Peers have the same chimerical foundation; for the only one which treats of the war in the East was first discovered by the Abbé de la Rue, not in France, but in the British Museum. With regard to the other monorhythmic romances, far from being founded on the same event, the greater part of them do not even belong to the age of Charlemagne. Thus, *Gerars de Roussillon*, of which nothing now remains but an imitation of a later date, records the wars of Charles Martel; *Garin le Loherain, Girbert*, and *Berte aus Grans Piés* embrace the reign of Pepin-le-Bref; *Raoul de Cambray, Guillaume au Cornez, Gerars de Nevers*, transport us to the days of Louis-le-Débonnaire; and others refer back to the age of Charles-le-Chauve. Of the poems which embrace the age of Charlemagne, the most ancient and authentic are the following: *Agolant*, or the expulsion of the Saracens from Italy;—*Jean de Lanson*, or the Lombard war;—*Guiteclin de Sassoigne*, or the wars of Saxony against Witikind;—*Les Quatre Fils Aymon* and *Girard de Vianne*, or the wars of Auvergne and Dauphiny; and *Ogier le Danois* and *Roncevaux*, or the expedition to Spain. In all these there is not one word about Jerusalem,—not even so much as an allusion to that chimerical pilgrimage. We must not, then, condemn these romances because "they are all founded on the pretended journey of Charlemagne to Jerusalem."

I now come to the last charge. And are the *Romances of the Twelve Peers* a paraphrase of the chronicle of Turpin, and consequently of a later date than this chronicle?

All your friends are well aware that you have been long engaged in preparing a valuable edition of the work of the Archbishop of Rheims. You have consulted the various manuscripts and the numerous translations of this work; you have compared the most correct texts and the most ancient readings. It is then for you to decide, whether our ancient poems, being only an imitation of this chronicle, are to be dated no farther back than the thirteenth, or, at farthest, than the twelfth century. And if I venture to offer you, in anticipation of your judgment, my own imperfect views upon this subject, I am urged to this step by the conviction, that my researches, though far less enlightened than your own, will notwithstanding coincide with them.

The author of this chronicle, whoever he may be, is very far from having made good the title of his work,—*De Vitâ et Gestis Caroli Magni*. With the exception of a few sentences which are bestowed upon the first exploits and upon the death of Charlemagne, the whole work is taken up in describing the crusade against the Saracens of Spain, and the defeat of the French rear-guard near Roncesvalles. According to the chronicler, the true motive of this expedition was a dream, in which Saint James commanded the Emperor to go and rescue his precious relics from the hands of the Saracens. In return for this, the Saint promised him victory on earth and paradise in heaven. The first care of Charlemagne was, therefore, to build churches to Saint James, and to honor his relics. Notwithstanding all this, his rear-guard, as everybody knows, was cut to pieces; but this, according to the same chronicler, was the fault of the French themselves, who were enticed from their duty by the allurements of the Moorish maidens. At all events, he declares that Charlemagne would have been damned after death, had it not been for the great number of churches which he built or endowed.

This brief analysis of the famous chronicle affords us a glimpse of its design. The author was, without doubt, a monk; and Geoffrey, Prior of Saint-André-de-Vienne, who first brought it from Spain, was living in the year 1092. Until that time the very existence of that legend was un known in France; and there can be little doubt, that even the protection of the monk of Dauphiny would not have rescued it from the obscurity into which all the pious frauds of the same kind have so justly fallen, had it not been for the infallible recommendation which Pope Calixtus II., formerly Archbishop of Vienne, let fall upon it from the height of his pontifical throne. But after all, the Holy Father never declared that this chronicle gave birth to the old French romances, and we may therefore, with all due respect to his decision, maintain that the greater part of these romances are anterior in date to the chronicle.

Indeed, who does not perceive that, if free scope had been given to the pious chronicler,—if he had not been restrained by the necessity of adapting his work to the exigency of traditions generally adopted, he would have omitted the defeat at Roncesvalles, which so unfortunately deranges the promises made to Charlemagne by Monseigneur Saint Jacques?

But there are other proofs even more incontestable than these. In the epistle which the Prior of Vienne wrote to the clergy of Limoges when he sent them the chronicle of Turpin, he observes that he had been the more anxious to procure the work from Spain, because that, previous to that time, the expedition of Charlemagne was known in France by the songs of the Troubadours only. It would seem, then, that these Troubadours, or Jongleurs, did not wait for the inspiration of the Spanish legend in order to enable them to celebrate the exploits of Roland, and to sing the sad but glorious day of Roncesvalles.

In the course of this miserable monkish chronicle the fictitious Turpin happens to name the principal leaders of the army of Charlemagne. In doing this he confounds, with the most singular ignorance, the poetic heroes of different generations; as, for example, Garin le Loherain and Oliver, the former of whom lived at the commencement of the reign of Pepin, and the latter in the last years of the reign of Charlemagne. On the same occasion he speaks of the valiant Ogier le Danois, who, says he, did such marvels, "that his praise is sung in ballads even down to the present day." The chansons of Roland and of Ogier, which are still preserved, are not, then, mere imitations of the legend of Turpin.

I feel that all further proof would be superfluous. Still, I cannot refrain from mentioning the fact that this Turpin, whom the forger of these writings has transformed into an historian, far from being cited in the *Chanson de Roland*, as the guaranty of the circumstances accompanying the death of this Paladin, expires covered with wounds some time before the death of Roland. But in the chronicle, which was made for and by the monks, and with the simple design of exciting the zeal of the pilgrims to the shrine of Saint James, Turpin appears only in order to confess the dying, and afterwards to carry to Charlemagne the story of the disastrous defeat. Surely, if the poets had followed this chronicle, and had taken it, as has been pretended, for the foundation of their poems, they would have represented the good Archbishop in the same manner in which he has represented himself. And if his testimony had been of any importance in their opinion, as it was in that of all the analysts of the twelfth and thirteenth centuries, they surely would not have begun by entirely overthrowing the authority of this testimony.

The following is the description given in the famous *Chanson de Roland* of the death of Turpin. I have praised these ancient poems so highly, that I might be accused of prejudice in their favor, if I brought forward no quotations to sustain my opinion.

The Archbishop, whom God loved in high degree,
Beheld his wounds all bleeding fresh and free;
And then his cheek more ghastly grew and wan,
And a faint shudder through his members ran.
Upon the battle-field his knee was bent;
Brave Roland saw, and to his succor went,
Straightway his helmet from his brow unlaced,
And tore the shining hauberk from his breast.
Then raising in his arms the man of God,
Gently he laid him on the verdant sod.
"Rest, Sire," he cried,—"for rest thy suffering needs."
The priest replied, "Think but of warlike deeds!
The field is ours well may we boast this strife!
But death steals on,—there is no hope of life
In paradise, where Almoners live again,
There are our couches spread, there shall we rest from pain."

Sore Roland grieved; nor marvel I, alas!
That thrice he swooned upon the thick green grass.
When he revived, with a loud voice cried he,
"O Heavenly Father! Holy Saint Marie!
Why lingers death to lay me in my grave!
Beloved France! how have the good and brave
Been torn from thee, and left thee weak and poor!"
Then thoughts of Aude, his lady-love, came o'er
His spirit, and he whispered soft and slow,
"My gentle friend!—what parting full of woe!
Never so true a liegeman shalt thou see;—

Whate'er my fate, Christ's benison on thee!
Christ, who did save from realms of woe beneath,
The Hebrew Prophets from the second death."
Then to the Paladins, whom well he knew,
He went, and one by one unaided drew
To Turpin's side, well skilled in ghostly lore;—
No heart had he to smile, but, weeping sore,
He blessed them in God's name, with faith that he
Would soon vouchsafe to them a glad eternity.

The Archbishop, then, on whom God's benison rest,
Exhausted, bowed his head upon his breast;—
His mouth was full of dust and clotted gore,
And many a wound his swollen visage bore.
Slow beats his heart, his panting bosom heaves,
Death comes apace,—no hope of cure relieves.
Towards heaven he raised his dying hands, and prayed
That God, who for our sins was mortal made,
Born of the Virgin, scorned and crucified,
In paradise would place him by his side.

Then Turpin died in service of Charlon,
In battle great and eke great orison;—
'Gainst Pagan host alway strong champion;
God grant to him his holy benison.[19]

One question more remains to be touched upon. To what century do these historic songs, or *Romances of the Twelve Peers,* belong? Some have been so sceptical in regard to their antiquity as to fix their date as late as the thirteenth century;—let us not fall into the opposite extreme, by referring them back to so early a period as that in which occurred the events they celebrate. But this discussion would demand a more profound erudition and a more experienced judgment than I can bring to the task, and above all a more extended view of the whole ground of controversy than my present limits allow. Nor shall I ever

[19] The stanzas of this extract, like those of the extract from *Gerard de Nevers,* are monorhythmic. This peculiarity it was not thought necessary to preserve in the translation, as the preceding extract will serve as an example of that kind of verse.

undertake this task, unless more skilful critics should be backward in maintaining the good cause; a supposition which is by no means probable, for on all sides a taste, nay a passion, for these earliest monuments of modern literature is springing up. Even before a professorship has been endowed in the Collége de France, for the purpose of thoroughly investigating the early stages of the French language, the public welcomes with avidity whatever is thus dug up from the fruitful soil of our ancient country. The mine is hardly open, and yet every day we hear of the publication of some old manuscript before unknown. Immediately subsequent to the publication of *Le Roman de Renard*, appeared under your own auspices our earliest comic opera, *Le Jeu de Robin et Marion*, and our earliest drama, *Le Jeu d'Adam le Bossu d'Arras*. M. de Roquefort has presented, as his offering, the poems of Marie de France; and M. Chapelet, the agreeable romance of *Le Châtelain dc Coucy*. M. F. Michel, not satisfied with having published the romance of *Le Comte de Poitiers,* is about bringing forward, with the assistance of an able Orientalist, a poem entitled *Mahomet*, which will show us in what light the religion and the person of the Arab lawgiver were regarded in the East during the thirteenth century. M. Bourdillon, who has long felt all the historic and literary importance of the *Chanson de Ronceveauaux*, is now occupied in preparing an edition for the press; and M. Robert, already favorably known by his work upon La Fontaine, will soon publish edition of the fine old romance of *Partenopex de Blois*. Meanwhile the celebrated M. Raynouard is about completing his *Glossaire des Langues Vulgaires*; and the Abbé de la Rue is superintending the publication of a large work on *les Bardes, les Jongleurs, et les Trouvères*. Thus the knowledge of our ancient literature develops itself more and more daily; and thus will arise, if indeed it has not already arisen, a sober and enlightened judgment concerning the productions of the human mind during that long period bounded on one side by antiquity and on the other by the sixteenth century, the epoch of the revival of the arts and sciences.

The author of the romance of *Berte aus Grans Piés* flourished about the close of the thirteenth century. His name was Adans or Adenès, according to the general custom of designating an individual indifferently by his patronymic name or by its diminutive. The greater part of the manuscripts give him the surname of *Roi*, or *King*; and M. Roquefort thinks that it was bestowed upon him because one of his poems bore off the palm at a *puy d'amour*, or *Court of Love*;[20] whilst the learned authors of the *Histoire Littéraire de la France* suppose that Adenès was indebted for this title to the justice of his contemporaries and to the superiority of his poetic talent. I shall hazard an opinion of my own, which does not conform to either of these. We are acquainted with several Trouvères, whose works obtained prizes in the *Puys* of Valenciennes or Cambray;—they all took the surname of *couronné*, and not that of *roi*.

But in the twelfth and thirteenth centuries there was a King of the Minstrels (*Roi des Ménestrels*). This pacific sovereign had the direction of the Jongleurs or Troubadours of the court, and I am inclined to think that his duties bore no inconsiderable resemblance to those of a modern leader of an orchestra. To him people addressed themselves, when they wanted a good singer, a good lute-player, or a good harper; and the King of the Minstrels, as the most skilful of all, directed and animated the concert by voice and gesture. Such were probably the prerogatives and functions of *le Roi Adenès*.

However this may be,—and although no one can doubt, on running over the names of his numerous and illustrious protectors, that Adenès enjoyed a high reputation as Trouvère and minstrel,—yet I do not find that any contemporary writer makes mention of him. It is true, that in one of the copies of the fables of Marie de France, this poetess designates *le Roi Adans* as the author of the first English translation of the fables of Esop:—

> Esop call we this book;
> King Adans did highly rate it,
> And into English did translate it.

But this copy deceived the learned author of the catalogue of the La Vallière manuscripts. All other copies of Marie de France read *Li rois Henrys*, instead of *Li rois Adans*. At all events, as many of the manuscripts of Marie de France belong to the commencement of the thirteenth century, it is evident that they

---

[20] The *puys d'amour* were assemblies in which questions of love and gallantry were discussed in poetry. The name of *puy* comes from the low Latin *podium*, "balcony" or "stage," as the poets on these occasions recited their verses from an elevated place. For an account of these *Puys or Cours d'Amour*, see Roquefort, *De la Poésie Françoise*, p. 93.—Raynouard, *Choix de Poésies des Troubadours*, tom. ii. p. 79 et seq.

can make no mention of the works of Adenès, who did not flourish till near its close.

It is, then, to the writings of Adenès, and particularly to his romance of *Cléomadès* that we must look for information respecting the time in which he flourished, and for some circumstances of his life.

Adenès was born in the duchy of Brabant, about 1240. He doubtless exhibited, at an early age, a remarkable talent for poetry; for Henry III., then Duke of Brabant, the warm friend of poets, and yet a poet himself, had him educated with care, and afterward chose him for his minstrel. It is very possible that the pretty songs of Henry III., which are still preserved in the Royal Library, were submitted to the correction of the young Adenès, before they were sung in public. Nearly all the princes of the thirteenth century give proofs of great talent, and sometimes of true poetic genius. But perhaps their highest, their most indisputable merit was mainly owing to the choice of their minstrels. Thus, Blondel was distinguished by the patronage of Richard Cœur-de-Lion, and Gaces Brulés by that of the king of Navarre; Charles d'Anjou, king of Naples, was accompanied by the Bossu d'Arras, and we have seen that Adenès had merited the good graces of the Duke of Brabant.

Minstrel was l to the good Duke Henry;
He it was that brought me up and nourished me,
And made me learn the art of minstrelsy.

Henry died in 1260, regretted by his subjects, and above all by the poets, whose labors he liberally rewarded. Adenès, who, after the death of his benefactor, took every opportunity of praising his virtues, soon gained the affection of the Duke's children. Jean and Guyon preserved the poet from the ills of penury, and when Marie de Brabant became queen of France, she took him with her to Paris. There, in his double capacity of poet and courtier, he was honored with the most marked distinction. In those days, poets were permitted to eulogize the great, and to celebrate their numerous virtues. In doing this Adenès had no peer; but whilst he rendered due homage to those whom fortune surrounded with all the splendor of power, he listened also to the natural promptings of his heart, and both respected and cherished all self-acquired renown. He somewhere says in *Buevon de Comarchis*:—

If it please God and his saints, through all my earthly days,
Of good men and of valiant, I will gladly speak in praise;
What good I hear of them, I will record it in my lays,
If aught I hear that's ill, I will hold my peace always.

The precise date of the death of Adenès is unknown. The last poem to which he has prefixed his name is *Cléomadès*, whose story transports us back to the reign of Diocletian. This is the longest of the author's poems, and contains no less than nineteen thousand octosyllabic lines. The principal narrative is often interrupted by agree able episodes, such as the history of the miraculous deeds of the poet Virgil, "the greatest magician of Rome." Among other marvels, which unfortunately time hath put into his wallet as "aims for oblivion," Adenès mentions the baths of Pozzuoli. On each of these Virgil had inscribed the name of that disease which was instantly cured by the virtue of its waters.

But the Physicians every one,
Who much ill and much good have done,
All of these writings did decry;—
For nothing could they gain thereby.
And if those baths existed now,
They'd like them little enough, I trow.

A great number of copies of *Cléomadès* are still extant,—some of them under the title of *Cheval de Fust*. This *cheval de fust*, or wooden horse, takes a very active part in the romance. He traversed the air, you know, with inconceivable rapidity, and was guided in his course by turning a peg, which is sufficient to prove that this famous courser is the type of the horse on which Pierre de Provence carried away the fair Maguelonne, and which, at a later period, under the name of *Clavileño*, bore the divine Sancho so high in air as to make him confound the earth with a grain of mustard-seed, and its inhabitants with filberts.

Cléomadès was written at the joint request of Marie de Brabant and Blanche de France, who was married in 1269 to the Infante of Castile. The names of these two princesses determine very nearly the date of its composition. Marie de Brabant was married in 1274 to Philippe-le-Hardi; and Blanche, on the death of her husband, returned to France in 1275. *Cléomadès* must, therefore, have been written between 1275 and 1283, the year in which Philippe-le-Hardi died.

I have one word more to say of this romance. It thus commences:—

> He who did write *Ogier the Dane*,
> And *She of the wood*, yelept *Bertaine*,
> And *Bueron of Comarchis* make,
> Another book doth undertake.

These three romances are still preserved in the Royal Library, all of them complete, except *Bueron de Comarchis*, of which the first part only remains. *Bueron de Comarchis* is a kind of appendage to the old romances which immortalize the family of Guillaume au Cornez; in the same manner that the *Enfances Ogier* are the sequel of the romances of Ogier. It has been often supposed that Adenès was the author of all the poems of Guillaume au Gomez and also of Ogier le Danois; but this is an error; for the origin of the greater part of these romances can be traced back to the very cradle of French poetry,—to a period far beyond the thirteenth century.

Adenès, on the contrary, is one of the last poets who sang, in monorhythmic verse, the traditions of our fabulous and heroic ages. His versification is pure and correct; but it may be said that the subject of his narratives is the less poetic in proportion as his style is the more so.

But this letter is already a thousand times too long; and I therefore close these desultory remarks upon Adenès and his works, leaving it to the romance of *Berte aus Grans Piés* to plead its own cause, and to justify the importance which I attach to its publication.

FRITHIOF'S SAGA.

The paper on *Frithiof's Saga* was contributed to the *North American Review*, and published in the number for July, 1837. The description of rural life in Sweden served afterward as a preface to the translation of Tegnér's *Nattvardsbarnen* (*The Children of the Lord's Supper*), when that poem first appeared in *Ballads and other Poems*. Mr. Longfellow spent the summer of 1835 in Sweden, and there made the acquaintance of Tegnér's *Saga*. In reprinting the article he took the opportunity to revise it, and especially to improve the translations.

HERE beginneth the Legend of Frithiof the Valiant. He was the son of Thorsten Vikingsson, a thane, and loved fair Ingeborg, the daughter of a king. His fame was great in the North, and his name in the song of bards. His marvellous deeds on land and sea are told in tradition; and his history is written in the old Icelandic Saga that bears his name. This Saga is in prose, with occasionally a few stanzas of verse. Upon the events recorded in it the poem of Tegnér is founded.

Esaias Tegnér, Bishop of Wexiö and Knight of the Order of the North Star, was born in 1782 and died in 1846. He stands first among the poets of Sweden; a man of beautiful imagination,—a poetic genius of high order. His countrymen are proud of him, and rejoice in his fame. If you speak of their literature, Tegnér will be the first name upon their lips. They will tell you with enthusiasm of Frithiof's Saga, and of Axel, and Svea, and the Children of the Lord's Supper. The modern Scald has written his name in immortal runes: not on the bark of trees alone, in the "unspeakable rural solitudes" of pastoral song, but on the mountains of his fatherland, and the cliffs that overhang the sea, and on the tombs of ancient heroes, whose histories are epic poems.

The Legend of Frithiof is an epic poem, composed of a series of ballads, each describing some event in the hero's life, and each written in a different measure, according with the action described in the ballad. This is a novel idea, and perhaps thereby the poem loses something in sober, epic dignity. But the loss is more than made up by the greater spirit of the narrative; and it seems a laudable innovation thus to describe various scenes in various metres, and not to employ the same for a game of chess and a storm at sea.

It may be urged against Tegnér, with some show of truth, that he is too profuse and elaborate in his use of figurative language, and that the same figures are sometimes repeated with little variation. But the reader must bear in mind that the work before him is written in the spirit of the Past; in the spirit of that old poetry of the North in which the same images and expressions are oft repeated, and the sword is called the Lightning's Brother; a banner, the Hider of Heaven; gold, the Daylight of Dwarfs; and the grave, the Green Gate of Paradise. The old Scald smote the strings of his harp with as bold a hand as the Berserk smote his foe. When heroes fell in battle, he sang of them in his Drapa, or Death-Song, that they had gone to drink beer with the gods. He lived in a credulous age, in the dim twilight of the Past. He was

> The skylark in the dawn of years,
> The poet of the morn.

In the vast solitudes around him "the heart of Nature beat against his own." From the midnight gloom of groves the melancholy pines called aloud to the neighboring sea. To his ear these were not the voices of dead, but of living things. Demons rode the ocean like a weary steed, and the gigantic pines flapped their sounding wings to smite the spirit of the storm.

With this same baptism has the soul of the modern Scald been baptized. He dwells in that land where the sound of the sea and the midnight storm are the voices of tradition, and the great forests beckon to him, and in mournful accents seem to say, "Why hast thou tarried so long?" They have not spoken in vain. In this spirit the poem has been written, and in this spirit it must be read. We must visit, in imagination at least, that distant land, and converse with the Genius of the place. It points us to the great mounds, which are the tombs of kings. Their bones are within; skeletons of warriors mounted on the skeletons of their steeds, and Vikings sitting gaunt and grim on the plankless ribs of their pirate ships. There is a wooden statue in the Cathedral of Upsala. It is an image of the god Thor, who in Valhalla holds seven stars in his hand,

and Charles's Wain.[21] In the village of Gamla Upsala there is an ancient church. It was once a temple, in which the gods of the old mythology were worshipped. In every mysterious sound that fills the air, the peasant still hears the trampling of Odin's steed, which many centuries ago took fright at the sound of a church bell. The memory of Balder is still preserved in the flower that bears his name, and Freja's spinning-wheel still glimmers in the stars of the constellation Orion. The sound of Strömkarl's flute is heard in tinkling brooks, and his song in waterfalls. In the forest the Skogsfrun, of wondrous beauty, leads young men astray; and Tomtgubbe hammers and pounds away, all night long, at the peasant's unfinished cottage.

Almost primeval simplicity reigns over this Northern land,—almost primeval solitude and stillness. You pass out from the gate of the city, and, as if by magic, the scene changes to a wild, woodland landscape. Around you are forests of fir. Overhead hang the long fan-like branches trailing with moss, and heavy with red and blue cones. Underfoot is a carpet of yellow leaves, and the air is warm and balmy. On a wooden bridge you cross a little silver stream. Anon you come forth into a pleasant and sunny land of farms. Wooden fences divide the adjoining fields. Across the road are gates, which are opened for you by troops of flaxen-haired children. The peasants take off their hats as you pass. You sneeze, and they cry, "God bless you!" The houses in the villages and smaller cities are all built of hewn timber, and for the most part painted red. The floors of the taverns are strewn with the fragrant tips of fir boughs. In many villages there are no taverns, and the peasants take turns in receiving travellers. The thrifty housewife shows you into the best chamber, the walls of which are hung round with rude pictures from the Bible; and brings you her heavy silver spoons—an heirloom—to dip the curdled milk from the pan. You have oaten cakes baked some months before; or bread with anise-seed and coriander in it, and perhaps a little pine-bark.[22]

---

[21] Thor Gudh war högsten aff them
Han satt naken som ett Barn
Siv stiemor i handen och Karlewagn.

Old Swedish Rhyme—Chronicle

[22] Speaking of Dalekarlia a Swedish writer says: "In the poorer parishes the inhabitants are forced, even in good years, to mingle some bark in their bread." Of Elfdalen he says: "The

Meanwhile the sturdy husband has brought his horses from the plough, and harnessed them to your carriage. Solitary travellers come and go in uncouth one-horse chaises. Most of them have pipes in their mouths, and, hanging around their necks in front, a leathern wallet, wherein they carry tobacco, and the great bank-notes of the country as large as your two hands. You meet, also, groups of Dalekarlian peasant-women, travelling homeward or city-ward in pursuit of work. They walk barefoot, carrying in their hands their shoes, which have high heels under the hollow of the foot, and the soles of birch-bark.

Frequent, too, are the village churches standing by the roadside, each in its own little garden of Gethsemane. In the parish register great events are doubtless recorded. Some old king was christened or buried in that church; and a little sexton, with a great rusty key, shows you the baptismal font, or the coffin. In the churchyard are a few flowers and much green grass; and daily the shadow of the church spire, with its long, tapering finger, counts the tombs, thus representing an index of human life, on which the hours and minutes are the graves of men. The stones are flat, and large, and low, and perhaps sunken, like the roofs of old houses. On some are armorial bearings; on others, only the initials of the poor tenants, with a date, as on the roofs of Dutch cottages. They all sleep with their heads to the westward. Each held a lighted taper in his hand when he died, and in his coffin were placed his little heart-treasures, and a piece of money for his last journey. Babes that came lifeless into the world were carried in the arms of gray-haired old men to the only cradle they ever slept in; and in the shroud of the dead mother were laid the little garments of the child that lived and died in her bosom. And over this scene the village pastor looks from his window in the stillness of midnight, and says in his heart, "How quietly they rest, all the departed!"

Near the churchyard gate stands a poor-box, fastened to a post by iron bands, and secured by a padlock, with a sloping wooden roof to keep off the rain. If it be Sunday the peasants sit on the church steps and con their psalm-books. Others are coming down the road with their beloved pastor, who talks

---

people are poor; without bark-bread they could not live the year out. The traveller who visits these regions, and sees by the roadside long rows of young pines stripped of their bark, in answer to his question wherefore this is so, bears, and truly not without emotion, his postilion's reply: 'To make bread for ourselves and for our children.'"

to them of holy things from beneath his broad-brimmed hat. He speaks of fields and harvests, and of the parable of the sower that went forth to sow. He leads them to the Good Shepherd, and to the pleasant pastures of the spirit land. He is their patriarch, and, like Melchisedek, both priest and king, though he has no other throne than the church pulpit. The women carry psalm-books in their hands, wrapped in silk handkerchiefs, and listen devoutly to the good man's words. But the young men, like Gallio, care for none of these things. They are busy counting the plaits in the kirtles of the peasant-girls, their number being an indication of the wearer's wealth. It may end in a wedding.

I must describe a village wedding in Sweden. It shall be in summer time, that there may be flowers, and in a southern province, that the bride may be fair. The early song of the lark and of chanticleer are mingling in the clear morning air; and the sun, the heavenly bridegroom with golden locks, arises in the east, just as Olof Olofsson, our earthly bridegroom with yellow hair, arises in the south. In the yard there is a sound of voices and trampling of hoofs, and horses are led forth and saddled. The steed that is to bear the bridegroom has a bunch of flowers upon his forehead, and a garland of corn-flowers around his neck. Friends from the neighboring farms come riding in, their blue cloaks streaming to the wind; and finally, the happy bridegroom, with a whip in his hand, and a monstrous nosegay in the breast of his black jacket, comes forth from his chamber; and then to horse and away, towards the village where the bride already sits and waits.

Foremost rides the Spokesman, followed by some half-dozen village musicians, all blowing and drumming and fifing away like mad. Then comes the bridegroom between his two groomsmen, and then forty or fifty friends and wedding guests, half of them perhaps with pistols and guns in their hands. A kind of baggage-wagon brings up the rear, laden with meat and drink for these merry pilgrims. At the entrance of every village stands a triumphal arch, adorned with flowers and ribbons and ever greens; and as they pass beneath it the wedding guests fire a salute, and the whole procession stops. And straight from every pocket flies a black-jack, filled with punch or brandy. It is passed from hand to hand among the crowd; provisions are brought from the wagon of the sumpter horse; and after eating and drinking and loud hurrahs, the procession moves forward again, and at length draws near the house of the bride. Four heralds ride forward to announce that a knight and his attendants are in the neighboring forest, and pray for hospitality. "How many are you?" asks the bride's father. "At least three hundred," is the answer; and to this the host replies, "Yes; were you seven times as many you should all be welcome, and in token thereof receive this cup." Whereupon each herald receives a can of ale, and soon after the whole jovial company come storming into the farmer's yard, and, riding round the May-pole, which stands in the centre, alight amid a grand salute and flourish of music.

In the hall sits the bride, with a crown upon her head and a tear in her eye, like the Virgin Mary in old church paintings. She is dressed in a red bodice and kirtle, with loose linen sleeves. There is a gilded belt around her waist; and around her neck, strings of golden beads and a golden chain. On the crown rests a wreath of wild roses, and be low it another of cypress. Loose over her shoulders falls her flaxen hair; and her blue innocent eyes are fixed upon the ground. O thou good soul! thou hast hard hands, but a soft heart! Thou art poor. The very ornaments thou wearest are not thine. They have been hired for this great day. Yet art thou rich; rich in health, rich in hope, rich in thy first, young, fervent love. The blessing of Heaven be upon thee! So thinks the parish priest, as he joins together the hands of bride and bride groom, saying, in deep, solemn tones: "I give thee in marriage this damsel, to be thy wedded wife in all honor, and to share the half of thy bed, thy lock and key, and every third penny which you two may possess, or may inherit, and all the rights which Upland's laws provide, and the holy King Erik gave."

The dinner is now served, and the bride sits between the bridegroom and the priest. The Spokesman delivers an oration, after the ancient custom of his fathers. He interlards it well with quotations from the Bible, and invites the Saviour to be present at this marriage feast, as he was at the marriage feast in Cana of Galilee. The table is not sparingly set forth. Each makes a long arm, and the feast goes cheerly on. Punch and brandy are served up between the courses, and here and there a pipe smoked while waiting for the next dish. They sit long at table; but, as all things must have an end, so must a Swedish dinner. Then the dance begins. It is led off by the bride and the priest, who perform a solemn minuet together. Not till after midnight comes the Last Dance. The girls form a ring around the bride to keep her from the hands of the married women, who endeavor to break through the magic circle and seize their new sister. After long struggling, they succeed; and the crown is taken from her head and the jewels from her neck, and her bodies is unlaced and her kirtle taken off; and like a vestal virgin clad in white she goes, but it is to her marriage chamber, not to her grave; and the wedding guests follow her with lighted candles in their hands. And this is a village bridal.

Nor must we forget the sudden changing seasons of the Northern clime. There is no long and lingering spring, unfolding leaf and blossom one by one no long and lingering autumn, pompous with many-colored leaves and the glow of Indian summers. But winter and summer are wonderful, and pass into each other. The quail has hardly ceased piping in the corn, when winter, from the folds of trailing clouds, sows broadcast over the land snow, icicles, and rattling hail. The days wane apace. Erelong the sun hardly rises above the horizon, or does not rise at all. The moon and the stars shine through the day; only at noon they are pale and wan, and in the southern sky a red, fiery glow, as of sunset, burns along the horizon, and then goes out. And pleasantly under the silver moon, and under the silent, solemn stars, ring the steel shoes of the skaters on the frozen sea, and voices and the sound of bells.

And now the Northern Lights begin to burn, faintly at first, like sunbeams playing in the waters of the blue sea. Then a soft crimson glow tinges the heavens. There is a blush on the cheek of night. The colors come and go, and change from crimson to gold, from gold to crimson. The snow is stained with rosy light. Twofold from the zenith, east and west, flames a fiery sword; and a broad band passes athwart the heavens like a summer sunset. Soft purple clouds come sailing over the sky, and through their vapory folds the winking stars shine white as silver. With such pomp as this is Merry Christmas ushered in, though only a single star heralded the first Christmas. And in memory of that day the Swedish peasants dance on straw and the peasant-girls throw straws at the timbered roof of the hall, and for every one that sticks in a crack shall a groomsman come to their wedding. Merry Christmas indeed! For pious souls church songs shall be sung, and sermons preached;—

> And all the bells on earth shall ring,
> And all the angels in heaven shall sing,
>   On Christmas day in the morning.

But for Swedish peasants brandy and nut-brown ale in wooden bowls; and the great Yule-cake crowned with a cheese, and garlanded with apples, and upholding a three-armed candlestick over the Christmas feast. They may tell tales, too, of Jöns Lundsbracka, and Lunkenfus, and the great Riddar Finke of Pingsdaga. [23]

And now the glad, leafy midsummer, full of blossoms and the song of nightingales, is come! Saint John has taken the flowers and festival of heathen Balder; and in every village there is a May-pole fifty feet high, with wreaths and roses and ribbons streaming in the wind, and a noisy weathercock on top, to tell the village whence the wind cometh and whither it goeth. The sun does not set till ten o'clock at night, and the children are at play in the streets an hour later. The windows and doors are all open, and you may sit and read till midnight without a candle. Oh, how beautiful is the summer night, which is not night, but a sunless yet unclouded day, descending upon earth with dews, and shadows, and refreshing coolness! How beautiful the long, mild twilight, which like a silver clasp unites today with yesterday! How beautiful the silent hour, when Morning and Evening thus sit together, hand in hand, beneath the starless sky of midnight! From the church tower in the public square the bell tolls the hour, with a soft, musical chime; and the watchman, whose watch-tower is the belfry, blows a blast in his horn for each stroke of the hammer, and four times to the four corners of the heavens, in a sonorous voice, he chants:—

Ho! watchman, ho!
Twelve is the clock!
God keep our town
From fire and brand,
And hostile hand!
Twelve is the clock!

From his swallow's nest in the belfry he can see the sun all night long; and farther north the priest stands at his door in the warm midnight, and lights his pipe with a common burning-glass.

And all this while the good Bishop of Wexiö is waiting, with his poem in his hand. And such a poem, too! Alas! I am but too well aware that a brief analysis and a few scattered extracts can give only a faint idea of the original, and that

[23] Titles of Swedish popular tales.

consequently the admiration of my readers will probably lag somewhat behind my own. If the poem itself should ever fall into their hands, I hope that the foregoing remarks on Sweden, which now may seem to them a useless digression, will nevertheless enable them to enter more easily into the spirit of the poem, and to feel more truly the influences under which it was written.

I.

The first canto describes the childhood and youth of Frithiof and Ingeborg the fair, as they grew up together under the humble roof of Hilding, their foster-father. They are two plants in the old man's garden;—a young oak, whose stem is like a lance, and whose leafy top is rounded like a helm; and a rose, in whose folded buds the spring still sleeps and dreams. But the storm comes, and the young oak must wrestle with it; the sun of spring shines warm in heaven, and the red lips of the rose open. The sports of their childhood are described. They sail together on the deep blue sea; and when he shifts the sail, she claps her small white hands in glee. For her he plunders the highest bird's-nests, and the eagle's eyry, and bears her through the rushing mountain brook; it is so sweet when the torrent roars to be pressed by small white arms.

But childhood and the sports thereof soon pass away, and Frithiof becomes a mighty hunter. He fights the bear without spear or sword, and lays the conquered monarch of the forest at the feet of Ingeborg. And when, by the light of the winter-evening hearth, he reads the glorious songs of Valhalla, no goddess, whose beauty is there celebrated, can compare with Ingeborg. Freya's golden hair may wave like a wheat-field in the wind, but Ingeborg's is a net of gold around roses and lilies. Iduna's bosom throbs full and fair beneath her silken vest, but beneath the silken vest of Ingeborg two Elves of Light leap up with rose-buds in their hands. And she embroiders in gold and silver the wondrous deeds of heroes; and the face of every champion that looks up at her from the woof she is weaving is the face of Frithiof; and she blushes and is glad;—that is to say, they love each other a little. Ancient Hilding does not favor their passion, but tells his foster-son that the maiden is the daughter of King Bele, and be but the son of Thorsten Vikingsson, a Thane; he should not aspire to the love of one who has descended in a long line of ancestors from the star-clear hall of Odin himself. Frithiof smiles in scorn, and replies that he has slain the shaggy king of the forest, and inherits his ancestors with his hide; and moreover that he will possess his bride, his white lily, in spite of the very god of thunder, for a puissant wooer is the sword.

II.

Thus closes the first canto. In the second, old King Bele stands leaning on his sword in his hall, and with him is his faithful brother in arms, Thorsten Vikingsson, the father of Frithiof, silver-haired, and scarred like a runic stone. The king complains that the evening of his days is drawing near, that the mead is no longer pleasant to his taste, and that his helmet weighs heavily upon his brow. He feels the approach of death. Therefore he summons to his presence his two sons, Helge and Halfdan, and with them Frithiof, that he may give a warning to the young eagles before the words slumber on the dead man's tongue. Foremost advances Helge, a grim and gloomy figure, who loves to dwell among the priests and before the altars, and now comes, with blood upon his hands, from the groves of sacrifice. And next to him approaches Halfdan, a boy with locks of light, and so gentle in his mien and bearing that he seems a maiden in disguise. And after these, wrapped in his mantle blue, and a head taller than either, comes Frithiof, and stands between the brothers, like midday between the rosy morning and the shadowy night. Then speaks the king, and tells the young eaglets that his sun is going down, and that they must rule his realm after him in harmony and brotherly love; that the sword was given for defence and not for offence; that the shield was forged as a padlock for the peasant's barn; and that they should not glory in their fathers' honors, as each can hear his own only. If we cannot bend the bow, he says, it is not ours; what have we to do with worth that is buried? The mighty stream goes into the sea with its own waves. These and many other wise sayings fall from the old man's dying lips; and then Thorsten Vikingsson, who means to die with his king as he has lived with him, arises and addresses his son Frithiof. He tells him that old age has whispered many warnings in his ear, which he will repeat to him; for as the birds of Odin descend upon the sepulchres of the North, so words of manifold wisdom descend upon the lips of the old. Then follows much sage advice: that he should serve his king, for one alone shall reign,—the dark Night has many eyes, but the Day has only one; that he should not praise the day until the sun had set, nor his beer until he had drunk it; that he should not trust to ice but one night old, nor snow in spring, nor a sleeping snake, nor the words of a maiden on his knee,—sagacious hints from the High Song of Odin. Then the old men speak together of their long-tried friendship, and the king praises the valor and heroic strength of Frithiof, and Thorsten has much to say of the glory which crowns the Kings of the North-land, the sons of the gods. Then the king speaks to his sons again, and bids them greet his daughter, the rosebud. In retirement, says he, as it behoved her, has she grown up; protect her; let not the storm come and fix upon his helmet my delicate flower. And he bids them bury him and his ancient friend by the seaside, by the billow blue, for its song is pleasant to the spirit evermore, and, like a funeral dirge, its blows ring against the strand.

III.

And now King Bele and Thorsten Vikingsson are gathered to their fathers; Helge and Halfdan share the throne between them, and Frithiof retires to his ancestral estate at Framnäs; of which a description is given in the third canto, conceived and executed in a truly Homeric spirit.

> Three miles extended around the fields of the homestead, on three sides
> Valleys and mountains and hills, but on the fourth side was the ocean.
> Birch woods crowned the summits, but down the slope of the hillsides
> Flourished the golden corn, and man-high was waving the ryefield.
> Lakes, full many in number, their mirror held up for the mountains,
> Held for the forests up, in whose depths the high-horned reindeers
> Had their kingly walk, and drank of a hundred brooklets.
> But in the valleys widely around, there fed on the greensward
> Herds with shining hides and udders that longed for the milk-pail
> 'Mid these scattered, now here and now there, were numberless flocks of
> Sheep with fleeces white, as thou seest the white-looking stray clouds,
> Flock-wise spread o'er the heavenly vault, when it bloweth in spring-time.
> Coursers two times twelve, all mettlesome, fast fettered stormwinds,
> Stamping stood in the line of stalls, and tugged at their fodder.
> Knotted with red were their manes, and their hoofs all white with steel shoes.
> Th' banquet-hall, a house by itself, was timbered of hard fir.

Not five hundred men (at ten times twelve to the hundred[24])
Filled up the roomy hall, when assembled for drinking, at Yuletide.
Thorough the hall, as long as it was, went a table of holm-oak
Polished and white, as of steel; the columns twain of the High-seat
Stood at the end thereof, two gods carved out of an elm-tree;
Odin[25] with lordly look, and Frey[26] with the sun on his frontlet.
Lately between the two, on a bear-skin (the skin it was coal-black,
Scarlet-red was the throat, but the paws were shodden with silver),
Thorsten sat with his friends, Hospitality sitting with Gladness.
Oft, when the moon through the cloud-rack flew, related the old man
Wonders from distant lands he had seen, and cruises of Vikings[27]
Far away on the Baltic, and Sea of the West, and the White Sea.
Hushed sat the listening bench, and their glances hung on the graybeard's
Lips, as a bee on the rose; but the Scald was thinking of Brage, [28]
Where, with his silver beard, and runes on his tongue, he is seated
Under the leafy beech, and tells a tradition by Mimer's[29]
Ever-murmuring wave, himself a living tradition.
Midway the floor (with thatch was it strewn) burned ever the fire-flame
Glad on its stone-built hearth; and thorough the wide-mouthed smoke-flue
Looked the stars, those heavenly friends, down into the great hall.
Round the walls, upon nails of steel, were hanging in order
Breastplate and helmet together, and here and there among them
Downward lightened a sword, as in winter evening a star shoots.
More than helmets and swords the shields in the hall were resplendent,
White as the orb of the sun, or white as the moon's disk of silver.
Ever and anon went a maid round the board, and filled up the drink-horns,
Ever she cast down her eyes and blushed; in the shield her reflection
Blushed, too, even as she; this gladdened the drinking champions.

Among the treasures of Frithiof's house are three of transcendent worth. The first of these is the sword Angurvadel, brother of the lightning, handed

---

[24] An old fashion of reckoning in the North.

[25] Odin, the All-father; the Jupiter of the Scandinavian mythology.

[26] Frey, the god of Fertility; the Bacchus of the North.

[27] The old pirates of the North.

[28] Brage, the god of Song; the Scandinavian Apollo.

[29] Mimer, the Giant, who possessed the Well of Wisdom, under one of the roots of the Ash Igrasil.

down from generation to generation, since the days of Björn Blåtand, the Blue-toothed Bear. The hilt thereof was of beaten gold, and on the blade were wondrous runes, known only at the gates of the sun. In peace these runes were dull, but in time of war they burned red as the comb of a cock when he fights; and lost was he who in the night of slaughter met the sword of the flaming runes!

The second in price is an arm-ring of pure gold, made by Vaulund, the limping Vulcan of the North, and containing upon its border the signs of the zodiac,—the Houses of the Twelve Immortals. This ring had been handed down in the family of Frithiof from the days when it came from the hands of Vaulund, the founder of the race. It was once stolen and carried to England by Viking Sote, who there buried himself alive in a vast tomb, and with him his pirate-ship and all his treasures. King Bele and Thorsten pursue him, and through a crevice of the door look into the tomb, where they behold the ship, with anchor and masts and spars; and on the deck, a fearful figure, clad in a mantle of flame, sits, gloomily scouring a blood-stained sword. The ring is upon his arm. Thorsten bursts the doors of the great tomb asunder with his lance, and, entering, does battle with the grim spirit, and bears home the ring as a trophy of his victory.[30]

The third great treasure of the house of Frithiof is the dragon-ship Ellida. It was given to one of Frithiof's ancestors by a sea-god, whom this ancestor saved from drowning, somewhat as Saint Christopher did the angel. The ancient mariner was homeward bound, when at a distance on the wreck of a ship he espied an old man with sea-green locks, a beard white as the foam of waves, and a face which smiled like the sea when it plays in sunshine. Viking takes this Old Man of the Sea home with him, and entertains him in hospitable guise; but at bedtime the green-haired guest, instead of going quietly to his rest like a Christian man, sets sail again on his wreck, like a hobgoblin, having, as he says, a hundred miles to go that night, at the same time telling the Viking to look the next morning on the sea-shore for a gift of thanks. And the next morning, behold! the dragon-ship Ellida comes sailing up the harbor, like a phantom ship, with all her sails set, and not a man on board. Her prow is a dragon's head, with jaws of gold; her stern, a

[30] Not unlike the old tradition of the ring of Gyges; which was found on a dead man's finger in the flank of a brazen horse, deep buried in a chasm of the earth.

dragon's tail, twisted and scaly with silver; her wings black, tipped with red; and when she spreads them all, she flies a race with the roaring storm, and the eagle is left behind.

These were Frithiof's treasures, renowned in the North; and thus in his hall, with Björn, his bosom friend, he sat, surrounded by his champions twelve, with breasts of steel and furrowed brows, the comrades of his father, and all the guests that had gathered together to pay the funeral rites to Thorsten, the son of Viking. And Frithiof, with eyes full of tears, drank to his father's memory, and heard the song of the Scalds, a dirge of thunder.

IV.

Frithiof's Courtship is the title of the fourth canto.

High sounded the song in Frithiof's hall,
And the Scalds they praised his fathers all;
But the song rejoices
Not Frithiof, he hears not the Scalds' loud voices.

And the earth has clad itself green again,
And the dragons swim once more on the main,
But the hero's son
He wanders in woods, and looks at the moon.

He had lately made a banquet for Helge and Halfdan, and sat beside Ingeborg the fair, and spoke with her of those early days when the dew of morning still lay upon life; of the reminiscences of childhood; their names carved in the birch-tree's bark; the well-known valley and woodland, and the hill where the great oaks grew from the dust of heroes. And now the banquet closes, and Frithiof remains at his homestead to pass his days in idleness and dreams. But this strange mood pleases not his friend the Bear.

It pleased not Björn these things to see:
"What ails the young eagle now," said he,
"So still, so oppressed?
Have they plucked his wings? have they pierced his
breast?

"What wilt thou? Have we not more than we need
Of the yellow lard and the nut-brown mead?
And of Scalds a throng?
There's never an end to their ballads long.

"True enough, the coursers stamp in their stall,
For prey, for prey, scream the falcons all;
But Frithiof only
Hunts in the clouds, and weeps so lonely."

* * *

Then Frithiof set the dragon free,
And the sails swelled full, and snorted the sea.
Right over the bay
To the sons of the King he steered his way.

He finds them at the grave of their father, King Bele, giving audience to the people, and promulgating laws, and he boldly asks the hand of their sister Ingeborg, this alliance being in accordance with the wishes of King Bele. To this proposition Helge answers, in scorn, that his sister's hand is not for the son of a thane; that he needs not the sword of Frithiof to protect his throne, but if he will be his serf, there is a place vacant among the house-folk which he can fill. Indignant at this reply, Frithiof draws his sword of the flaming runes, and at one blow cleaves in twain the golden shield of Helge as it hangs on a tree, and, turning away in disdain, departs over the blue sea homeward.

V.

In the next canto the scene changes. Old King Ring pushes back his golden chair from the table, and arises to speak to his heroes and Scalds,—old King Ring, a monarch renowned in the North, beloved by all as a father to the land he governs, and whose name each night goes up to Odin with the prayers of his people. He announces to them his intention of taking to himself a new queen as a mother to his infant son, and tells them he has fixed his choice upon Ingeborg, the lily small, with the blush of morn on her cheeks. Messengers are forthwith sent to Helge and Halfdan, bearing golden gifts, and attended by a long train of Scalds, who sing heroic ballads to the sound of their harps. Three days and three nights they revel at the court, and on the fourth morning receive from Helge a solemn refusal and from Halfdan a taunt, that King Graybeard should ride forth in person to seek his bride. Old King Ring is wroth at the reply, and straightway prepares to avenge his wounded pride with his sword. He smites his shield as its hangs on the bough of the high linden-tree, and the dragons swim forth on the waves with blood-red combs, and the helms nod in the wind. The sound of the approaching war reaches the ears of the royal brothers, and they place their sister for protection in the temple of Balder[31].

VI.

In the next canto, which is the sixth, Frithiof and Björn are playing chess together, when old Hilding comes in, bringing the prayer of Helge and Halfdan, that Frithiof would aid them in the war against King Ring. Frithiof, instead of answering the old man, continues his game, making allusions as it goes on to the king's being saved by a peasant or pawn, and the necessity of rescuing the queen at all hazards. Finally, he tells the ancient Hilding to return to Bele's sons and tell them that they have wounded his honor, that no ties unite them together, and that he will never be their bondman. So closes this short and very spirited canto.

VII.

The seventh canto describes the meeting of Frithiof and Ingeborg in Balder's temple, when silently the high stars stole forth, like a lover to his maid, on tiptoe. Here all passionate vows are retold; he swears to protect her with his sword while here on earth, and to sit by her side here after in Valhalla, when the champions ride forth to battle from the silver gates, and maidens bear round the mead-horn mantled with golden foam.

VIII.

The eighth canto commences in this wise. Ingeborg sits in Balder's temple, and waits the coming of Frithiof, till the stars fade away in the morning sky. At

---

[31] Blader, the god of the Summer Sun.

length he arrives, wild and haggard. He comes from the Ting, or council, where he has offered his hand in reconciliation to King Helge, and again asked of him his sister in marriage, before the assembly of the warriors. A thousand swords hammered applause upon a thousand shields, and the ancient Hilding with his silver beard stepped forth and held a talk full of wisdom, in short, pithy language, that sounded like the blows of a sword. But all in vain. King Helge says him nay, and brings against him an accusation of having profaned the temple of Balder by daring to visit Ingeborg there. Death or banishment is the penalty of the law; but instead of being sentenced to the usual punishment, Frithiof is ordered to sail to the Orkney Islands, in order to force from Jarl Angantyr the payment of an annual tribute, which, since Bele's death, he has neglected to pay. All this does Frithiof relate to Ingeborg, and urges her to escape with him to the lands of the South, where the sky is clearer, and the mild stars shall look down with friendly glance upon them through the warm summer nights. By the light of the winter-evening's fire, old Thorsten Vikingsson had told them tales of the Isles of Greece, with their green groves and shining billows;—where, amid the ruins of marble temples, flowers grow from the runes that utter forth the wisdom of the past, and golden apples glow amid the leaves, and red grapes hang from every twig. All is prepared for their flight; already Ellida spreads her shadowy eagle-wings, but Ingeborg refuses to escape. King Bele's daughter will not deign to steal her happiness. In a beautiful and passionate appeal, she soothes her lover's wounded pride, and at length he resolves to undertake the expedition to Jarl Angantyr. He gives her the golden arm-ring of Vaulund, and they part, she with mournful forebodings, and he with ardent hope of ultimate success. This part of the poem is a dramatic sketch in blank verse. It is highly wrought, and full of poetic beauties.

IX.

Ingeborg's Lament is the subject of the ninth canto. She sits by the seaside, and watches the westward-moving sail, and speaks to the billows blue, and the stars, and to Frithiof's falcon, that sits upon her shoulder,—the gallant bird whose image she has worked into her embroidery, with wings of silver and golden claws. She tells him to greet again and again her Frithiof, when he returns and weeps by her grave.

X.

And now follows the ballad of Frithiof at Sea, one of the most spirited and characteristic cantos of the poem. The versification, likewise, is managed with great skill, each strophe consisting of three several parts, each in its respective metre. King Helge stands by the sea-shore and prays to the fiends for a tempest; and soon Frithiof hears the wings of the storm flapping in the distance, and, as wind-cold Ham and snowy Heid beat against the flanks of his ship, he sings:—

Fairer was the journey,
In the moonbeam's shimmer,
O'er the mirrored waters
Unto Balder's grove;
Warmer than it here is,
Close by Ingeborg's bosom;—
Whiter than the sea-foam
Swelled the maiden's breast.

But the tempest waxes sore; it screams in the shrouds, and cracks in the keel, and the dragon ship leaps from wave to wave like a goat from cliff to cliff. Frithiof fears that witchcraft is at work, and calling Björn, he bids him gripe the tiller with his bear-paw while he climbs the mast to look out upon the sea. From aloft he sees the two fiends riding on a whale; Heid with snowy skin, and in shape like a white bear,—Ham, with outspread, sounding wings, like the eagle of the storm. A battle with these sea-monsters ensues. Ellida hears the hero's voice, and with her copper keel smites the whale so that he dies; and the whale-riders learn how bitter it is to bite blue steel, being transfixed with Northern spears hurled from a hero's hand. And thus the storm is stilled, and Frithiof reaches at length the shores of Angantyr.

XI.

In the eleventh canto Jarl Angantyr sits in his ancestral hall carousing with his friends. In merry mood he looks forth upon the sea, where the sun is sinking into the waves like a golden swan. At the window the ancient Halvar stands sentinel, watchful alike of things within doors and without;

for ever and anon he drains the mead horn to the bottom, and, uttering never a word, thrusts the empty horn in at the window to be filled anew. At length he announces the arrival of a tempest-tost ship, and Jarl Angantyr looks forth, and recognizes the dragon-ship Ellida, and Frithiof, the son of his friend. No sooner has he made this known to his followers, than the Viking Atle springs up from his seat and screams aloud: "Now will I test the truth of the tale that Frithiof can blunt the edge of hostile sword, and never begs for quarter." Accordingly he and twelve other champions seize their arms, and rush down to the sea-shore to welcome the stranger with war like sword-play. A single combat ensues between Frithiof and Atle. Both shields are cleft in twain at once; Angurvadel bites full sharp, and Atle's sword is broken. Frithiof, disdaining an unequal contest, throws his own away, and the combatants wrestle together unarmed. Atle falls, and Frithiof, as he plants his knee upon the breast of his foe, says that, if he had his sword, the Viking should feel its sharp edge and die. The haughty Atle bids him go and recover his sword, promising to lie still and await death, which promise he fulfils. Frithiof seizes Angurvadel, and when he re turns to smite the prostrate Viking, he is so moved by his courage and magnanimity that he stays the blow, seizes the hand of the fallen, and they return together as friends to the banquet-hall of Angantyr. This hall is adorned with more than wonted splendor. Its walls are not wainscoted with rough-hewn planks, but covered with gold leather, stamped with flowers and fruits. No hearth glows in the centre of the floor, but a marble fireplace leans against the wall. There is glass in the windows, there are locks on the doors; and instead of torches, silver chandeliers stretch forth their arms with lights over the banquet-table, whereon is a hart roasted whole, with larded haunches, and gilded hoofs lifted as if to leap, and green leaves on its branching antlers. Behind each warrior's seat stands a maiden, like a star behind a stormy cloud. And high on his royal chair of silver, with helmet shining like the sun, and breastplate inwrought with gold, and mantle star-spangled, and trimmed with purple and ermine, sits the Viking Angantyr, Jarl of the Orkneys. With friendly salutations he welcomes the son of Thorsten, and in a goblet of Sicilian wine, foaming like the sea, drinks to the memory of the departed; while Scalds, from the hills of Morven, sing heroic songs. Frithiof relates to him his adventures at sea, and makes known the object of his mission; whereupon

Angantyr declares that he was never tributary to King Bele; that, although he pledged him in the wine-cup, he was not subject to his laws; that his sons he knew not; but that, if they wished to levy tribute, they must do it with the sword, like men. And then he bids his daughter bring from her chamber a richly embroidered purse, which he fills with golden coins of foreign mint, and gives to Frithiof as a pledge of welcome and hospitality. And Frithiof remains his guest till spring.

XII.

In the twelfth canto we have a description of Frithiof's return to his native land. He finds his homestead at Framnäs laid waste by fire; house, fields, and ancestral forests are all burnt over. As he stands amid the ruins, his falcon perches on his shoulder, his dog leaps to welcome him, and his snow-white steed comes with limbs like a hind and neck like a swan. He will have bread from his master's hands. At length old Hilding appears from among the ruins, and tells a mournful tale: how a bloody battle had been fought between King Ring and Helge; how Helge and his host had been routed, and in their flight through Framnäs, from sheer malice, had laid waste the lands of Frithiof; and finally, how, to save their crown and kingdom, the brothers had given Ingeborg to be the bride of King Ring. He describes the bridal, as the train went up to the temple, with virgins in white, and men with swords, and Scalds, and the pale bride seated on a black steed like a spirit on a cloud. At the altar the fierce Helge had torn the bracelet, the gift of Frithiof, from Ingeborg's arm, and adorned with it the image of Balder. And Frithiof remembers that it is now mid-sum mer, and festival time in Balder's temple. Thither he directs his steps.

XIII.

The sun stands, at midnight, blood-red on the mountains of the North. It is not day, it is not night, but something between the two. The fire blazes on the altar in the temple of Balder. Priests with silver beards and knives of flint in their hands stand there, and King Helge with his crown. A sound of arms is heard in the sacred grove without, and a voice commanding Björn to guard the door. Then Frithiof rushes in like a storm in autumn. "Here is your tribute from the Western seas," he cries; "take it, and then be there a battle for life and death between us twain, here by the light of Balder's altar;—shields behind us, and bosoms bare;—and the first blow be thine, as king; but forget not that mine is the second. Look not thus toward the door; I have caught the fox in his den. Think of Framnäs, think of thy sister with golden locks!" With these words he draws from his girdle the purse of Angantyr, and throws it into the face of the king with such force that the blood gushes from his mouth, and he falls senseless at the foot of the altar. Frithiof then seizes the bracelet on Balder's arm, and in trying to draw it off he pulls the wooden statue from its base, and it falls into the flames of the altar. In a moment the whole temple is in a blaze. All attempts to extinguish the conflagration are vain. The fire is victorious. Like a red bird the flame sits upon the roof, and flaps its loosened wings. Mighty was the funeral pyre of Balder!

XIV.

The fourteenth canto is entitled Frithiof in Exile. Frithiof sits at night on the deck of his ship, and chants a song of welcome to the sea, which, as a Viking, he vows to make his home in life and his grave in death. "Thou knowest naugh" he sings, "thou Ocean free, of a king who oppresses thee at his own will."

Thy king is he
Among the free,
Who trembles never,
How high soever
Heaves in unrest
Thy foam-white breast.
Blue fields like these
The hero please.
His keels go thorough
Like plough in the furrough,
But steel-bright are
The seeds sown there.

He turns his prow from shore, and is putting to sea, when King Helge, with ten ships, comes sailing out to attack him. But anon the ships sink down into the sea, as if drawn downward by invisible hands, and Helge saves himself by swimming ashore. Then Björn laughed aloud, and told how the night before he had bored holes in the bottom of each of Helge's ships. But the king now stood on a cliff, and bent his mighty how of steel against the rock with such force that it snapped in twain. And Frithiof jeering cried that it was rust that had broken the bow, not Helge's strength; and to show what nerve there was in a hero's arm, he seized two pines, large enough for the masts of ships, but shaped into oars, and rowed with such marvellous strength that the two pines snapped in his hands like reeds. And now uprose the sun, and the land-breeze blew off shore; and bidding his native land farewell, Frithiof the Viking sailed forth to scour the seas.

XV.

The fifteenth canto contains the Viking's Code, the laws of the pirate-ship. No tent upon deck, no slumber in house, but the shield must be the Viking's couch, and his tent the blue sky overhead. The hammer of victorious Thor is short, and the sword of Frey but an ell in length; and the warrior's steel is never too short if he goes near enough to the foe. Hoist high the sail when the wild storm blows; 't is merry in stormy seas; onward and ever onward; he is a coward who strikes; rather sink than strike. There shall be neither maiden nor drunken revelry on board. The freighted merchantman shall be protected, but must not refuse his tribute to the Viking; for the Viking is king of the waves, and the merchant a slave to gain, and the steel of the brave is as good as the gold of the rich. The plunder shall be divided on deck, by lot and the throwing of dice; but in this the sea-king takes no share; glory is his prize; he wants none other. They shall be valiant in fight, and merciful to the conquered, for he who begs for quarter has no longer a sword, is no man's foe, and Prayer is a child of Valhalla,—they must listen to the voice of the pale one. With such laws sailed the Viking over the foaming sea for three weary years, and came at length to the Isles of Greece, which in days of yore his father had so oft described to him, and whither he had wished to flee with Ingeborg. And thus the forms of the absent and the dead rose up before him, and seemed to beckon him to his home in the North. He is weary of sea-fights, and of hewing men in twain, and the glory of battle. The flag at the masthead pointed northward; there lay the beloved land; be resolved to follow the course of the winds of heaven, and steer back again to the North.

XVI.

Canto sixteenth is a dialogue between Frithiof and his friend Björn, in which the latter gentleman exhibits some of the rude and uncivilized tastes of his namesake, Bruin the Bear. They have again reached the shores of their fatherland. Winter is approaching. The sea begins to freeze around their keel. Frithiof is weary of a Viking's life. He wishes to pass the Yule-tide on land, and to visit King Ring and his bride of the golden locks, his beloved Ingeborg. Björn, dreaming all the while of bloody exploits, offers himself as a companion, and talks of firing the king's palace at night, and bearing off the queen by force. Or if his friend deems the old king worthy of a holmång,[32] or of a battle on the ice, he is ready for either. But Frithiof tells him that only gentle thoughts now fill his bosom. He wishes only to take a last farewell of Ingeborg. These delicate feelings cannot penetrate the hirsute breast of Bruin. He knows not what this love may be—this sighing and sorrow for a maiden's sake. The world, he says, is full of maidens, and he offers to bring Frithiof a whole ship-load from the glowing South, all red as roses and gentle as lambs. But Frithiof will not stay. He resolves to go to King Ring, but not alone, for his sword goes with him.

XVII.

The seventeenth canto relates how King Ring sat in his banquet-hall at Yule-tide and drank mead. At his side sat Ingeborg his queen, like Spring by the side of Autumn. And an old man, and unknown, all wrapped in skins, entered the hall, and humbly took his seat near the door. And the courtiers looked at each other with scornful smiles, and pointed with the finger at the hoary bear-skin man. At this the stranger waxed angry, and seizing with one hand a young

---

[32] A duel between the Vikings of the North was called a *holmgång*, because the two combatants met on an island to decide their quarrel. Fierce battles were likewise fought by armies on the ice: the frozen bays and lakes of a mountainous country being oftentimes the only plains large enough for battle-fields.

coxcomb, he "twirled him up and down." The rest grew silent; he would have done the same with them. "Who breaks the peace?" quoth the king. "Tell us who thou art, and whence, old man." And the old man answered,

> In Anguish was I nurtured, Want is my homestead hight,
> Now come I from the Wolf's den, I slept with him lastnight.

But King Ring is not so easily duped, and bids the stranger lay aside his disguise. And straight the shaggy bear-skin fell from the head of the unknown guest, and down from his lofty forehead, over his shoulders broad and full, floated his shining ringlets like a wave of gold. Frithiof stood before them in a rich mantle of blue velvet, with a hand-broad silver belt around his waist; and the color came and went in the cheek of the queen like the Northern light on fields of snow,

> And as two water-lilies, beneath the tempest's might,
> Lie heaving on the billow, so heaved her bosom white.

And now a horn blew in the hall, and kneeling on a silver dish, with haunch and shoulder hung "with garlands gay and rosemary," and holding an apple in his mouth, the wild-boar was brought in.[33]

And King Ring rose up in his hoary locks, and, laying his hand upon the boar's head, swore an oath that he would conquer Frithiof, the great champion, so help him Frey and Odin, and the mighty Thor. With a disdainful smile Frithiof threw his sword upon the table so that the hall echoed to the clang, and every warrior sprang up from his seat, and turning to the king he said: "Young Frithiof is my friend; I know him well, and I swear to protect him, were it against the world; so help me Destiny and my good sword." The king was pleased at this great freedom of speech, and invited the stranger to remain their guest till spring, bidding Ingeborg fill a

---

[33] "The old English custom of the boar's head at Christmas dates from a far antiquity. It was in use at the festivals of Yule-tide among the pagan Northmen. The words of Chaucer in the Franklein's Tale will apply to the old hero of the North:—

> "And he drinketh of his bugle-horn the wine,
> Before him standeth the brawne of the tusked swine."

goblet with the choicest wine for the stranger. With downcast eyes and trembling hand she presented Frithiof a goblet, which two men, as men are now, could not have drained, but he, in honor of his lady-love, quaffed it at a single draught. And then the Scald took his harp and sang the song of Hagbart and Fair Signe, the Romeo and Juliet of the North. And thus the Yule-carouse was prolonged far into the night, and the old fellows drank deep, till at length

> They all to sleep departed, withouten pain or care,
> But old King Ring, the graybeard, slept with Ingeborg the fair.

XVIII.

The next canto describes a sledge-ride on the ice. It has a cold breath about it. The short, sharp stanzas are like the angry gusts of a northwester.

> King Ring with his queen to the banquet did fare,
> On the lake stood the ice so mirror-clear.
>
> "Fare not o'er the ice," the stranger cries;
> "It will burst, and full deep the cold bath lies."
>
> "The king drowns not easily," Ring outspake;
> "He who's afraid may go round the lake."
>
> Threatening and dark looked the stranger round,
> His steel shoes with haste on his feet he bound.
>
> The sledge-horse starts forth strong and free;
> He snorteth flames, so glad is he.
>
> "Strike out," screamed the king, "my trotter good,
> Let us see if thou art of Sleipner's[34] blood."
>
> They go as a storm goes over the lake,
> No heed to his queen doth the old man take.

[34] The steed of Odin.

But the steel-shod champion standeth not still,
He passeth them by as swift as he will.
He carves many runes in the frozen tide,
Fair Ingeborg o'er her own name doth glide.

Thus they speed away over the ice, but beneath them the treacherous Ran[35] lies in ambush. She breaks a hole in her silver roof, the sledge is sinking, and fair Ingeborg is pale with fear, when the stranger on his skates comes sweeping by like a whirlwind. He seizes the steed by his mane, and at a single pull places the sledge upon firm ice again. They return together to the king's palace, where the stranger, who is none else than Frithiof, remains a guest till spring.

XIX.

The nineteenth canto is entitled Frithiof's Temptation. It is as follows:—

Spring is coming, birds are twittering, forests leaf, and smiles the sun,
And the loosened torrents downward, singing, to the ocean run;
Glowing like the cheek of Freya, peeping rosebuds 'gin to ope,
And in human hearts awaken love of life, and joy, and hope.

Now will hunt the ancient monarch, and the queen shall join the sport:
Swarming in its gorgeous splendor, is assembled all the court;

Bows ring loud, and quivers rattle, stallions paw the ground alway,
And, with hoods upon their eyelids, scream the falcons for their prey.

See, the Queen of the chase advances! Frithiof, gaze not at the sight!
Like a star upon a spring-cloud sits she on her palfrey white.
Half of Freya[36], half of Rota [37]yet more beauteous than these two,
And from her light hat of purple wave aloft the feathers blue.

Gaze not at her eye's blue heaven, gaze not at her golden hair!
Oh beware! her waist is slender, full her bosom is, beware!

---

[35] A giantess holding dominion over the waters.
[36] The goddess of Love and Beauty; the Venus of the North.
[37] One of the Valkyrs, or celestial virgins, who bear off the souls of the slain in battle.

Look not at the rose and lily on her check that shifting play,
List not to the voice beloved, whispering like the wind of May.

Now the huntsman's band is ready. Hurrah! over hill and dale!
Horns ring, and the hawks right upward to the hall of Odin sail.
All the dwellers in the forest seek in fear their cavern homes,
But, with spear outstretched before her, after them the Valkyr comes.

The old king cannot keep pace with the chase. Frithiof rides beside him, silent and sad. Gloomy musings rise within him, and he hears continually the mournful voices of his own dark thoughts. Why had he left the ocean, where all care is blown away by the winds of heaven? Here he wanders amid dreams and secret longings. He cannot forget Balder's grove. But the grim gods are no longer friendly. They have taken his rosebud and placed it on the breast of Winter, whose chill breath covers bud and leaf and stalk with ice. And thus they come to a lonely valley shut in by mountains, and overshadowed by beeches and alders. Here the king alights; the quiet of the place invites to slumber.

Then threw Frithiof down his mantle, and upon the greensward spread,
And the ancient king so trustful laid on Frithiof's knee his head,
Slept as calmly as the hero sleepeth, after war's alarm,
On his shield, or as an infant sleeps upon its mother's arm.

As he slumbers, hark! there sings a coal-black bird upon the bough:
"Hasten, Frithiof, slay the old man, end your quarrel at a blow;
Take his queen, for she is thine, and once the bridal kiss she gave,
Now no human eye beholds thee, deep and silent is the grave."

Frithiof listens; hark! there sings a snow-white bird upon the bough:
"Though no human eye beholds thee, Odin's eye beholds thee now.
Coward! wilt thou murder sleep, and a defenceless old man slay!
Whatsoe'er thou winn'st, thou canst not win a hero's fame this way."

Thus the two wood-birds did warble: Frithiof took his war-sword good,
With a shudder hurled it from him, far into the gloomy wood.
Coal-black bird flies down to Nastrand[38] but on light, unfolded wings,
Like the tone of harps, the other, sounding towards the sun, upsprings.

---

[38] The Strand of Corpses; a region in the Niffelhem, or Scandinavian hell.

Straight the ancient king awakens. "Sweet has been my sleep," he said;
"Pleasantly sleeps one in the shadow, guarded by a brave man's blade.
But where is thy sword, O stranger? Lightning's brother, where is he?
Who thus parts you, who should never from each other parted be!"

"It avails not," Frithiof answered; "in the North are other swords:
Sharp, O monarch! is the sword's tongue, and it speaks not peaceful words;
Murky spirits dwell in steel blades, spirits from the Niffelhem;
Slumber is not safe before them, silver locks but anger them."

To this the old king replies, that he has not been asleep, but has feigned sleep, merely to put Frithiof—for he has long recognized the hero in his guest—to the trial. He then upbraids him for having come to his palace in disguise, to steal his queen away; he had expected the coming of a warrior with an army; he beheld only a beggar in tatters. But now he has proved him, and forgiven; has pitied, and forgotten. He is soon to be gathered to his fathers. Frithiof shall take his queen and kingdom after him. Till then he shall remain his guest, and thus their feud shall have an end. But Frithiof answers, that he came not as a thief to steal away the queen, but only to gaze upon her face once more. He will remain no longer. The vengeance of the offended gods hangs over him. He is an outlaw. On the green earth he seeks no more for peace, for the earth burns beneath his feet, and the trees lend him no shadow. "Therefore," he cries, "away to sea again! Away, my dragon brave, to bathe again thy pitch-black breast in the briny wave! Flap thy white wings in the clouds, and cut the billow with a whistling sound; fly, fly, as far as the bright stars guide thee, and the subject billows bear. Let me hear the lightning's voice again, and on the open sea, in battle, amid clang of shields and arrowy rain, let me die, and go up to the dwelling of the gods!"

XX.

In the twentieth canto the death of King Ring is described. The sunshine of a pleasant spring morning plays into the palace-hall, when Frithiof enters to bid his royal friends a last farewell. With them he bids his native land good-night.

No more shall I see
In its upward motion

The smoke of the Northland. Man is a slave:
The fates decree.
On the waste of the ocean
There is my fatherland, there is my grave.

Go not to the strand,
Ring, with thy bride,
After the stars spread their light through the sky.
Perhaps in the sand,
Washed up by the tide,
The bones of the outlawed Viking may lie.

Then, quoth the king,
"'T is mournful to hear
A man like a whimpering maiden cry.
The death-song they sing
Even now in urine ear.
What avails it? He who is born must die."

He then says that he himself is about to depart for Valhalla; that a death on the straw becomes not a King of the Northmen. He would fain die the death of a hero, and he cuts on his arms and breasts the runes of death,—runes to Odin. And while the blood drops from among the silvery hairs of his naked bosom, he calls for a flowing goblet, and drinks a health to the glorious North; and in spirit hears the Gjallar Horn,[39] and goes to Valhalla, where glory, like a golden helmet, crowns the coming guest.

XXI.

The next canto is the Drapa, or Dirge of King Ring, in the unrhymed alliterative stanzas of the old Icelandic poetry. The Scald sings how the high-descended monarch sits in his tomb, with his shield on his arm and his battle-

---

[39] The Gjallar Horn was blown by Heimdal, the watchman of the gods. He was the son of nine virgins, and was called "the God with the Golden Teeth." His watch-tower was upon the rainbow, and he blew his horn whenever a fallen hero rode over the Bridge of Heaven to Valhalla.

sword by his side. His gallant steed, too, neighs in the tomb, and paws the ground with his golden hoofs.[40] But the spirit of the departed rides over the rainbow, which bends beneath its burden, up to the open gates of Valhalla. Here the gods receive him, and garlands are woven for him of golden grain with blue flowers intermingled, and Brage sings a song of praise and welcome to the wise old Ring.

Now rideth royal
Ring over Bifrost[41],
Sways with the burden
The bending bridge.
Open spring Valhall's
Vaulted doors widely;
Asanar's[42] hands are
Hanging in hrs.

* * *

Brage, the graybeard,
Gripeth the gold string,
Stiller now soundeth
Song than before.
Listening leaneth
Vanadi's[43] lovely
Breast at the banquet,
Burning to hear.

* * *

"High sings the sword-blade
Steady on helmet;
Boisterous the billows, and
Bloody alway.
Strength, of the gracious

[40] It was a Scandinavian, as well as a Seythian custom, to bury the favorite steed of a warrior in the same tomb with him.

[41] The rainbow.

[42] The great gods.

[43] Freya.

Gods is the gift, and
Bitter as Berserk
Biteth in shield.

* * *

"Welcome, thou wise one,
Heir of Valhalla!
Long learn the Northland
Land to thy name.
Brage doth hail thee,
Honored with horn-drink,
Nornoma's herald
Now from the North."

XXII.

The twenty-second canto describes, in a very spirited and beautiful style, the election of a new king. The yeoman takes his sword from the wall, and, with clang of shields and sound of arms, the people gather together in a public assembly, or Ting, whose roof is the sky of heaven. Here Frithiof harangues them, bearing aloft on his shield the little son of Ring, who sits there like a king on his throne, or a young eagle on the cliff, gazing upward at the sun. Frithiof hails him as King of the Northmen, and swears to protect his kingdom; and when the little boy, tired of sitting on the shield, leaps fearlessly to the ground, the people raise a shout, and acknowledge him for their monarch, and Jarl Frithiof as regent, till the boy grows older. But Frithiof has other thoughts than these. He must away to meet the Fates at Balder's ruined temple, and make atonement to the offended god. And thus he departs.

XXIII.

Canto twenty-third is entitled Frithiof at his Father's Grave. The sun is sinking like a golden shield in the ocean, and the hills and vales around him, and the fragrant flowers, and song of birds, and sound of the sea, and shadow of trees, awaken in his softened heart the memory of other days. And he calls aloud to the gods for pardon of his crime, and to the spirit of his father that he should come from his grave and bring him peace and for giveness from the city of the gods. And lo! amid the evening shadows, from the western wave up rising, landward floats the Fata Morgana, and, sinking down upon the spot where Balder's temple once stood, assumes itself the form of a temple, with columns of dark blue steel, and an altar of precious stone. At the door, leaning upon their shields, stand the Destinies. And the Destiny of the Past points to the solitude around, and the Destiny of the Future to a beautiful temple newly risen from the sea. While Frithiof gazes in wonder at the sight, all vanishes away, like a vision of the night. But the vision is interpreted by the hero without the aid of prophet or of soothsayer.

XXIV.

Canto twenty-fourth is the Atonement. The temple of Balder has been rebuilt, and with such magnificence that the North beholds in it the image of Valhalla. And two by two, in solemn procession, walk therein the twelve virgins, clad in garments of silver tissue, with roses upon their cheeks, and roses in their innocent hearts. They sing a solemn song of Balder, how much beloved he was by all that lived, and how he fell, by Höder's arrow slain, and earth and sea and heaven wept. And the sound of the song is not like the sound of a human voice, but like the tones which come from the halls of the gods; like the thoughts of a maiden dreaming of her lover, when the nightingale is singing in the midnight stillness, and the moon shines over the beech-trees of the North. Frithiof listens to the song, and as he listens, all thoughts of vengeance and of human hate melt within him, as the icy breastplate melts from the bosom of the fields when the sun shines in spring. At this moment the high-priest of Balder enters, venerable with his long, silver beard; and, welcoming the Viking to the temple he has built, he delivers for his special edification a long homily on things human and divine, with a short catechism of Northern mythology. He tells him, likewise, very truly, that more acceptable to the gods than the smoke of burnt-offerings is the sacrifice of one's own vindictive spirit, the hate of a human soul; and then speaks of the Virgin's Son,—

> Sent by All-father to declare aright the runes
> On Destiny's black shield-rim, unexplained till now.

Peace was his battle-cry, and his white sword was love,
And innocence sat dove-like on his silver helm.
Holy he lived and taught, he died and he forgave,
And under distant palm-trees stands his grave in light.
His doctrine, it is said, wanders from dale to dale,
Melting the hard of heart, and laying hand in hand,
And builds the realm of Peace on the atonèd earth.
I do not know his lore aright, but darkly still
In better hours I have presentiment thereof,
And every human heart feeleth alike with mine.
One day, that know I, shall it come, and lightly wave
Its white and dove-like wings over the Northern hills.
But there shall be no more a North for us that day,
And oaks shall whisper soft o'er the graves of the forgotten.

He then speaks of Frithiof's hatred to Bele's sons; and tells him that Helge is dead, and that Halfdan sits alone on Bele's throne, urging him at the same time to sacrifice to the gods his desire of vengeance, and proffer the hand of friendship to the young king. This is done straightway, Halfdan opportunely coming in at that moment, and the priest removes forthwith the ban from the Varg-i-Veum, the sacrilegious and outlawed man. And then Ingeborg enters the vaulted temple, followed by maidens, as the moon is followed by stars in the vaulted sky, and from the hand of her brother Frithiof receives the bride of his youth, and they are married in Balder's temple.

And here endeth the Legend of Frithiof the Valiant, the noblest poetic contribution which Sweden has yet made to the literary history of the world.

TWICE-TOLD TALES.

The same number of the *North American Review*, July, 1837, which contained the article on *Frithiof's Saga* contained also a review of Hawthorne's *Twice-Told Tales*. The reprint here is of the general part of the review revised and slightly pruned; it was followed by several pages of extracts with a few running comments. Hawthorne, as is well known, was a classmate of Mr. Longfellow, but the intimate acquaintance of the two men seems to have begun at the time, and with the occasion, of the review. In sending the book to Mr. Longfellow, Hawthorne wrote: "We were not, it is true, so well acquainted at college that I can plead an absolute right to inflict my twice-told tediousness upon you but I have often regretted that we were not better known to each other, and have been glad of your success in literature and in more important matters. ... The present volumes contain such articles as seemed best worth offering to the public a second time; and I should like to flatter myself that they would repay you some part of the pleasure which I have derived from your own *Outre-Mer*." After the review appeared Hawthorne wrote to the author: "I have to-day received and read with huge delight your review of *Twice-Told Tales*. I frankly aver that I was not without hopes that you would do this kind office for the book, though I could not have anticipated how very kindly it would be done. Whether or not the public will agree to the praise which you bestow on me, there are at least five per sons who think you the most sagacious critic on earth; viz., my mother and two sisters, my old maiden aunt, and finally, the sturdiest believer of the whole five,—my own self. If I doubt the sincerity and correctness of any of my critics, it shall be of those who censure me. Hard would be the lot of the poor scribbler if he may not have this privilege."

WHEN a new star rises in the heavens, people gaze after it for a season with the naked eye, and with such telescopes as they can find. In the stream of thought which flows so peacefully deep and clear through the pages of this book, we see the bright reflection of a spiritual star, after which men will be fain to gaze "with the naked eye, and with the spy-glasses of criticism." This star is but newly risen, and erelong the observations of numerous star-gazers, perched upon arm chairs and editors' tables, will inform the world of its magnitude and its place in the heaven of poetry, whether it be in the paw of the Great Bear, or on the forehead of Pegasus, or on the strings of the Lyre, or in the wing of the Eagle. My own observations are as follows.

To this little work let us say, as was said to Sidney's "Arcadia:" "Live ever, sweet, sweet book! the simple image of his gentle wit, and the golden pillar of his noble courage; and ever notify unto the world that thy writer was the secretary of eloquence, the breath of the Muses, the honeybee of the daintiest flowers of wit and art." It comes from the hand of a man of genius. Everything about it has the freshness of morning and of May. These flowers and green leaves of poetry have not the dust of the highway upon them. They have been gathered fresh from the secret places of a peaceful and gentle heart. There flow deep waters, silent, calm, and cool; and the green trees look into them and "God's blue heaven."

This book, though in prose, is written nevertheless by a poet. He looks upon all things in the spirit of love, and with lively sympathies; for to him external form is but the representation of internal being, all things having a life, an end and aim. The true poet is a friendly man. He takes to his arms even cold and inanimate things, and rejoices in his heart, as did St. Francis of old, when he kissed his bride of snow. To his eye all things are beautiful and holy; all are objects of feeling and of song, from the great hierarchy of the silent, saint-like stars, that rule the night, down to the little flowers which are "stars in the firmament of the earth."

It is one of the attributes of the poetic mind to feel a universal sympathy with Nature, both in the material world and in the soul of man. It identifies itself likewise with every object of its sympathy, giving it new sensation and poetic life, whatever that object may be, whether man, bird, beast, flower, or star. As to the pure mind all things are pure, so to the poetic mind all things are poetical. To such souls no age and no country can be utterly dull and prosaic. They make unto themselves their age and country, dwelling in the universal mind of man, and in the universal forms of things. Of such is the author of this book.

There are many who think that the ages of poetry and romance are gone by. They look upon the Present as a dull, unrhymed, and prosaic translation of a brilliant and poetic Past. Their dreams are of the days of eld; of the Dark Ages, the ages of Chivalry, and Bards, and Troubadours, and Minnesingers; and the times of which Milton says: "The villages also must have their visitors to inquire what lectures the bagpipe, and the rebbec reads even to the ballatry, and the gammuth of every municipal fiddler, for these are the countryman's Arcadia and his Monte Mayors."

We all love ancient ballads. Pleasantly to all ears sounds the voice of the people in song, swelling fitfully through the desolate chambers of the Past like the wind of evening among ruins. And yet this voice does not persuade us that the days of balladry were more poetic than our own. The spirit of the Past pleads for itself, and the spirit of the Present likewise. If poetry be an element of the human mind, and consequently in accordance with nature and truth, it would be strange indeed if, as the human mind advances, poetry should recede. The truth is, that, when we look back upon the Past, we see only its bright and poetic features. All that is dull, prosaic, and commonplace is lost in the shadowy distance. We see the moated castle on the hill, and,

Golden and red, above it
The clouds float gorgeously;

but we see not the valley below, where the patient bondman toils like a beast of burden. We see the tree-tops waving in the wind, and hear the merry birds singing under their green roofs; but we forget that at their roots there are swine feeding upon acorns. With the Present it is not so. We stand too near to see objects in a picturesque light. What to others, at a distance, is a bright and folded summer cloud, is to us, who are in it, a dismal, drizzling rain. Thus has it been since the world began. Ours is not the only Present which has seemed dull, commonplace, and prosaic.

The truth is, the heaven of poetry and romance still lies around us and within us. So long as truth is stranger than fiction, the elements of poetry and romance will not be wanting in common life. If, invisible ourselves, we could follow a single human being through a single day of his life, and know all his secret thoughts and hopes and anxieties, his prayers and tears and good resolves, his passionate delights and struggles against temptation,—all that excites, and all that soothes the heart of man,—we should have poetry enough to fill a volume. Nay, set the imagination free, like another bottle-imp, and bid it lift for you the roofs of the city, street by street, and after a single night's observation you may sit down and write poetry and romance for the rest of your life.

The Twice-Told Tales are so called from having been first published in various annuals and magazines, and now collected together and told a second time in a volume. And a very delightful volume they make;—one of those which excite in you a feeling of personal interest for the author. A calm, thoughtful face seems to be looking at you from every page, with now a pleasant smile, and now a shade of sadness stealing over its features. Sometimes, though not often, it glares wildly at you, with a strange and painful expression, as, in the German romance, the bronze knocker of the Archivarius Lindhorst makes up faces at the Student Anselmus.

One of the prominent characteristics of these tales is, that they are national in their character. The author has chosen his themes among the traditions of New England, the dusty legends of "the good old Colony times, when we lived under a king." This is the right material for story. It seems as natural to make tales out of old, tumble-down traditions, as canes and snuff-boxes out of old steeples, or trees planted by great men. The dreary old Puritanical times begin to look romantic in the distance. Who would not like to have strolled through the city of Agamenticus, where a market was held every week, on Wednesday, and there were two annual fairs at St. James's and St. Paul's? Who would not like to have been present at the court of the worshipful Thomas Gorges, in those palmy days of the law when Tom Heard was fined five shillings for being drunk, and John Payne the same, "for swearing one oath"? Who would not like to have seen Thomas Taylor presented to the grand jury "for abusing Captain Raynes, being in authority, by thee-ing and thou-ing him;" and John Wardell likewise, for denying Cambridge College to be an ordinance of God; and people fined for winking at comely damsels in church; and others for being common sleepers there on the Lord's day? Truly, many quaint and quiet customs, many comic scenes and strange adventures, many wild and wondrous things, fit for humorous tale and soft, pathetic story, lie all about us here in New England. There is no tradition of the Rhine nor of the Black Forest which surpasses in beauty that of the Phantom Ship of New Haven. The Flying Dutchman of the Cape, and the Klabotermann of the Baltic, are nowise superior. The story of Peter Rugg, the man who could not find

Boston, is as good as that told by Gervase of Tilbury, of a man who gave himself to the devils by an unfortunate imprecation, and was used by them as a wheelbarrow; and the Great Carbuncle of the White Mountains shines with no less splendor than that which illuminated the subterranean palace in Rome, as related by William of Malmesbury.

Another characteristic of this writer is the exceeding beauty of his style. It is as clear as running waters. Indeed, he uses words as mere stepping-stones, upon which, with a free and youthful bound, his spirit crosses and recrosses the bright and rushing stream of thought. Some writers of the present day have introduced a kind of Gothic architecture into their style. All is fantastic, vast, and wondrous in the outward form, and within is mysterious twilight, and the swelling sound of an organ, and a voice chanting hymns in Latin, which need a translation for many of the crowd. To this I do not object. Let the priest chant in what language he will, so long as he understands his own Mass-book. But if he wishes the world to listen and be edified, he will do well to choose a language that is generally understood.

THE GREAT METROPOLIS.

The Great Metropolis is the title of a book by James Grant, editor of the *London Morning Advertiser*, which was reviewed by Mr. Longfellow in the *North American Review* for April, 1837. Mr. Longfellow characterized the book as vulgar and having bad manners, with no strength, no dignity, no grace, and no refinement. "To us, however," he adds, "the title of the book is attractive," and then proceeds with the passages which here follow. After this half-personal sketch of London, he returns, in his article, to the book in question, and gives long extracts with brief comments.

I HAVE an affection for a great city. I feel safe in the neighborhood of man, and enjoy "the sweet security of streets." The excitement of the crowd is pleasant to me. I find sermons in the stones of the pavement, and in the continuous sound of voices and wheels and footsteps hear the "sad music of humanity." I feel that life is not a dream, but a reality; that the beings around me are not the insects of an hour, but the pilgrims of an eternity; each with its history of thousand-fold occurrences, insignificant it may be to others, but all-important to himself; each with a human heart, whose fibres are woven into the great web of human sympathies and none so small that, when he dies, some of the mysterious meshes are not broken. The green earth, and the air, and the sea, all living and all lifeless things, preach the gospel of a good providence; but most of all does man, in his crowded cities, and in his manifold powers and wants and passions and deeds, preach this same gospel. The greatest works of his handicraft delight me hardly less than the greatest works of Nature. They are "the masterpieces of her own masterpiece." Architecture, and painting, and sculpture, and music, and epic poems, and all the forms of art, wherein the hand of genius is visible, please me evermore, for they conduct me into the fellowship of great minds. And thus my sympathies are with men, and streets, and city gates, and towers from which the great bells sound solemnly and slow, and cathedral doors, where venerable statues, holding books in their hands, look down like sentinels upon the church-going multitude, and the birds of the air come and build their nests in the arms of saints and apostles.

And more than all this, in great cities we learn to look the world in the face. We shake hands with stern realities. We see ourselves in others. We become acquainted with the motley, many sided life of man, and finally learn, like Jean Paul, to "look upon a metropolis as a collection of villages; a village as some blind alley in a metropolis; fame as the talk of neighbors at the street door; a library as a learned conversation; joy as a second sorrow as a minute; life as a day; and three things as all in all, God, Creation, Virtue."

Forty-five miles westward from the North Sea, the lap of a broad and pleasant valley watered by the Thames, stands the Great Metropolis. It comprises the City of London and its Liberties, with the City and Liberties of Westminster, the Borough of Southwark, and upwards of thirty of the contiguous villages of Middlesex and Surrey. East and west, its greatest length is about eight miles; north and south, its greatest breadth about five its circumference, from twenty to thirty. Its population is estimated at two millions. The vast living tide goes thundering through its ten thousand streets in one unbroken roar. The noise of the great thoroughfares is deafening. But you step aside into a by-lane, and anon you emerge into little green squares half filled with sunshine, half with shade, where no sound of living thing is heard, save the voice of a bird or a child, and amid solitude and silence you gaze in wonder at the great trees "growing in the heart of a brick and-mortar wilderness." Then there are the three parks, Hyde, Regent's, and St. James's, where you may lose yourself in green alleys, and dream you are in the country; Westminster Abbey, with its tombs and solemn cloisters, where, with George Herbert, you may think that, "when the bells do chime, 't is angels' music;" and high above all, half hidden in smoke and vapor, rises the dome of St. Paul's.

These are a few of the more striking features of London. More striking still is the Thames. Above the town, by Kingston and Twickenham, it winds through groves and meadows green, a rural, silver stream. The traveller who sees it here for the first time can hardly believe that this is the mighty river which bathes the feet of London. He asks, perhaps, the coachman what stream it is; and the coachman answers, with a stare of wonder and pity, "The Thames, sir." Pleasure-boats are gliding back and forth, and stately swans float, like water-lilies, on its bosom. On its banks are villages and church towers, beneath which, among the patriarchs of the hamlet, lie many gifted sons of song, "in sepulchres unhearsed and green."

In and below London the whole scene is changed. Let us view it by night. Lamps are gleaming along shore and on the bridges, and a full moon rising over the Borough of Southwark. The moonbeams silver the rippling, yellow tide, wherein also flare the shore lamps with a lambent, flickering gleam. Barges and wherries move to and fro; and heavy-laden luggers are sweeping up stream with the rising tide, swinging sideways, with loose, flapping sails. Both sides of the river are crowded with sea and river craft, whose black hulks lie in shadow, and whose tapering masts rise up into the moonlight. A distant sound of music floats on the air; a harp, and a flute, and a horn. It has an unearthly sound, and lo! like a shooting star, a light comes gliding on. It is a signal-lamp at the mast-head of a steam vessel, that flits by, cloud-like and indistinct. And from all this scene goes up a sound of human voices,—curses, laughter, and singing,—mingled with the monotonous roar of the city, the clashing and careering streams of life, hurrying to lose themselves in the impervious gloom of eternity."

And now the midnight is past, and amid the general silence the clock strikes,—one, two. Far distant, from some belfry in the suburbs, comes the first sound, so indistinct as hardly to be distinguished from the crowing of a cock. Then, close at hand, the great bell of St. Paul's, with a heavy, solemn sound,—one, two. It is answered from Southwark; then at a distance like an echo; and then all around you, with various and intermingling clang, like a chime of bells, the clocks from a hundred belfries strike the hour. But the moon is already sinking, large and fiery, through the vapors of morning. It is just in the range of the chimneys and house-tops, and seems to follow you with speed as you float down the river between unbroken ranks of ships. Day is dawning in the east, not with a pale streak in the horizon, but with a silver light spread through the sky almost to the zenith. It is the mingling of moonlight and day light. The water is tinged with a green hue, melting into purple and gold, like the brilliant scales of a fish. The air grows cool. It comes fresh from the eastern sea, toward which we are swiftly gliding; and, dimly seen in the uncertain twilight, behind us rises

A mighty mass of brick, and smoke, and shipping,
   Dirty and dusky, but as wide as eye
Could reach, with here and there a sail just skipping

In sight, then lost amidst the forestry
Of masts; a wilderness of steeples peeping
On tiptoe through their sea-coal canopy;
A huge, dun cupola, like a fool's-cap crown
On a fool's head and there is London town![44]

[44] *Don Juan*, Canto X. lxxxii.

ANGLO-SAXON LITERATURE.

Published in the *North American Review*, July, 1838. In the reprint, Mr. Longfellow omitted the special reference made to the several books which formed a text for the review. He also added to the translations.

WE read in history that the beauty of an ancient manuscript tempted King Alfred, when a boy at his mother's knee, to learn the letters of the Saxon tongue. A volume which that monarch minstrel wrote in after years now lies before me, so beautifully printed that it might tempt any one to learn not only the letters of the Saxon language, but the language also. The monarch himself is looking from the ornamented initial letter of the first chapter. He is crowned and careworn; having a beard, and long, flowing locks, and a face of majesty. He seems to have just uttered those remarkable words, with which his Preface closes: "And now he prays, and for God's name implores, every one of those whom it lists to read this book, that he would pray for him, and not blame him, if he more rightly understand it than he could; for every man must, according to the measure of his understanding, and according to his leisure, speak that which he speaketh, and do that which he doeth."

I would fain hope that the beauty of this and other Anglo-Saxon books may lead many to the study of that venerable language. Through such gateways will they pass, it is true, into no gay palace of song, but among the dark chambers and mouldering walls of an old national literature, weather-stained and in ruins. They will find, however, venerable names recorded on those walls; and inscriptions, worth the trouble of deciphering. To point out the most curious and important of these is my present purpose, and according to the measure of my understanding, and according to my leisure, I speak that which I speak.

The Anglo-Saxon language was the language of our Saxon forefathers in England, though they never gave it that name. They called it English. Thus King Alfred speaks of translating "from book-Latin into English;" Abbot Ælfric was requested by Æthelward "to translate the book of Genesis from

Latin into English;" and Bishop Leofric, speaking of the manuscript he gave to the Exeter Cathedral, calls it "a great English book." In other words, it is the old Saxon, a Gothic tongue, as spoken and developed in England. That it was spoken and written uniformly throughout the land is not to be imagined, when we know that Jutes and Angles were in the country as well as Saxons. But that it was essentially the same language everywhere is not to be doubted, when we compare pure West-Saxon texts with Northumbrian glosses and books of Durham. Hickes speaks of a Dano-Saxon period in the history of the language. The Saxon kings reigned six hundred years; the Danish dynasty, twenty only. And neither the Danish boors, who were earthlings in the country, nor the Danish soldiers, who were dandies at the court of King Canute, could, in the brief space of twenty years, have so overlaid or interlarded the pure Anglo-Saxon with their provincialisms as to give it a new character, and thus form a new period in its history, as was afterwards done by the Normans.

The Dano-Saxon is a dialect of the language, not a period which was passed through in its history. Down to the time of the Norman Conquest, it existed in the form of two principal dialects: namely, the Anglo-Saxon in the South; and the Dano-Saxon, or Northumbrian, in the North. After the Norman Conquest, the language assumed a new form, which has been called, properly enough, Norman-Saxon and Semi-Saxon.

This form of the language, ever flowing and filtering through the roots of national feeling, custom, and prejudice, prevailed about two hundred years; that is, from the middle of the eleventh to the middle of the thirteenth century, when it became English. It is impossible to fix the land marks of a language with any great precision, but only floating beacons, here and there.

It is oftentimes curious to consider the far-off beginnings of great events, and to study the aspect of the cloud no bigger than one's hand. The British peasant looked seaward from his harvest field, and saw, with wondering eyes, the piratical schooner of a Saxon Viking making for the mouth of the Thames. A few years—only a few years—afterward, while the same peasant, driven from his homestead north or west, still lives to tell the story to his grandchildren, another race lords it over the land, speaking a different language and living under different laws. This important event in his history is more important in the world's history. Thus began the reign of the Saxons in England; and the downfall of one nation and the rise of another seem to us at this distance only the catastrophe of a stage-play.

The Saxons came into England about the middle of the fifth century. They were pagans; they were a wild and warlike people, brave, rejoicing in sea-storms, and beautiful in person, with blue eyes and long, flowing hair. Their warriors wore their shields suspended from their necks by chains. Their horsemen were armed with iron sledge-hammers. Their priests rode upon mares, and carried into the battle-field an image of the god Irminsula—in figure like an armed man; his helmet crested with a cock; in his right hand a banner, emblazoned with a red rose; a bear carved upon his breast; and, hanging from his shoulders, a shield, on which was a lion in a field of flowers.

Not two centuries elapsed before this whole people was converted to Christianity. Ælfric, in his homily on the birthday of St. Gregory, informs us that this conversion was accomplished by the holy wishes of that good man, and the holy works of St. Augustine and other monks. St. Gregory, beholding one day certain slaves set for sale in the market-place of Rome, who were "men of fair countenance and nobly-haired," and learning that they were heathens, and called Angles, heaved a long sigh, and said: "Well-away! that men of so fair a hue should be subjected to the swarthy Devil! Rightly are they called Angles, for they have angels' beauty, and therefore it is fit that they in heaven should be companions of angels." As soon, therefore, as he undertook the popehood, the monks were sent to their beloved work. In the Witena Gemot, or Assembly of the Wise, convened by King Edwin of Northumbria to consider the propriety of receiving the Christian faith, a Saxon Ealdorman arose, and spoke these noble words: "Thus seemeth to me, O king, this present life of man upon earth, compared with the time which is unknown to us; even as if you were sitting at a feast, amid your Ealdorman and Thegns in winter-time. And the fire is lighted, and the hall warmed, and it rains and snows and storms without. Then cometh a sparrow, and flieth about the hall. It cometh in at one door, and goeth out at another. While it is within, it is not touched by the winter's storm, but that is only for a moment, only for the least space. Out of the winter it cometh, to return again into the winter eftsoon. So also this life of man endureth for a little space. What goeth before it and what followeth after, we know not. Wherefore, if this new lore bring aught more certain and more advantageous, then is it worthy that we should follow it."[45]

Thus the Anglo-Saxons became Christians. For the good of their souls, they built monasteries and went on pilgrimages to Rome. The whole country, to use Malmesbury's phrase, was "glorious and refulgent with relics." The priests sang psalms night and day, and so great was the piety of St. Cuthbert, that, according to Bede, he forgot to take off his shoes for months together,—sometimes the whole year round;—from which Mr. Turner infers that he had no stockings.[46] They also copied the Evangelists and illustrated them with illuminations, in one of which St. John is represented in a pea-green dress with red stripes. They also drank ale out of buffalo horns and wooden-knobbed goblets. A Mercian king gave to the Monastery of Croyland his great drinking-horn, that the elder monks might drink therefrom at festivals, and "in their benedictions remember sometimes the soul of the donor, Witlaf." They drank his health, with that of Christ, the Virgin Mary, the apostles, and other saints. Malmesbury says that excessive drinking was the common vice of all ranks of people. King Hardicanute died in a revel, and King Edmund in a drunken brawl at Pucklechurch, being, with all his court, much overtaken by liquor, at the festival of St. Augustine. Thus did mankind go reeling through the Dark Ages; quarrelling, drinking, hunting, hawking, singing psalms, wearing breeches,[47] grinding in mills, eating hot bread, rocked in cradles, buried in coffins,—weak, suffering, sublime. Well might King Alfred exclaim, "Maker of all creatures! help now thy miserable mankind."

A national literature is a subject which should always be approached with reverence. It is difficult to comprehend fully the mind of a nation; even when that nation still lives, and we can visit it, and its present history, and the lives of men we know, help us to a comment on the written text. But here the dead alone speak. Voices, half understood; fragments of song, ending abruptly, as

---

[45] [In the article as given in the North-American Review, Mr. Longfellow continued: "This brave man spoke well; and how like an American Indian!" In a footnote he called attention to the similarity of our Indian names with some of the Anglo-Saxon name when translated.]

[46] *History of the Anglo-Saxons, vol ii. P.61.*

[47] In an old Anglo-Saxon dialogue, a shoemaker says that he makes "slippers, shoes, and leather breeches" *(swyftleras, sceos, and lether-hose).*

if the poet had sung no further, but died with these last words upon his lips homilies, preached to congregations that have been asleep for many centuries; lives of saints, who went to their reward long before the world began to scoff at sainthood; and wonderful legends, once believed by men, and now, in this age of wise children, hardly credible enough for a nurse's tale;—nothing entire, nothing wholly understood, and no further comment or illustration than may be drawn from an isolated fact found in an old chronicle, or perchance a rude illumination in an old manuscript! Such is the literature we have now to consider. Such fragments, and mutilated remains has the human mind left of itself, coming down through the times of old, step by step, and every step a century. Old men and venerable accompany us through the Past; and put into our hands, at parting, such written records of themselves as they have. We should receive these things with reverence. We should respect old age.

> This leaf, is it not blown about by the wind?
> Woe to it for its fate! Alas! it is old.

What an Anglo-Saxon glee-man was, we know from such commentaries as are mentioned above. King Edgar forbade the monks to be ale-poets, and one of his accusations against the clergy of his day was, that they entertained glee-men in their monasteries, where they had dicing, dancing, and singing, till midnight. The illumination of an old manuscript shows how a glee-man looked. It is a frontispiece to the Psalms of David. The great Psalmist sits upon his throne, with a harp in his hand, and his masters of sacred song around him. Below stands the glee-man, throwing three balls and three knives alternately into the air, and catching them as they fall, like a modern juggler. But all the Anglo-Saxon poets were not glee-men. All the harpers were not dancers. The Sceop, the creator, the poet, rose, at times, to higher themes. He sang the deeds of heroes, victorious odes, death songs, epic poems; or, sitting in cloisters, and afar from these things, converted holy writ into Saxon chimes.

The first thing which strikes the reader of Anglo-Saxon poetry is the structure of the verse the short exclamatory lines, whose rhythm depends on alliteration in the emphatic syllables, and to which the general omission of the particles gives great energy and vivacity. Though alliteration predominates in all Anglo-Saxon poetry, rhyme is not wholly wanting. It had line-rhymes and final rhymes, which, being added to the alliteration, and brought so near together in the short, emphatic lines, produce a singular effect upon the ear. They ring like blows of hammers on an anvil. For example:—

Flah mah fliteth,
Flan man hwiteth,
Burg sorg biteth,
Bald ald thwiteth,
Wræc-fæc writheth,
Wrath ath smiteth.[48]

Other peculiarities of Anglo-Saxon poetry, which cannot escape the reader's attention, are its frequent inversions, its bold transitions, and abundant metaphors. These are the things which render Anglo-Saxon poetry so much more difficult than Anglo-Saxon prose. But upon these points I need not enlarge. It is enough to allude to them.

One of the oldest and most important remains of Anglo-Saxon literature is the epic poem of Beowulf. Its age is unknown, but it comes from a very distant and hoar antiquity, somewhere between the seventh and tenth centuries. It is like a piece of ancient armor, rusty and battered, and yet strong. From within comes a voice sepulchral, as if the ancient armor spoke, telling a simple, straightforward narrative, with here and there the boastful speech of a rough old Dane, reminding one of those made by the heroes of Homer. The style, likewise, is simple,—perhaps one should say austere. The bold metaphors, which characterize nearly all the Anglo-Saxon poems, are for the most part wanting in this. The author seems mainly bent upon telling us how his Sea-Goth slew the Grendel and the Fire-drake. He is too much in earnest to multiply epithets and gorgeous figures. At times he is tedious, at times obscure, and he who undertakes to read the original will find it no easy task.

---

[48] Strong dart flitteth,
Spear-man whetteth,
Care the city biteth,
Age the bold quelleth,
Vengeance prevaileth,
Wrath a town smiteth.

The poem begins with a description of King Hrothgar the Scylding, in his great hall of Heort, which reëchoed with the sound of harp and song. But not far off, in the fens and marshes of Jutland, dwelt a grim and monstrous giant, called Grendel, a descendant of Cain. This troublesome individual was in the habit of occasionally visiting the Scylding's palace by night, to see, as the author rather quaintly says, "how the doughty Danes found themselves after their beer-carouse." On his first visit he destroyed some thirty Mates, all asleep, with beer in their brains, and ever afterwards kept the whole land in fear of death. At length the fame of these evil deeds reached the ears of Beowulf, the Thane of Higelac, a famous Viking in those days, who had slain sea-monsters, and wore a wild-boar for his crest. Straightway he sailed with fifteen followers for the court of Heort; unarmed, in the great mead-hall, and at midnight, fought the Grendel, tore off one of his arms, and hung it up on the palace wall as a curiosity; the fiend's fingers being armed with long nails, which the author calls the hand-spurs of the heathen hero. Retreating to his cave, the grim ghost departed this life, whereat there was great carousing at Heort. But at night came the Grendel's mother, and carried away one of the beer drunken heroes of the ale-wassail. Beowulf, with a great escort, pursued her to the fenlands of the Grendel; plunged, all armed, into a dark-rolling and dreary river, that flowed from the monster's cavern; slew worms and dragons manifold; was dragged to the bottom by the old-wife; and seizing a magic sword, which lay among the treasures of that realm of wonders, with one fell blow let her heathen soul out of its bone-house. Having thus freed the land from the giants, Beowulf, laden with gifts and treasures, departed homeward, as if nothing special had happened, and, after the death of King Higelac, ascended the throne of the Seyldings. Here the poem should end, and we doubt not, did originally end. But, as it has come down to us, eleven more cantos follow, containing a new series of adventures. Beowulf has grown old. He has reigned fifty years, and now, in his gray old age, is troubled by the devastations of a monstrous Fire-drake, so that his metropolis is beleaguered, and he can no longer fly his hawks and merles in the open country. He resolves, at length, to fight with this Fire-drake; and, with the help of his attendant, Wiglaf, overcomes him. The land is made rich by the treasures found in the dragon's cave, but Beowulf dies of his wounds.

Thus departs Beowulf, the Sea-Goth; of the world-kings the mildest to men, the strongest of hand, the most element to his people, the most desirous of glory. And thus closes the oldest epic in any modern language, written in forty-three cantos of some six thousand lines. The outline here given is filled up with abundant episodes and warlike details. We have ale-revels, and giving of bracelets, and presents of mares, and songs of bards. The battles with the Grendel and the Firedrake are minutely described, as likewise are the dwellings and rich treasure-houses of these monsters. The fire-stream flows with lurid light; the dragon breathes out flame and pestilential breath; the gigantic sword, forged by the Jutes of old, dis solves and thaws like an icicle in the hero's grasp; and the swart raven tells the eagle how he fared with the fell wolf at the death-feast. Such is, in brief, the machinery of the poem. It possesses great epic merit, and in parts is strikingly graphic in its descriptions. As we read, we can almost smell the brine, and hear the sea-breeze blow, and see the mainland stretch out its jutting promontories, those sea-noses, as the poet calls them, into the blue waters of the solemn ocean.

The next work to which I would call the attention of my readers is very remarkable, both in a philological and in a poetical point of view, being written in a more ambitious style than Beowulf. It is Cædmon's *Paraphrase of Portions of Holy Writ*. Cædmon was a monk in the Minster of Whitby. He lived and died in the seventh century. The only account we have of his life is that given by the Venerable Bede in his *Ecclesiastical History*.

By some he is called the Father of Anglo-Saxon Poetry, because his name stands first in the history of Saxon song-craft; by others, the Milton of our Forefathers, because he sang of Lucifer and the Loss of Paradise.

The poem is divided into two books. The first is nearly complete, and contains a paraphrase of parts of the Old Testament and the Apocrypha. The second is so mutilated as to be only a series of unconnected fragments. It contains scenes from the New Testament, and is chiefly occupied with Christ's descent into the lower regions,—a favorite theme in old times, and well known in the history of miracle-plays, as the Harrowing of Hell. The author is a pious, prayerful monk, "an awful, reverend, and religious man." He has all the simplicity of a child. He calls his Creator Blithe-heart King: the patriarchs, Earls, and their children, Noblemen. Abraham is a wise-heedy man, a guardian of bracelets, a mighty earl; and his wife Sarah, a woman of elfin beauty. The sons of Reuben are called Sea-Pirates. A laugher is a laughter-smith; the Ethiopians, a people brown with the hot coals of heaven.

Striking poetic epithets and passages are not wanting in his works. They are sprinkled here and there throughout the narrative. The sky is called the roof of nations, the roof adorned with stars. After the overthrow of Pharaoh and his folk, he says, the blue air was with corruption tainted, and the bursting ocean whooped a bloody storm. Nebuchadnezzar is described as a naked, unwilling wanderer, a wondrous wretch and weed less. Horrid ghosts, swart and sinful,

Wide through windy halls
Wail woful.

And, in the sack of Sodom, we are told how many a fearful, pale-faced damsel must trembling go into a stranger's embrace, and how fell the defenders of brides and bracelets, sick with wounds. Indeed, whenever the author has a battle to describe, and hosts of armbearing and warfaring men draw from their sheaths the ring-hilted sword of edges doughty, he enters into the matter with so much spirit that one almost imagines he sees, looking from under that monkish cowl, the visage of no parish priest, but of a grim war-wolf, as the great fighters were called, in the days when Cædmon wrote.

Such are the two great narrative poems of the Anglo-Saxon tongue. Of a third, a short fragment remains. It is a mutilated thing, a mere *torso*. Judith of the Apocrypha is the heroine. The part preserved describes the death of Holofernes in a fine, brilliant style, delighting the hearts of all Anglo-Saxon scholars. But a more important fragment is that on the Death of Byrhtnoth at the battle of Maldon. It savors of rust and of antiquity, like *Old Hildebrand* in German. What a fine passage is this, spoken by an aged vassal over the dead body of the hero, in the thickest of the fight!

> Byrhtwold spoke; he was an aged vassal; he raised his shield; he brandished his ashen spear; he full boldly exhorted the warriors. "Our spirit shall be the hardier, our heart shall be the keener, our soul shall be the greater, the more our forces diminish. Here lieth our chief all mangled; the brave one in the dust; ever may he lament his shame that thinketh to fly from this play of weapons! Old am I in life, yet will I not stir hence; but I think to lie by the side of my lord, by that much loved man!"

Shorter than either of these fragments is a third on the Fight of Finsborough. Its chief value seems to be, that it relates to the same action which formed the theme of one of Hrothgar's bards in Beowulf. In addition to these narrative poems and fragments, there are two others, founded on lives of saints. They are the Life and Passion of St. Juliana, and the Visions of the Hermit Guthlac.

There is another narrative poem, which I must mention here on account of its subject, though of a much later date than the foregoing. It is the Chronicle of King Lear and his daughters, in Norman-Saxon; not rhymed throughout, but with rhymes too often recurring to be accidental. As a poem, it has no merit, but shows that the story of Lear is very old, for, in speaking of the old king's death and burial, it refers to a previous account, "as the book telleth." Cordelia is married to Aganippus, king of France, and, after his death, reigns over England, though Maglaudus, king of Scotland, declares that it is a "muckle shame that a queen should be king in the land."[49]

Besides these long, elaborate poems, the Anglo-Saxons had their odes and ballads. Thus, when King Canute was sailing by the Abbey of Ely, he heard the voices of the monks chanting their vesper hymn. Whereupon he sang, in the best Anglo-Saxon he was master of, the following rhyme:—

Merie sungen the muneches binnen Ely,
Tha Cnut ching reuther by;
Roweth, cnihtes, noer the land,
And here we thes muneches sang.[50]

The best, and, properly speaking, perhaps the only, Anglo-Saxon odes, are those preserved in the Saxon Chronicle, in recording the events they celebrate. They are five in number: Æthelstan's Victory at Brunanburh; the Victories of

[49] For hit was swithe mochel same,
and eke hit was mochel grame,
that a cwene solde
be king in thisse land.

[50] Merry sang the monks in Ely,
As King Canute was steering by;
Row, ye knights, near the land,
And hear we these monks' song.

Edmund Ætheling; the Coronation of King Edgar; the Death of King Edgar; and the Death of King Edward. The Battle of Brunanburh is already pretty well known by the numerous English versions, and attempts thereat, which have been given of it.

This ode is one of the most characteristic specimens of Anglo-Saxon poetry. What a striking picture is that of the lad with flaxen hair, mangled with wounds; and of the seven earls of Anlaf, and the five young kings, lying on the battle-field, lulled asleep by the sword! Indeed, the whole ode is striking, bold, graphic. The furious onslaught; the cleaving of the wall of shields; the hewing down of banners; the din of the fight; the hard hand-play; the retreat of the Northmen, in nailed ships, over the stormy sea and the deserted dead, on the battle-ground, left to the swart raven, the war-hawk, and the wolf;—all these images appeal strongly to the imagination. The bard has nobly described this victory of the illustrious war smiths, the most signal victory since the coming of the Saxons into England; so say the books of the old wise men.

And here I would make due and honorable mention of the Poetic Calendar, and of King Alfred's Version of the Metres of Boëthius. The Poetic Calendar is a chronicle of great events in the lives of saints, martyrs, and apostles, referred to the days on which they took place. At the end is a strange poem, consisting of a series of aphorisms, not unlike those that adorn a modern almanac.

In addition to these narratives and odes and didactic poems, there are numerous minor poems on various subjects, some of which have been published, though for the most part they still lie buried in manuscripts,—hymns, allegories, doxologies, proverbs, enigmas, paraphrases of the Lord's Prayer, poems on Death and the Day of Judgment, and the like. A large quantity of them is contained in the celebrated Exeter Manuscript,—a folio given by Bishop Leofric to the Cathedral of Exeter in the eleventh century, and called by the donor "a great English book about everything, composed in verse." Among them is a very singular and striking poem, entitled "The Soul's Complaint against the Body," in which the departed spirit is described as returning, ghastly and shrieking, to upbraid the body it had left.

Much it behoveth
Each one of mortals,
That he his soul's journey

In himself ponder,
How deep it may be.
When Death cometh,
The bonds he breaketh
By which were united
The soul and the body.

Long it is thenceforth
Ere the soul taketh
From God himself
Its woe or its weal;
As in the world erst,
Even in its earth-vessel,
It wrought before.

The soul shall come
Wailing with loud voice,
The soul, to find
The body
That it erst dwelt in;—
Three hundred winters,
Unless ere that worketh
The Eternal Lord,
The end of the world.

Crieth then, so care-worn,
With cold utterance,
And speaketh grimly,
The ghost to the dust:
"Dry dust! thou dreary one!
How little didst thou labor for me!
In the foulness of earth
Thou all wearest away
Like to the loam!
Little didst thou think
How thy soul's journey
Would be thereafter,
When from the body
It should be led forth."

But perhaps the most curious poem in the Exeter Manuscript is the Rhyming Poem, to which I have before alluded.[51]

Still more spectral is the following Norman-Saxon poem, from a manuscript volume of Homilies in the Bodleian Library. The subject is the grave. It is Death that speaks.

For thee was a house built
Ere thou wast born;
For thee was a mould meant
Ere thou of mother camest.
But it is not made ready,
Nor its depth measured,
How long it shall be.
Now I bring thee
Where thou shalt be.
Now I shall measure thee,
And the mould afterwards.

Thy house is not
Highly timbered;
It is unhigh and low,
When thou art therein,
The heel-ways are low,
The side-ways unhigh;
The roof is built
Thy breast full nigh.
So thou shalt in mould
Dwell full cold,
Dimly and dark.

Doorless is that house,
And dark it is within;
There thou art fast detained,
And Death hath the key.
Loathsome is that earth-house,
And grim within to dwell;

[51] Since this paper was written, the Exeter Manuscript has been published, with a translation by Mr. Thorpe.

There thou shalt dwell,
And worms shall divide thee.

Thus thou art laid
And leavest thy friends;
Thou hast no friend
Who will come to thee,
Who will ever see
How that house pleaseth thee,
Who will ever open
The door for thee,
And descend after thee;
For soon thou art loathsome
And hateful to see.

We now come to Anglo-Saxon Prose. At the very boundary stand two great works, like landmarks. These are the Saxon Laws, promulgated by the various kings that ruled the land; and the Saxon Chronicle, in which all great historic events, from the middle of the fifth to the middle of the twelfth century, are recorded by contemporary writers, mainly, it would seem, the monks of Winchester, Peterborough, and Canterbury.[52] Setting these aside, doubtless the most important remains of Anglo-Saxon prose are the writings of King Alfred the Great.

What a sublime old character was King Alfred! Alfred, the Truth-teller! Thus the ancient historian surnamed him, as others were surnamed the Unready, Ironside, Harefoot. The principal events of his life are known to all men—the nine battles fought in the first year of his reign; his flight to the marshes and forests of Somersetshire; his poverty and suffering, wherein was fulfilled the prophecy of St. Neot, that he should "be bruised like the ears of wheat;" his life with the swineherd, whose wife bade him turn the cakes, that they might not be burnt, for she saw daily that he was a great eater; his

[52] The style of this Chronicle rises at times far above that of most monkish historians. For instance, in recording the death of William the Conqueror, the writer says: "Sharp Death, that passes by neither rich men nor poor, seized him also. Alas! how false and how uncertain is this world's weal! He that was before a rich king, and lord of many lands, had not then of all his land more than a space of seven feet! and he that was whilom enshrouded in gold and gems lay there covered with mould." A. D. 1087.

successful rally; his victories and his future glorious reign;—these things are known to all men. And not only these, which are events in his life, but also many more, which are traits in his character, and controlled events; as, for example, that he was a wise and virtuous man, a religious man, a learned man for that age. Perhaps. they know, even, how he measured time with his six horn lanterns; also, that he was an author and wrote many books. But of these books how few persons have read even a single line! And yet it is well worth our while, if we wish to see all the calm dignity of that great man's character, and how in him the scholar and the man outshone the king. For example, do we not know him better, and honor him more, when we hear from his own lips, as it were, such sentiments as these? "God has made all men equally noble in their original nature. True nobility is in the mind, not in the flesh. I wished to live honorably whilst I live and, after my life, to leave to the men who were after me my memory in good works!"

The chief writings of this royal author are his translations of Gregory's *Pastoralis*, Boëthius's *Consolations of Philosophy*, Bede's *Ecclesiastical History*, and the *History of Orosius*, known in manuscripts by the mysterious title of *Hormesta*. Of these works the most remarkable is the Boëthius, so much of his own mind has Alfred infused into it. Properly speaking, it is not so much a translation as a gloss or paraphrase, for the Saxon king, upon his throne, had a soul which was near akin to that of the last of the Roman philosophers in his prison. He had suffered, and could sympathize with suffering humanity. He adorned and carried out still further the reflections of Boëthius. He begins his task, however, with an apology, saying, "Alfred, king, was translator of this book, and turned it from book-Latin into English, as he most plainly and clearly could, amid the various and manifold worldly occupations which often busied him in mind and body;" and ends with a prayer, beseeching God, "by the sign of the holy cross, and by the virginity of the blessed Mary, and by the obedience of the blessed Michael, and by the love of all the saints and their merits," that his mind might be made steadfast to the Divine will and his own soul's need.

Other remains of Anglo-Saxon prose exist in the tale of Apollonius of Tyre; the Bible-translations and Colloquies of Abbot Ælfric; Glosses of the Gospels, at the close of one of which the conscientious scribe has written, "Aldred, an unworthy and miserable priest, with the help of God and St. Cuthbert, overglossed it in English;" and, finally, various miscellaneous treatises, among which the most curious is a Dialogue between Saturn and Solomon. I cannot refrain from giving a few extracts from this very original and curious document, which bears upon it some of the darkest thumb-marks of the Middle Ages.

> Tell me, what man first spake with a dog?
>
> I tell thee, Saint Peter.
>
> Tell me, what man first ploughed the earth with a plough?
>
> I tell thee, it was Ham, the son of Noah.
>
> Tell me, wherefore stones are barren?
>
> I tell thee, because Abel's blood fell upon a stone, when Cain his brother slew him with the jawbone of an ass.
>
> * * *
>
> Tell me, what made the sea salt?
>
> I tell thee, the ten commandments that Moses collected in the old law,—the commandments of God. He threw the ten commandments into the sea, and he shed tears into the sea, and the sea became salt.
>
> * * *
>
> Tell me, what man first built a monastery?
>
> I tell thee, Elias, and Elisha the prophet, and after baptism, Paul and Anthony, the first anchorites.
>
> Tell me, what were the streams that watered Paradise?
>
> I tell thee, they were four. The first was called Pison; the second, Geon; the third, Tigris; the fourth, Euphrates; that is, milk, and honey, and ale, and wine.
>
> Tell me, why is the sun red at evening?
>
> I tell thee, because he looks into Hell.
>
> Tell me, why shineth he so red in the morning?
>
> I tell thee, because he doubteth whether he shall or shall not shine upon this earth, as he is commanded.
>
> Tell me, what four waters feed this earth?
>
> I tell thee, they are snow, and rain, and hail, and dew.
>
> Tell me, who first made letters?
>
> I tell thee, Mercury the Giant.

Hardly less curious, and infinitely more valuable, is a *Colloquy* of Ælfric, composed for the purpose of teaching boys to speak Latin. The Saxon is an interlinear translation of the Latin. In this Colloquy various laborers and handicraftsmen are introduced,—ploughmen, herdsmen, huntsmen, shoemakers, and others; and each has his say, even to the blacksmith, who dwells in his smithy amid iron fire-sparks and the sound of beating sledge-hammers and blowing bellows. I translate the close of this Colloquy, to show our readers what a poor school-boy had to suffer in the Middle Ages. They will hardly wonder that Erigena Scot should have been put to death with penknives by his scholars.

Magister. Well, boy, what hast thou been doing today?

Discipulus. A great many things have I been doing. Last night, when I heard the knell, I got out of my bed and went into the church, and sang the matin-song with the friars; after that we sang the hymn of All Saints and the morning songs of praise; after these Prime, and the seven Psalms, with the litanies and the first Mass; then the nine-o'clock service and the mass for the day, and after this we sang the service of mid-day, and ate, and drank, and slept, and got up again, and sang Nones, and now are here before thee, ready to hear what thou hast to say to us.

Magister. When will you sing Vespers or the Compline?

Discipulus. When it is time.

Magister. Hast thou had a whipping to-day?

Discipulus. I have not, because I have behaved very warily.

Magister. And thy playmates?

Discipulus. Why dost thou ask me about them? I dare not tell thee our secrets. Each one of them knows whether he has been whipped or not.

Magister. What dost thou eat every day?

Discipulus. I still eat meat, because I am a child, living under the rod.

Magister. What else dost thou eat?

Discipulus. Greens and eggs, fish and cheese, butter and beans, and all clean things, with much thankfulness.

Magister. Exceedingly voracious art thou, for thou devourest everything that is set before thee.

Discipulus. Not so very voracious either, for I don't eat all kinds of food at one meal.

Magister. How then?

Discipulus. Sometimes I eat one kind, and sometimes another, with soberness, as becomes a monk, and not with voracity; for I am not a glutton.

Magister. And what dost thou drink?

Discipulus. Beer, when I can get it, and water when I cannot get beer.

Magister. Dost thou not drink wine?

Discipulus. I am not rich enough to buy wine, and wine is not a drink for boys and ignorant people, but for old men and wise.

Magister. Where dost thou sleep?

Discipulus. In the dormitory, with the friars.

Magister. Who wakes thee for matins?

Discipulus. Sometimes I hear the knell and get up; sometimes my master wakes me sternly with a rod.

Magister. O ye good children, and winsome learners! Your teacher admonishes you to follow godly lore, and to behave yourselves decently everywhere. Go obediently, when you hear the chapel bell, enter into the chapel, and bow suppliantly at the holy altars, and stand submissive, and sing with one accord, and pray for your sins, and then depart to the cloister or the school-room without levity.

I cannot close this sketch of Anglo-Saxon Literature without expressing the hope, that what I have written may "stir up riper wits than mine to, the perfection of this rough-hewn work." The history of this literature still remains to be written. How strange it is that so interesting a subject should wait so long for its historian!

PARIS IN THE SEVENTEENTH CENTURY

This sketch served as introduction to a college lecture on Molière, which was first delivered, apparently, in 1838. This and kindred lectures were used by Mr. Longfellow when preparing *The Poets and Poetry of Europe*, and the pages which follow were incorporated in the essay on *French Language* and *Poetry* which introduces the translations from the French given in that volume. When the Blue and Gold Edition of the Prose writings was prepared in 1857, this sketch was separated from its context and made an independent paper.

THE age of Louis the Fourteenth is one of the most brilliant in history; illustrious by its reign of seventy-two years and its hundred authors known to fame. The government of this monarch has been called "a satire upon despotism." His vanity was boundless: his magnificence equally so. The palaces of Marly and Versailles are monuments of his royal pride; equestrian statues, and his figure on one of the gates of Paris, represented as a naked Hercules, with a club in his hand and a flowing wig on his head, are monuments of his vanity and self-esteem.

His court was the home of etiquette and the model of all courts. "It seemed," says Voltaire, "that Nature at that time took delight in producing in France the greatest men in all the arts; and of assembling at court the most beautiful men and women that had ever existed. But the king bore the palm away from all his courtiers by the grace of his figure and the majestic beauty of his countenance; the noble and winning sound of his voice gained over the hearts that his presence intimidated. His carriage was such as became him and his rank only, and would have been ridiculous in any other. The embarrassment he inspired in those who spoke with him flattered in secret the self-complacency with which he recognized his own superiority. The old officer, who became agitated and stammered in asking a favor from him, and not being able to finish his discourse, exclaimed, 'Sire, I do not tremble so before your enemies!' had no difficulty in obtaining the favor he asked."

All about him was pomp and theatrical show. He invented a kind of livery, which it was held the greatest honor to wear; a blue waistcoat embroidered with gold and silver;—a mark of royal favor. To all around him he was courteous; towards women chivalrous. He never passed even a chambermaid without touching his hat; and always stood uncovered in the presence of a lady. When the disappointed Duke of Lauzun insulted him by breaking his sword in his presence, he raised the window, and threw his cane into the courtyard, saying, "I never should have forgiven myself if I had struck a gentleman."

He seems, indeed, to have been a strange mixture of magnanimity and littleness;—his gallantries veiled always in a show of decency; severe, capricious, fond of pleasure, hardly less fond of labor. One day we find him dashing from Vincennes to Paris in his hunting-dress, and standing in his great boots, with a whip in his hand, dismissing his Parliament as he would a pack of hounds. The next he is dancing in the ballet of his private theatre, in the character of a gypsy, and whistling or singing scraps of opera-songs; and then parading at a military review, or galloping at full speed through the park of Fontainebleau, hunting the deer, in a calash drawn by four ponies. Towards the close of his life he became a devotee. "It is a very remarkable thing," says Voltaire, "that the public, who forgave him all his mistresses, could not forgive him his father confessor." He outlived the respect of his subjects. When he lay on his death-bed,—those godlike eyes that had overawed the world now grown dim and lustreless,—all his courtiers left him to die alone, and thronged about his successor, the Duke of Orleans. An empiric gave him an elixir, which suddenly revived him. He ate once more, and it was said he could recover. The crowd about the Duke of Orleans diminished very fast. "If the king eats a second time, I shall be left all alone," said he. But the king ate no more. He died like a philosopher. To Madame de Maintenon he said, "I thought it was more difficult to die!" and to his domestics, "Why do you weep? Did you think I was immortal?"

Of course the character of the monarch stamped itself upon the society about him. The licentious court made a licentious city. Yet everywhere external decency and decorum prevailed. The courtesy of the old school held sway. Society, moreover, was pompous and artificial. There were pedantic scholars about town, and learned women, and *Précieuses Ridicules*, and Euphuism. With all its greatness, it was an effeminate age.

The old city of Paris, which lies in the Marais, was once the court end of the town. It is now entirely deserted by wealth and fashion. Travellers even seldom find their way into its broad and silent streets. But sightly mansions and garden walls, over which tall, shadowy trees wave to and fro, speak of a more splendid age, when proud and courtly ladies dwelt there, and the frequent wheels of gay equipages chafed the now grass-grown pavements.

In the centre of this part of Paris, within pistol-shot of the Boulevard St. Antoine, stands the Place Royale. Old palaces of a quaint and uniform style, with a low arcade in front, run quite round the square. In its centre is a public walk, with trees, an iron railing, and an equestrian statue of Louis the Thirteenth. It was here that monarch held his court. But there is no sign of a court now.

Under the arcade are shops and fruit-stalls, and in one corner sits a cobbler, seemingly as old and deaf as the walls around him. Occasionally you get a glimpse through a grated gate into spacious gardens, and a large flight of steps leads up into what was once a royal palace, and is now a tavern. In the public walk, old gentlemen sit under the trees on benches, and enjoy the evening air. Others walk up and down, buttoned in long frock coats. They have all a provincial look. Indeed, for a time you imagine yourself in a small French town, not in Paris; so different is everything there from the Paris you live in. You are in a quarter where people retire to live genteelly on small incomes. The gentlemen in long frock-coats are no courtiers, but retired tradesmen.

Not far off is the Rue des Tournelles; and the house is still standing in which lived and loved that Aspasia of the seventeenth century,—the celebrated Ninon de l'Enclos. From the Boulevard you look down into the garden, where her illegal and ill-fated son, on discovering that the object of his passion was his own mother, put end to his miserable life. Not very remote from this is the house once occupied by Madame de Sévigné. You are shown the very cabinet where she composed those letters which beautified her native tongue, and "make us love the very ink that wrote them." In a word, you are here in the centre of the Paris of the seventeenth century; the gay, the witty, the licentious city, which in Louis the Fourteenth's time was like Athens in the age of Pericles. And now all is changed to solitude and silence. The witty age, with its brightness and licentious heat, all burnt out,—puffed into darkness by the breath of time. Thus passes an age of libertinism and sedition, and bloody, frivolous wars, and fighting bishops, and devout prostitutes, and "factious *beaux esprits* improvising epigrams in the midst of seditions, and madrigals on the field of battle."

Westward from this quarter, near the Seine and the Louvre, stood the ever famous Hôtel de Rambouillet, the court of Euphuism and false taste. Here Catherine de Vivonne, Marchioness of Rambouillet, gave her æsthetical soirées in her bed-chamber, and she herself in bed, among the curtains and mirrors of a gay alcove. The master of ceremonies bore the title of the *Alcoviste*. He did the honors of the house and directed the conversation, and such was the fashion of the day, that, impossible as it may seem to us, no evil tongue soiled with malignant whisper the fair fame of the Précieuses, as the ladies of the society were called. Into this bedchamber came all the most noted literary personages of the day;—Corneille, Malherbe, Bossuet, Fléchier, La Rochefoucault, Balzac, Bussy-Rabutin, Madame de Sévigné, Mademoiselle de Scudéri, and others of less note, though hardly less pretension. They paid their homage to the Marchioness, under the title of Arthénice, Éracinthe, and Corinthée, anagrams of the name of Catherine. There, as in the Courts of Love of a still earlier age, were held grave dissertations on frivolous themes: and all the metaphysics of love, and the subtilties of exaggerated passion, were discussed with most puerile conceits and a vapid sentimentality. "We saw, not long since," says La Bruyère, "a circle of persons of the two sexes, united by conversation and mental sympathy. They left to the vulgar the art of speaking intelligibly. One obscure expression brought on another still more obscure, which in turn was capped by something truly enigmatical, attended with vast applause. With all this so-called delicacy, feeling, and refinement of expression, they at length went so far that they were neither under stood by others nor could understand themselves. For these conversations one needed neither good sense, nor memory, nor the least capacity; only *esprit*, and that not of the best, but a counterfeit kind, made up chiefly of imagination."

Looking back from the present age, how very absurd all these things seem to us! Nevertheless, the minds of some excellent men were seriously impressed with their worth; and the pulpit-orator, Fléchier, in his funeral oration upon the death of Madame de Montausier, exclaimed, in pious enthusiasm: "Remember, my brethren, those cabinets which are still regarded with so much veneration, where the mind was purified, where virtue was revered under the name of the incomparable Arthénice, where were gathered together so many personages of quality and merit, forming a select court, numerous without confusion, modest without constraint, learned without pride, polished without affectation."

Table-Talk.

These paragraphs were first printed when *Drift-Wood* was arranged in the Blue and Gold Edition of 1857. Mr. Longfellow was in the habit of setting down single thoughts in this form in his note-book, and illustrations are to be found in his *The Blank Book of a Country Schoolmaster* and in the thirteenth chapter of *Kavanagh*. It is possible that he meditated a similar chapter when writing *Hyperion*, since he notes in his diary that he wrote and then threw aside a chapter entitled *St. Clair's Note-Book*, St. Clair being the first form of his hero's name.

If you borrow my books, do not mark them; for I shall not be able to distinguish your marks from my own, and the pages will become like the doors in Bagdad marked by Morgiana's chalk.

Don Quixote thought he could have made beautiful bird-cages and toothpicks if his brain had not been so full of ideas of chivalry. Most people would succeed in small things, if they were not troubled with great ambitions.

A torn jacket is soon mended; but hard words bruise the heart of a child.

Authors, in their Prefaces, generally speak in a conciliatory, deprecating tone of the critics, whom they hate and fear; as of old the Greeks spake of the Furies as the Eumenides, the benign Goddesses.

Doubtless criticism was originally benignant, pointing out the beauties of a work, rather than its defects. The passions of men have made it malignant, as the bad heart of Procrustes turned the bed, the symbol of repose, into an instrument of torture.

Popularity is only, in legal phrase, the "instantaneous seisin" of fame.

The Mormons make the marriage ring, like the ring of Saturn, fluid, not solid, and keep it in its place by numerous satellites.

In the mouths of many men soft words are like roses that soldiers put into the muzzles of their muskets on holidays.

We often excuse our own want of philanthropy by giving the name of fanaticism to the more ardent zeal of others.

Every great poem is in itself limited by necessity,—but in its suggestions unlimited and in finite.

If we could read the secret history of our enemies, we should find in each man's life sorrow and suffering enough to disarm all hostility.

As turning the logs will make a dull fire burn, so change of studies a dull brain.

The Laws of Nature are just, but terrible. There is no weak mercy in them. Cause and consequence are inseparable and inevitable. The elements have no forbearance. The fire burns, the water drowns, the air consumes, the earth buries. And perhaps it would be well for our race if the punishment of crimes against the Laws of Man were as inevitable as the punishment of crimes against the Laws of Nature,—were Man as unerring in his judgments as Nature.

Round about what is, lies a whole mysterious world of might be,—a psychological romance of possibilities and things that do not happen. By going out a few minutes sooner or later, by stop ping to speak with a friend at a corner, by meeting this man or that, or by turning down this street instead of the other, we may let slip some great occasion of good, or avoid some impending evil, by which the whole current of our lives would have been changed. There is no solution to the dark enigma but the one word, "Providence."

The Helicon of too many poets is not a hill crowned with sunshine and visited by the Muses and the Graces, but an old, mouldering house, full of gloom and haunted by ghosts.

"Let us build such a church, that those who come after us shall take us for madmen," said the old canon of Seville, when the great cathedral was planned. Perhaps through every mind passes some such thought, when it first entertains the design of a great and seemingly impossible action, the end of which it dimly foresees. This divine madness enters more or less into all our noblest undertakings.

I feel a kind of reverence for the first books of young authors. There is so much aspiration in them, so much audacious hope and trembling fear, so much of the heart's history, that all errors and short-comings are for a while lost sight of in the amiable self-assertion of youth.

Authors have a greater right than any copy right, though it is generally unacknowledged or disregarded. They have a right to the reader's civility. There are favorable hours for reading a book, as for writing it, and to these the author has a claim. Yet many people think that when they buy a book they buy with it the right to abuse the author.

A thought often makes us hotter than a fire.

Black seals upon letters, like the black sails of the Greeks, are signs of bad tidings and ill success.

Love makes its record in deeper colors as we grow out of childhood into manhood; as the Emperors signed their names in green ink when under age, but when of age, in purple.

Some critics are like chimney-sweepers; they put out the fire below, or frighten the swallows from their nests above they scrape a long time in the chimney, cover themselves with soot, and bring nothing away but a bag of cinders, and then sing from the top of the house as if they had built it.

When we reflect that all the aspects of Nature, all the emotions of the soul, and all the events of life, have been the subjects of poetry for hundreds and thousands of years, we can hardly wonder that there should be so many resemblances and coincidences of expression among poets, but rather that they are not more numerous and more striking.

The first pressure of sorrow crushes out from our hearts the best wine; afterwards the constant weight of it brings forth bitterness,—the taste and stain from the lees of the vat.

The tragic element in poetry is like Saturn in alchemy,—the Malevolent, the Destroyer of Nature; but without it no true Aurum Potabile, or Elixir of Life, can be made.

APPENDIX

I. List of Miscellaneous Papers.

As stated in the note heading *Drift-Wood*, Mr. Longfellow designed at one time to publish "a volume of old matters collected from corners of reviews and magazines, to be called *Driftwood*." It is hardly likely however that he would have included in that volume all of his miscellaneous prose papers. During the early years of his professorship, down to the date of his first collection of poems, his pen was busy with subjects connected with his academic work, and even after it was clear that the poetic was the literary form most congenial to him, he continued to write critical and biographical essays upon subjects related to his work of setting forth foreign literature,—a work which in the shape of translation occupied him all his life. The following is a list of his several prose writings so far as traced, exclusive of his *Outre-Mer* and his work in fiction.

The Lay Monastery: 1. Authors and Writers. 2. Winter Months. 3. The Literary Spirit of our Country: *The United States Literary Gazette*, March 1, March 15, April 1, 1825.

The Schoolmaster: *The New England Magazine*, 1831 -1833. See Introductory Note to *Outre-Mer, ante*, reference page 1.

Origin and Progress of the French Language: *The North American Review*, April, 1831. See *ante*, reference page 4.

The Defence of Poetry: *The North American Review*, January, 1832. See *ante*, reference page 4.

The Devotional Poetry of Spain: *The North American Review*, April, 1832. See *ante*, reference page 4.

History of the Italian Language and Dialects: *The North American Review*, October, 1832.

Review of Mancinelli's *Dialoghi: The American Monthly Review*, October, 1832.

Ancient French Romances: *The Select Journal of Foreign Periodical Literature*, January, 1833. See *ante*, reference page 195.

Review of Dana's Poems and Prose Writings: *The American Monthly Review*, December, 1833.

The Blank-Book of a Country Schoolmaster: *The Knicker-bocker* Magazine, 1834, 1835. See *ante*, reference page 6, and *post*, reference page 295.

Spanish Language and Literature: *The North American Review*, April, 1833.

Old English Romances: *The North American Review*, October, 1833. See *ante*, reference page 5.

The Great Metropolis: *The North American Review*, April, 1837. See *ante*, reference page 262.

Hawthorne's Twice-Told Tales: *The North American Review*, July, 1837. See *ante*, reference page 257.

Tegnér's Frithiof's Saga: *The North American Review*, July, 1837 See *ante*, reference page 222.

Anglo-Saxon Literature: *The North American Review*, July, 1838. See *ante*, reference page 265.

The French Language in England: *The North American Review*, October, 1840.

Review of C. C. Felton's translation of Menzel's History of German Literature: *The New World*, 1840.

Translations from Jean Paul: *Boston Nation*, March 13, 1841.

The Literary Remains of Willis Gaylord Clark: *The North American Review*, October, 1844.

The Poets and Poetry of Europe. With Introductions and Biographical Notices. Philadelphia: Carey and Hart. 1845. This volume, besides including portions of some of the North American Review articles, contained the paper on Dante which was published in the first edition of the Prose Works.

Dante's Divina Commedia; from the German of Schelling: *Graham's Magazine*, June, 1850. Afterward published in the first edition of the Prose Works.

II. The Blank Book of a Country Schoolmaster.

I. Saturday Afternoon.

It is Saturday afternoon. Once more the school-house door has creaked upon its hebdomadal hinges; the dogeared book yawns upon the deserted desk; the flies are buzzing and bumping their heads against the sunny window; the school-boy is abroad in the woods, and the schoolmaster has laid his birchen sceptre upon the shelf, and with it the cares and solicitudes of another week.

Saturday afternoon! Delightful season, when the mind, like a tired artisan, lays down its implements of toil, and leaves the long-accustomed handicraft! How sweet, amid the busy avocations of the week, to look forward to this short interval of repose, when, for a time at least, the grinding shall cease, and the heart be permitted to indulge its secret longings, and listen to the soft whispers of its own wayward fancies! Surely the feelings of the school boy linger around me still. I love the *dolce far niente* of Saturday afternoon!

It is an interlude between the swift-succeeding acts of life; the close of a seven-days' journey; a golden clasp, that shuts each weekly volume of our history; a goal, where Time pauses to rest his wing, and turn his glass; a type of that longer interval of rest, when our evening sun shall be going down, when our lengthening shadows shall "point towards morning," and we shall be looking forward to an eternal Sabbath!

II. An Old Saying.

The vulgar saying, to *"wet your whistle,"* is of Norman pedigree, and as old as the thirteen century. Henri d'Andeli thus commences his poem on "The battle of the Wines."

> Volez oïr une grant fable,
> Qu'il avint l'autrier sus la table
> Au bon Roi qui ot non Phelippe,

Qui volontiers *moilloit sa pipe*
Du bon vin qui estoit du blanc.

Will you hear of a great fable,
That happened the other day at table
To good king Philip, who did decline
To *wet his whistle* with good white wine.

III. A Passage from Dante.

In the translation of Dante by the Rev. Henry Boyd, the following passage in the Inferno, Canto 2,

O, donna di virtù sola per cui
L'umana specie eccede ogni contento
Da quel ciel ch' ha minori i cerchi sui;

is thus rendered:

Spirit benign! whose disentangled soul
Thy brethren taught to spurn the nether goal,
Pierce the blue mundane shell, and claim the sky.

This interpolation upon the *Gran Padre* of Italian poetry renders the whole passage burlesque, by comparing the soul in its upward flight to a chicken breaking from its shell!

IV. The Happy Man and the Lucky Dog.

In this strange world of ours, where each pursues his own golden bubble, and laughs at his neighbor for doing the same, he is the Happy Man who, blessed with modest case, a wife and children,—sits enthroned in the hearts of his family, and knows no other ambition than that of making those around him happy. But the Lucky Dog is he who, free from all domestic cares, saunters up and down his room in morning gown and slippers, drums on the window of a rainy day, and as he stirs his evening fire snaps his fingers at the world, and says, "I have no wife nor children, good or bad, to provide for."

Mankind are like a pendulum; they vibrate from one extreme to the other. It was so with my friend Quibble, who is now no more. He was taken away in the bloom of life by a very rapid—widow. Before this untimely event, he was by preëminence *the* Bold Bachelor, the "good knight without fear and without reproach," as the old chronicles say. He was by birth and by profession a beau;—born with a quizzing-glass and a cane. Cock of the walk, he flapped his wings, and crowed among the feathered tribe. But alas a fair, white partlet has torn his crest out, and he shall crow no more.

You will generally find him of a morning nosing round a beef-cart, with domestic felicity written in every line of his countenance; and sometimes meet him in a cross-street at noon, hurrying homeward, with a beef-steak on a wooden skewer, or a fresh fish, with a piece of tarred twine run through its gills. In the evening he rocks the cradle, and gets up in the night, when the child cries. Like a Goth of the Dark Ages, he consults his wife on all mighty matters, and looks upon her as a being of more than human good ness and wisdom. In return, she sweetens his coffee for him, puts in his breast-pin, ties his cravat in a bow-knot, and never lets him go out alone after dark. In short, the ladies all say he is a very domestic man, and makes a good husband; which, under the rose, is only a more polite way of saying he is henpecked.

Quibble is a Happy Man.

Not so Dribble. He is a sexagenary bachelor, and a Lucky Dog. He has one of those well-oiled dispositions which turn upon the hinges of the world without creaking. The heyday of life is over with him; but his old age is sunny and chirping, and a merry heart still nestles in his tottering frame, like a swallow that builds in a tumble-down chimney.

Dribble is a professed Squire of Dames. The rustle of a silk gown is music to his ears, and his imagination is continually lantern-led by some will-with-a-wisp in the shape of a lady's stomacher. In his devotion to the fair sex—"the muslin" as he calls it—he is the "gentle flower of chivalry." It is amusing to see how quick he strikes into the scent of a lady's handkerchief. When once fairly in pursuit, there is no such thing as throwing him out. His heart looks out at his eye, and his inward delight tingles down to the tail of his coat. He loves to bask in the sunshine of a smile; when he can breathe the sweet atmosphere of kid gloves and cambric handkerchiefs his soul is in its element; and his supreme delight is to pass the morning, to use his own quaint language, "in making dodging calls, and wiggling round among the ladies!"

Dribble is a Lucky Dog!

V. Midnight Devotion.

If there be one hour more fitted to devotion than the rest, it is this,—the silent, solemn, solitary hour of midnight in mid-winter. Not a light can be seen in the village—the world is asleep around me. How breathless and how still! Not air enough to shake down the feathery snow from the branches of thetrees, and the leafless vine at my window.

—The moon, a Virgin Queen,
Reigns absolute in her celestial city.
One lonely star, beside the western gate,
Stands sentinel. All else around her throne
Submissive veil their faces; for in her
Reflected shine the majesty and light
Of her departed lord, the glorious sun.
The air itself is awed into a whisper!
And yet amid the stillness comes a sound,
Like the sad music of a muffled drum,—
Distant and indistinct. It is the voice
Of many waters, down the shelving rock
Falling, still falling through the silent night,
Fit music for the solemn march of Time.

FATHER, who art in heaven! With contrite heart
I bow before thee! Hallowed be thy name!
I have fled from thee, but thou hast not left me;
I have scoffed at thee, but thou hast not cursed me;
I have forsaken thee, yet thou hast blessed me—
Forgotten thee, yet thou hast loved me still!

VI. Intellect.

To be infatuated with the power of one's own intellect is an accident which seldom happens but to those who are remarkable for the want of intellectual power. Whenever Nature leaves a hole in a person's mind, she generally plasters it over with a thick coat of self-conceit.

VII. Imitation.

To a careless observer, a shallow mind may sometimes appear profound, by reflecting the higher thoughts of other minds, that stand infinitely above it; even as to the passing eye a drop of water seems thousands of fathoms deep, by holding within it a reflection of the sky;—and yet it is but a drop of water.

VIII. An Obituary.

Epitaphs and obituary notices are not fit themes for merriment; but at times they are so solemnly ludicrous, that sorrow and sadness change into a smile. I have one now before me which commences thus: "The death of Mr. ——— cannot fail to *draw a deep chasm* on the society of his numerous friends." The following is so surpassingly comic, that it seems a figment of a waggish fancy, though I find it in a provincial newspaper; it is no invention of my own. Shakespeare has seldom been so travestied. He little thought, when he made Mark Antony speak of the "rent the envious Casca made," that he should be so misunderstood, as in the following lines:—

"The spoiler came. Disease rioted on her vitals; and when she thought to taste again the dear enjoyments of domestic peace, death—cold, cruel, and relentless death—with his *envious casca closed the scene!*"

IX. A Cure for Celibacy.

The following wonderful cure is copied verbatim from the advertisement of a notorious Botanic Physician:—

"A lady—deplorable state of mental derangement—attended by the celebrated Dr.—and by him pronounced beyond the reach of medical aid, and advised that she be immediately removed to the Insane Hospital, or Mad House, Pepperell, (Mass)—cured in one week and *married in three months.*"

X.

Some poetic lover in the reign of King John thus quaintly addresses his mistress, whom he calls the fairest maid "bituene Lyncolne and Lyndeseye":—

When the nightegale singes the wodes waxen grene,
Lef and gras and hlosme springes in Avril y wene,
And love is to myn herte gon *with one spere so kene*,
Nighte and day my blod hit drynkes, my herte doth me tene.

XI. The Christian Fathers.

I love at times to turn over the pages of the early Christian Fathers. When I open one of their sombre-looking tomes, and my eye loiters down the long and weather-stained column, something of the same feeling comes over me as if I were passing along the gloomy aisles of an old cathedral, and listening to the sage monitions of the past. The names of Justin Martyr, Tertullian, Lactantius, Origen, Chrysestome, and others are familiar to our ears; but how few at the present day ever think of looking into their worm-eaten tomes either for delight or instruction! And yet they contain passages of startling eloquence trains of singular, but close-pressing argument—and touches of ludicrous home-preaching, which remind one of what he has heard and read of Whitfield.

The following specimen of the kind last mentioned, I copy from St. Cyprian, "Of the habit of Virgins." Works, part I. pp. 55:—

"God, we consider, made not sheep of a purple or a scarlet color; nor was it from his instruction that we were taught to tincture our wool with the juices of herbs or of fishes; nor did he form these ranges of pearl and precious stones, which make those necklaces, where with the neck, which was truly of his forming, is in a manner covered and hid and thus in truth his workmanship is made to disappear, in favor of an invention of Satan's, which is suffered to dangle over it. Can we think it the will of God, that the ears should be bored and wounded, and poor harmless infants, ignorant as yet of all worldly wickedness, be thereby tormented? ... All these mischievous inventions, those wicked spirits introduced among us, who, sinking into the dregs of worldly pollution, lost thereby the vigor of their heavenly state; and then instructed us, after their deceitful manner, in the arts of blackening our eyebrows, painting our faces, changing the color of our hair, and in short of disguising every feature.

"Your Lord and Master hath told you, that you cannot make one hair white or black; but you must needs confute his assertion, and prove yourselves capable of doing what he has pronounced impracticable. You presumptuously adventure to dye your hair, and *with a very ill omen to your future condition, you labor to make it flame-colored!* ... I wonder you are not afraid, that the great divine artist, who made and fashioned you, should refuse to acknowledge you at the general resurrection, and reject you from the hope of his promises, with the sarcasm of a satirist, and the censure of a judge, in some such manner as this which follows: 'This is none of my workmanship, nor my image; you have quite altered the countenance which I made for you; nor hair, nor face, nor features are the same; you cannot therefore see God, with those eyes which he did not make, but which the devil hath new-colored. Him indeed you have followed, and have taken for your pattern the red and fiery eyes of the serpent; and since you have taken your dress from him, you may e'en take up your abode with him, and dwell together in eternal fire.'"

XII. Plagiarists.

We read in an old story book,—the Gesta Romanorum,—that a law once prevailed in a certain city, requiring that every knight should be buried in his armor; and that if any one should rob the grave, and deprive the dead man of his armor, he should suffer death. It once happened, when this city was closely besieged, that a poor cavalier transgressed the law, by borrowing the harness of a dead knight from his sepulchre, and though he thereby saved the city from destruction, he was, nevertheless, condemned to death, in order to satisfy the noisy populace, who were jealous of his fame. Petrus Berchorius, the putative father of this story, appends a ghostly moral to it. Will it not likewise bear a literary application? Let the reader say whether an author who robs the grave, and borrows the weapons of the dead, even to do his country service, does not deserve to be put to death as a literary felon, and is not in danger of suffering such a fate.

XIII. Poetry.

Helicon was once a fountain, but has now become a sea; and he must dive deep, who would search for pearls of price. How many are contented to play with the pebbles on the shore!

XIV. Where is Peter Grimm?

(A Mid-Summer's Day-Dream.)

Two or three years ago, on a lazy, sultry, Saturday afternoon, as I was poring over the columns of a German newspaper, published in Philadelphia, my eye was caught by an advertisement headed:—

"Who ist Petter Grimm?"

This singular title struck my fancy by its novelty, and I read on as follows:—

"Peter Grimm, from Bingen, on the Rhine, who embarked for America in 1829, is requested to give information concerning his present place of residence. His family and friends are in great anxiety on his account, having received neither letter nor information of any kind from him since his departure. A letter from Bingen for Peter Grimm lies at this office."

Straightway I fell into a day-dream. What man of feeling would not have done so? The thermometer stood at 98°, and it was after dinner. Perhaps I was asleep. At all events fancy took wing; and shadows came and went before my mind's eye, like the shadows of a camera-obscura,—living—moving—well-defined.

Where is Peter Grimm?

Sure enough, where is he? Where—who—what is he? What golden dream allured this solitary wanderer from the father-land—from the glorious Rhine—from the peaceful shades of home? Bingen! I well remember Bingen on the Rhine. A beautiful little city, and all around it as green as an emerald;—placed, too, in the very centre of the most romantic scenery of the whole Rhein-gegend. It leans against the eastern slope of the Rochusberg, with one foot in the waters of the Nahe, and the other in the kingly Rhine. Over against it lie the rich vineyards of Ruedesheim, and Geisenheim and Johannisberg, remembered with a sigh by the lovers of Rhenish flagons. Above, the green meadows of Greifenklau, and the sloping hills of Lange Winkel bask luxuriantly in the sun. Below, the river darts through a narrow pass, dark with overhanging crags, and on every crag the ruins of a castle. O glorious scene! O glorious river Rhine! There stand the towers of the Rossel; there the light and graceful castle of Vogtsberg, perched like a fairy palace in the air; and there—

But where is Peter Grimm?

Sure enough, where is he? How *could* he leave a scene like this? Perhaps he was poor, and not fond of beautiful scenery, belonging to other people. He cared not for Falkenberg, nor Sternberg, nor Drachenfels, nor Ehrenbreitstein. And yet how *could* he leave a home like this? Perhaps he took the steamboat down the Rhine, as I did. Perhaps he did not. There he lost a pleasant sail upon the most beautiful of rivers; a most lordly and majestic stream, whose rebellious waters, on entering Holland, divide into various channels, and that which bears the name of the Rhine, dwindled to a brook, sinks ere it reaches the sea, being buried, like the Captain Kidd's Bible, in the sand. There is a German song, and a fine one, too, upon this theme. I once translated it into our vernacular tongue; and thus runs this "Song of the Rhine:"—

Forth rolled the Rhine-stream strong and deep
Beneath Helvetia's Alpine steep,
And joined in youthful company
Its fellow-travellers to the sea.

In Germany embraced the Rhine,
The Neckar, the Mosel, the Lahn, and the Main,
And strengthened by each rushing tide,
Onward he marched in kingly pride.

But soon from his enfeebled grasp
    The satraps of his power,
The current's flowing veins unclasped—
    He moves in pride no more.

Forth the confederate waters broke
    On that rebellious day,

And, bursting from their monarch's yoke,
Each chose a separate way.

Wahl, Issel, Leck and Wecht, all, all
Flowed sidewards o'er the land,
And a nameless brook, by Leyden's wall,
The Rhine sank in sand.

Doggerel? Did you say Doggerel? Then a fig for your taste in poetry. The song is like the stream it celebrates: unequal, sometimes smooth, sometimes rough, but always beautiful. And if it should ever be your lot—

But where is Peter Grimm?

Sure enough, where is he? To be gone so long without sending home any information of his whereabout looks rather suspicious. And the whole family, too, in deep anxiety about him. No doubt he left them all in tears,—with many promises to write, if he could, and if he could not write, to make his mark; and yet up to this date has neither written nor marked—

Doch hat er nicht geschrieben
Ob er gesund geblieben.

No, not a single line to tell whether he is sick or well. Ah, Peter Grimm! Peter Grimm! Your heart must be as hard to move as Plaffendorferhoehe or Blickhobzhaeuserhof is to pronounce. But your friends are less unkind; there is a letter for you. In absence, when seas divide us from our friends, when time as well as distance cuts us off from those we love, there is no balm for the sick heart like tidings of our home. Next to the pressure of the lip, next to the pressure of the hand, is the unfolding of the white wings of that mysterious little messenger, that comes commissioned by love with tidings of the absent. Sweet is the fountain to the traveller of the desert, sweet is repose to the toil-worn laborer, sweet is the breath of spring after winter's biting winds, sweet are the shades of night after the burthen and heat of the day; but sweeter far than all to the stranger in a strange land is a letter from his home, particularly a letter of credit!

But where is Peter Grimm?

Sure enough, where is he? Perhaps he is in Albany—perhaps he is in Sing-Sing, in the State-prison, or in bed, or in debt, or in liquor, or in "a claret-colored coat." Who knows? Perhaps he is quietly smoking his pipe at Lancaster,—or in some little village on the banks of the Susquehanna is quietly reading himself to sleep in the "Berks County Adler." Perhaps he is dead and gone,—swept away by the cholera. Yes: that accounts for his long silence. The grave tells no tales. He was huddled into it like a malefactor, a handful of earth thrown over him—no tears shed, no bell tolled, no dirge sung. After all, what matters it where or how? "The way to heaven is the same from all places, and he that has no grave has the heavens still over him." For aught I know, he may have been one of those who think it easier to die away from home; for then there are no weeping friends to unman you; no painful leave-taking of those you love; at most it is only prolonging the separation a little, not commencing it; and as the Italians say, *Il piu duro passo è quel della soglia*,—the hardest step is that of the threshold. However, if—

But where is Peter Grimm?

"In his skin! When he jumps out, you may jump in!" answered a voice close by my car. It broke my day-dream like a thunder-clap; and yet it was nobody but my old matter-of-fact friend, Mr. Pipkins, a very commonplace man, who is always quoting silly sayings, which he learned in his boyhood. He is not half so romantic as I am. Now, I must have been thinking aloud; in a word, I must have been, where I mean to be again in five minutes from this time, and where I suppose my reader is already,—asleep.

XV. History.

The history of the past is a mere puppet-show. A little man comes out and blows a little trumpet, and goes in again. You look for something new; and lo! another little man comes out, and blows another little trumpet, and goes in again. And it is all over.

XVI. A Wise Saw.

Let gray heads sway
And green heads obey,

is an old saying, which has come floating down the stream of Time bottom upwards.

XVII. Autumn.

Magnificent is the Autumn of our fatherland! By what a subtle alchemy the green leaves are transmuted into gold, as if molten by the fiery blaze of the hot sun! A magic covering spreads over the whole forest, and brightens into more gorgeous hues. The tree-tops seem bathed with the gold and crimson of an Italian sunset. Here and there a shade of green, here and there a tinge of purple, and a stain of scarlet so deep and rich, that the most cunning artifice of man is pale beside it. A thousand delicate shades melt into each other. They blend fantastically into one deep mass. They spread over the forest like a tapestry woven with a thousand hues.

Magnificent Autumn! He comes not like a pilgrim, clad in russet weeds. He comes not like a hermit, clad in gray. But he comes like a warrior, with the stain of blood upon his brazen mail. His crimson scarf is rent. His scarlet banner drips with gore. His step is like a flail upon the threshing floor.

The scene changes.

It is the Indian Summer. The rising sun blazes through the misty air like a conflagration. A yellowish, smoky haze fills the atmosphere; and

—a filmy mist,
Lies like a silver lining on the sky.

The wind is soft and low. It wafts to us the odor of forest leaves, that hang wilted on the dripping branches, or drop into the stream. Their gorgeous tints are gone, as if the autumnal rains had washed them out. Orange, yellow, and scarlet, all are changed to one melancholy russet hue. The birds, too, have taken wing, and have left their roofless dwellings. Not the whistle of a robin, not the twitter of an eavesdropping swallow, not the carol of one sweet, familiar voice! All gone. Only the dismal cawing of a crow, as he sits and curses, that the harvest is over,—or the chit-chat of an idle squirrel,—the noisy denizen of a hollow tree,—the mendicant friar of a large parish,—the absolute monarch of a dozen acorns!

Another change.

The wind sweeps through the forest with a sound like the blast of a trumpet. The dry leaves whirl in eddies through the air. A fret-work of hear-frost covers the plain. The stagnant water in the pools and ditches is frozen into fantastic figures. Nature ceases from her labors, and pre pares for the great change. In the low-hanging clouds, the sharp air, like a busy shuttle, weaves her shroud of snow. There is a melancholy and continual roar in the t0ps of the tall pines, like the roar of a cataract. It is the funeral anthem of the dying year.

XVIII. The Death of the Young.

Beautiful is that season of life, when we can say in the language of Scripture, "Thou hast the dew of thy youth." But of these flowers, Death gathers many. He places them upon his bosom, and his form is changed to something less terrific than before. We learn to gaze and shudder not: for he carries in his arms the sweet blossoms of our earthly hopes. We shall see them all again, blooming in a happier land.

Yes: Death brings us again to our friends. They are waiting for us,—and we shall not be long. They have gone before us,—and are like the angels in heaven. They stand upon the borders of the grave, to welcome us with the countenance of affection, which they wore on earth, yet more lovely, more radiant, more spiritual.

Death has taken thee, too, sweet sister, and "thou hast the dew of thy youth." He hath placed thee upon his bosom, and his stern countenance wears a smile. The "far country" seems nearer, and the way less dark; for thou hast gone before,—passing so quickly to thy rest, that day itself dies not more calmly. And thou art there waiting to bid us welcome, when we shall have done here the work given us to do, and shall go hence to be seen no more on earth.

www.ingramcontent.com/pod-product-compliance
Lightning Source LLC
Chambersburg PA
CBHW031939110726
47902CB00001B/232